Write From The Start
The Beginner's Guide to Writing Professional Non-Fiction

Caroline Foster

In memory of Peter Whitbread

Without Peter's encouragement and support in the very early days of my Writers Bureau course my writing career would never have begun. It saddens me that Peter is not with us today to see the writing road I have travelled but I will be forever grateful for his help and advice.

About Caroline Foster

Caroline Foster has enjoyed a freelance writing career spanning more than 20 years, writing for national and regional publications on a variety of topics. In 2006, Caroline was selected for The Writers Bureau 'Writer of the Year Award,' and by 2008 she was one of the founding partners of a successful Copywriting, PR and Digital Marketing company based in the East of England.

Acknowledgements

Every book you read has not been written or published by just one person. It takes a dedicated team of people to help you, the author, through the process. These invisible friends and colleagues are invaluable to every writer, and quite rightly they should be given credit for their services.

I am sincerely grateful to all the following people who have helped me complete this book.

I would like to thank James Lumsden-Cook, my publisher, and the team at Bennion Kearny who made this book possible. My husband, Aaron, and my son, Ashley, my pre-readers, my supporters, and hopefully my biggest fans, along with Veronica Morris who has been my listening ear.

On a professional level, I would like to thank Diana Nadin of Writers Bureau and the following contributors: Kate Everett, *The Write Impression LLP*, Richard Young, editor of *Hertfordshire Life Magazine*, Aisleen Marley, *Marley Bird Communications*, Alison Withers, *Multimedia Reputations*, and Sarah Banham, *For the Love of Books*. And last but by no means least, authors Ruth Dugdall, Sheila Steptoe, Ben Smart, and Anne-Louise Hall.

Once again, thank you all!

Table of Contents

Chapter 1
What it Takes to Write Non-Fiction

Are you sitting comfortably?

Do you have plenty of tea, coffee, biscuits, chocolate or jelly beans to hand? According to most writers, these are the essential ingredients you need to be a successful writer. And, it's true, they will certainly help, as will a double dose of grit and determination and a whole lot of stubbornness. But, more important than all of that is your desire to be a great writer.

At this stage, it doesn't matter if you want to write in your spare time, whether you want to do it as a serious hobby, or if you plan to give up the day job and make a full-time career of it – the principles are the same.

Being a writer means sitting in front of a computer for hours on end. Being a writer also means you must love words, and playing with them. The words you choose and the order in which you place them will help you develop and improve your style. Reading other people's work will also help you improve your writing. You must not copy or imitate another writer's work, as you could be accused of plagiarism, but you might learn something from studying their techniques. As a writer, you will always be learning, and the knowledge you gain will elevate you from being a good writer to a great writer.

Can anybody be a writer?

With a reasonable level of understanding for your language, whether that's English or another one, anyone can be a writer. But to be a published writer you need to tailor your craft, develop your style, understand your reader, and accept that like a painter you have to know when to stop painting, or in this case writing. Equally, you have to give every piece of writing your absolute best attention, appreciate when it's not quite good enough, and do whatever it takes to improve it.

Chapter 1

Writing is not like other professions, but in some ways, it is exactly like other professions. Let me take you back to your school days. It is almost certainly the case that unless you were physically unable to participate, PE lessons would have been compulsory. But, to become a professional or Olympic athlete you would need more than a weekly lesson or two at school. A career as an elite athlete would take hours and hours of practice, weeks, even years to get to the point where you could compete. Through practice, training, and competition, you would look to improve your performance and become a better athlete.

Becoming a published writer or a professional writer, for that matter, will take you hour upon hour of writing and editing, even before you are ready to submit your work. And, just like an athlete who may not qualify for the county championships or get the chance to represent their country at the Olympic Games, you will have to face rejection and defeat. Rejection doesn't mean you're not a good writer; it just means you have to try harder to be better!

So why do so many people who aspire to be writers fail?

Many aspiring writers fail because they set their expectations too high. Let me ask you this. Would you expect to pick up a dart and throw it at a dartboard and hit the bullseye first time? Probably not. So, why would you sit in front of your computer and expect the first thing you write to be worthy of publication?

Because everyone can write?

Can everyone throw a dart?

We have the ability to achieve what we want to achieve, as long as we accept that we need to learn, practise, take advice and keep at it. If you are willing to do that, then read on; your writing journey is about to get a lot more exciting.

Writing non-fiction

There are obvious differences between writing fiction and non-fiction, and there are major differences on how you can sell your work, and to whom.

For an aspiring writer, in whatever genre you choose to write, building your confidence will be the key to success which – I hope – is to see your work published.

I have known many 'bottom drawer writers' as I call them, during my time as a creative writing tutor, and my goal was to see those writers pull their work out from their desks and let the world read them. If it's not a private journal or something therapeutic, why on earth would you write a piece then tuck it away where no one else will ever read it? It is my opinion, and only my opinion, that if you are not writing for your reader then don't waste your time writing – find something else to do!

If, on the other hand, it's a confidence boost you need, and if you really want to see your work in print, then *Write From The Start* is for you, and writing non-fiction can certainly help you build a portfolio of published work.

Seeing your work published for the first time is like waking up on Christmas morning and receiving the gift you wanted more than anything in the world. It gets even better when you read your name printed in the byline.

This book will give you a comprehensive reference guide to the markets available and how to write for those markets, and show you how to submit your work. Whether you are submitting the occasional piece of writing or sending work off on a more regular basis, the opportunities are boundless.

Magazines of all types, whether hardcopy (printed) or online, offer aspiring writers many opportunities to see their work published. Whether it's a reader's letter or a centre page spread, magazine editors are always looking for articles of interest to fill their pages, especially if you have specialist knowledge. If you're a keen hobbyist, many more opportunities lie in wait for you.

Commercial publications, and trade and industry publications, may not be the first types of magazine that spring to mind, but later on, we will explore how you can use knowledge from your job or career to contribute to these publications. Equally, copywriting, PR, and writing online offer a completely different dimension to writing for profit and publication.

Beyond magazines, writing a book on your specialist subject or based on your career is another opportunity. Books for business, self-help, and entrepreneurial success have been very popular reads over the past decades, but other untapped markets could include writing non-fiction for radio or television.

Chapter 1

By now, your thinking cap should be on and working overtime. Your pen should be poised in your hand ready to jot down notes and ideas. And, if you're even contemplating reading this book without at the very least a highlighter pen, sticky notes, or a notebook and pen, then I suggest you grab them and be quick about it. I have never read a book on or about writing that hasn't offered opportunities and ideas throughout. As a writer, everywhere you go, everything you do, and everyone you meet offers you potential content. Your notes will become your cuttings file and the contents of your next masterpiece.

Writer's Block

Your notes, together with other resources, will also help you avoid 'writer's block', a term widely used but really nothing to worry about.

Writer's block in the true sense of the word is the result of writing too much or too long for a concentrated period, resulting in mental fatigue. Rest and relaxation will help you overcome this. Even something as simple as a walk or other form of exercise can help relieve the symptoms of mental fatigue. If the symptoms persist, you may need to take a longer break away from your writing.

What others might consider as writer's block is when a writer is stumped for ideas – this should never, I repeat, never happen. It doesn't matter if you don't have any other hobbies or interests, it doesn't matter if you don't think you've got a very exciting job or career, and it doesn't matter if you're not well travelled. What matters is that you know how and where to generate ideas. Picking up a newspaper or magazine, people watching on a park bench, or talking to someone you haven't met before, are just a few idea triggers that will help keep writer's block away.

As a writer, you should keep an open mind. You should be aware of your surroundings and opportunities. Enquire and ask questions. And I promise you, if you are serious about writing, you will never read a newspaper, magazine, or book, or even watch a film, in the same way again. Writing can become a hugely rewarding part of your life.

Now let's get this journey started!

Chapter 2
Resources and Tools of the Trade

Being a writer will give you a natural thirst for knowledge. Whether adding depth to your content through research or discovering ways to improve your writing, abundant resources are not only at your fingertips but on your very doorstep.

Even with closures and cuts to facilities, your local library is still one of the best resources at your disposal. Irrespective of what topics you are writing about, your library is easily accessible and shouldn't be overlooked. It might seem easier to sit at your computer and search for everything online, but it is not – and should not be – your only option.

If you are writing something historically-based, for example, more books and information on the history of an area are likely to be found in the local library than online.

In the same way, flicking through a few pages on *Amazon* is not going to help you determine everything you need to know about writing for children. While buying lots of children's books might not be economical, spending time in the children's section of a library would, however, help you discover the type of books currently available for children. You would learn what topics or themes are most popular, as well as compare the content, language, and style of those books.

Library assistants are also worth their weight in gold. Engaging in conversation with them could help you find out more than you would ever accomplish by just combing the bookshelves.

If finding somewhere quiet to write is challenging, many libraries provide workstations with Internet-connected computers or areas where you can work using your own laptop. Using cloud storage facilities, you can safely store your work and easily retrieve it on another device. Most libraries also provide photocopying, and some have printing facilities, which could prove very useful too.

Then there's the British Library. Holding more than 14 million books, 150 million published articles from around the globe, and almost a million journals and newspapers, the British Library is the largest library in the world, in terms of the number of items it holds. Whatever conceivable information or research you need to do, the British Library can help you source it.

Your writers library

Being an avid reader will help you become a better writer. The best advice is to read widely, choosing different authors and different themes or genres. As a writer, you are likely to build your own library of books on topics that are of interest to you, or perhaps on topics you are interested in writing about.

Below are some recommended reads that no writer should be without. I am not, for one minute, suggesting that you hit *Amazon* or any other bookstore with a shopping list that maxes out your credit cards; instead, I would like to make recommendations on books that will help you improve your writing and help you find the markets in which to sell your work. Remember too that loved ones, family, and friends will almost certainly relish the idea of gifting you with books or book vouchers for special occasions. Charity shops and second-hand bookstores are also worth browsing; just keep an eye on the age of publication, as changes in technology and submission guidelines have changed dramatically in more recent years.

If you invest in just one book (besides this one) then it has to be the *Writers' & Artists' Yearbook* – this annual publication is a writer's bible, and jammed-packed with just about every resource you might need as a writer. In addition to hints, tips, and advice from respected industry professionals, writers, authors, and journalists, there are sections dedicated to newspaper and magazine listings, publishers, literary agents, plus pages and pages of other practical information.

Published by *Bloomsbury Publishing*, there are numerous *Writers' & Artists'* Companion titles worth considering too.

It is worth noting that however informative the *Writers' & Artists' Yearbook* might be, you should always back up your research with a secondary source. For example, if you have made a list of preferred publishers or agents to submit your manuscript to, visit the individual publisher or agent's websites for further instructions or more up-to-date information on their submission process.

Even a publication as widely respected as the *Writers' & Artists' Yearbook* is essentially out of date before printing. In essence, there is a delay between collating the information and publication, during which time some details may have changed. Businesses close, publishing houses often merge, editors move from one magazine to another, and it would be impossible to keep editing the yearbook, as it would never make it to publication. At some point, there is a cut-off date, a deadline, after which entries can no longer be modified.

That said, for me personally, the contents do not change enough between editions to warrant buying a new copy every year. I find a biennial purchase is usually adequate.

I also believe that no writer should be without a good English Dictionary and Thesaurus. Both have become less used in print format since being readily available as components of word processing packages. These applications do have their limitations, though, so you might want to consider using a more comprehensive online version. Do bear in mind, however, that good writing is not about filling your copy with 'big' or overly complex words, it's about the readability of your work; a topic covered in the language section of the next chapter. Dictionaries are, however, far more useful than for just checking the spelling or meaning of words; the age of words and etymology can be incredibly valuable, especially if you are writing period pieces or including local dialect in your work.

The more you write, the easier it is to spot weaknesses in your writing, thus enabling you to select reading material to help you improve. For that reason, I would like to suggest a couple of books that had a big impact on my writing.

On Writing Well: The Classic Guide to Writing Nonfiction by William Zinsser. If you want to understand 'how to write', this book offers you an insight into the fundamental principles of writing. It will, without a doubt, increase your awareness of the structure and style of your writing, help you improve your editing techniques, and show you how to spot those superfluous words.

Another recommendation is the similarly titled *On Writing* by Stephen King. Best known for his horror, science fiction, and supernatural fiction, King reveals the secrets to his success as one of

Chapter 2

America's best-selling storytellers. Part memoir, part masterclass on writing, if you can skip over King's obsession, rage, and anger at his near-fatal accident, he offers writers of all genres a look at the different aspects of being a writer. (I'm not suggesting his accident wasn't a truly awful experience, but if you are more interested in his methods than his life story, you will find his affliction woefully embedded throughout.)

Collins Complete Writing Guide by Graham King, covers just about every aspect of writing, including helpful advice on spelling, grammar, and punctuation. If you feel your English skills are a little rusty, *Collins* will certainly help you regain confidence in your writing abilities. More specifically, *Improve your punctuation* or *Improve your grammar* are further titles from the *Collins* collection of books, or you could try the *Oxford Guide to Plain English*.

In the previous chapter, I mentioned writer's block, and although you won't ever experience this through lack of inspiration (will you?) if you are looking for some quick ideas to warm up or to get those creative juices flowing, I highly recommend *The Five Minute Writer* by Margret Geraghty, and a cute little number *The Writer's Block: 786 Ideas to Jump-Start Your Imagination* by Jason Rekulak. The latter, published as it declares in the title – as a block – is a quirky must-have for your bookshelf that will fire up your imagination in no time.

At your fingertips

Ah! The age of the computer. What a revolution we have experienced since the launch of the personal computer. For some of you, using a computer, laptop, smartphone, tablet or other device will be second nature, and you'll think nothing of tweeting, Facebooking, messaging, texting, Instagramming, etc., and flashing your musings, blogs, and *YouTube* videos over the worldwide web. However, for some of us, sending handwritten letters or using early word-processing devices might not seem that long ago and, in tortoise-like fashion, the internet is still a little bit scary. However, what technology has done for everyone is to bring every conceivable tool to our fingertips to help us improve our writing.

I mentioned, above, the built-in dictionaries and thesauri of word processing applications, and through online searching more advanced dictionaries and dictionary applications are available, but another program worth adding is *Grammarly*.

Grammarly is an instant spelling and grammar checking application. There are other ones available but *Grammarly* is, in my view, one of the best and most trusted.

Even if you consider yourself to have excellent writing skills, everyone makes mistakes and running your copy through *Grammarly* before submission might just help pick-up some unexpected proofreading errors. Equally, if you are less confident about your grammar, *Grammarly* can help you improve. A word of warning here, once you understand the importance of style and readability, you will appreciate that not every recommendation by *Grammarly* should be automatically accepted. You have the choice to reject a revised word, a misspelling, or the passive content of your work, and in some cases, you will need to do so. Nevertheless, used properly, *Grammarly* can help you improve the structure of your sentences, which in turn can help improve your writing style and the readability of your work. At the very least, it should identify when you've typed the word *bear* essentials instead of *bare* essentials.

Important websites are also worth mentioning. *Amazon*, although primarily a shopping channel, is one of the first places to search for book titles, together with reviews, ranking/sales data, plus other related information. If you are writing a book on a particular topic, knowing what competition already exists, whether the books sell, and what they do well or fail to do (read the user reviews) will pay immense dividends down the line. They could even help you spot a gap in the market.

I mentioned the *Writers' & Artists' Yearbook* above. The *Writers' & Artists'* website: *www.writersandartists.co.uk* is equally as informative, with additional information on editorial services, events, and links to other websites too.

The *BBC* also supports new writers, and the *BBC Writersroom* [*www.bbc.co.uk/writersroom*] is well worth a browse. Although its focus is primarily fiction and script writing, it does sometimes offer opportunities for contributing to documentaries and other factual programs.

As reputable bodies supporting writers of all calibres, *The Society of Authors* [*www.societyofauthors.org*] and *The NUJ (The National Union of*

Journalists) [*www.nuj.org.uk*] are both worth considering. You do not have to be members of either society to access information on their respective websites, but being a member carries added benefits. The *Writers' and Artists' Yearbook* also provides a list of other writing organisations you might want to consider.

The final site I would like to mention is *Writers Online* [*www.writers-online.co.uk*]. From the publishers of *Writing Magazine* (worth buying a copy or two) this website is packed with information relating to writing and writing activities, including writers' groups, courses, and competitions. You can also use the site to buy books, sign up for a course or two, and enter writing competitions.

One last thing on this topic. If you type the keywords 'writers resources' into a search engine, it will provide a wonderful list of websites containing useful information and resources for writers. So search away!

Writer's groups, workshops, courses, and retreats

A writer's life can, at times, seem a lonely existence, especially when your head is down and you are concentrating on a writing project. For this very reason, writing groups or circles, workshops, and even writing retreats have become extremely popular. There is a lot to gain from sharing your experiences and your work with fellow writers, or taking the time to get to know others who have a passion for writing. Most writing courses and workshops are run by experienced writers and authors or, at the very least, invite published writers as guest speakers.

The most common, most accessible, and probably least expensive activity for some writers is to join a writer's group or circle. Some are discussion groups or forums, some undertake writing tasks during the meeting, while others give you a topic or theme to work on at home and bring to the next gathering.

Most writer's circles encourage writers to share their work with the rest of the group, and this can be extremely helpful and encouraging, and often confidence-boosting, but very few will give you actual constructive feedback or critique your work to help you improve it. And, to be fair, many of the attendees are not necessarily qualified to do so.

If you are thinking of joining a writer's circle, do your research. Find out who the other members are. If there are published writers in the group, when were they published? You will gain very little from the rather distinguished but aged gentleman who published a book 40 years ago, especially as the publishing industry has changed such a lot in recent years. Learning from other writers is invaluable but needs to be kept in perspective.

You may also find the majority of other members share their short stories or snippets of novels in the making. It won't harm your non-fiction writing if you diversify with a little fiction here and there (after all, any writing practice is good practice) but do ask if there's an opportunity to share something from an article you are writing or other non-fiction work.

Gather as much information as you can before you go, and keep an open mind. Go along to a meeting or two but don't be afraid to walk away or find a different group if it's not right for you; it could do you more harm than good.

Well-organised and well-attended writing workshops are a fantastic opportunity to write alongside other writers while improving your skills. You can learn a lot, not just from the 'expert' tutoring the workshop but also from your fellow attendees. From a couple of hours to full day events, the workshops often cover specific topics or themes. Pick workshops based on the subjects most relevant to you, or choose one based on location. Don't be afraid to study outside of your comfort zone!

Similarly, opportunities frequently arise for 'talks'. Guest speakers – often published authors or industry professionals – give up their time to share information on writing, getting published, the submissions process, what publishers and agents are looking for, and more. On occasion, you might be afforded the chance of a brief one-to-one with a publisher or agent, which, if it is one you want to work with, could prove invaluable.

Book launches, meet the author events, book festivals, and the like, also offer writers the opportunity to rub shoulders with published writers from all genres. Bookshops, such as *Waterstones*, often promote the launch of a new book with the author in attendance. They will often share their experiences, read from their books, and autograph purchases. Again, if it is an author who is writing in a similar genre to you, other attendees (book buyers) could impart essential information on why they like that particular writer or that genre, or perhaps more importantly, what they don't like. Inadvertently, you might hear valuable comments that could be of benefit when you come to write and edit your manuscript.

But, let's get back to your writing.

Home learning and online courses are also in abundance, helping you to study when it's convenient, without the constraints of a full-time course. Again, do your research. Have an idea about what you hope to gain from the course, what sort of qualification you might achieve, and if it is worth sparing your time. I'm an avid supporter of honing skills, and for developing and improving writing, but not at the expense of publication. I have known some very talented writers who attend course after course, workshop after workshop, and while they are gaining valuable knowledge and experience, this becomes procrastination and stops them from getting their work completed and published.

Less time-consuming than courses are 'textbook style' resources or 'writing guides'. Many contain exercises or assignments throughout, enabling you to improve your writing craft as you progress through each chapter. These resources can be useful, certainly for practicing your writing and for developing ideas, and if you're in the early stages of your writing career they could help you build a portfolio of work – but if nothing else, they will encourage you to write and to do so regularly.

Writing retreats often allow you the time to write in beautiful or peaceful surroundings while bringing you into contact with other writers from across the country or even the globe. While the aim of a writing retreat is to spend time writing alone, often at specified times, you will get the chance to mingle with other retreaters, even if it is just during mealtimes. There are many writing retreats held across the UK, but there are also plenty held in other countries around the world. If you have romantic notions of whisking yourself off somewhere exotic to write then, by all means, do it! Exploring different locations can be as inspiring as the people you meet.

However, before you go rushing off, signing up to every writer's circle in your area, or jetting off to somewhere exotic with nothing but your bikini and notebook, I need to keep you rooted to the spot for a little longer so we can delve into the techniques of writing.

Chapter 3
Writing Techniques

Writing techniques are the practices you adopt that determine the outcome of your work. Many of these practices are a subconscious part of your natural writing ability, and learned from an early age, probably at school. Over time, and depending on the type of writing you do regularly, your methods will have developed and your writing style will have evolved.

But what are those techniques?

In essence, the words you choose – simple or complex, formal or informal – and the order in which you place them will form the basis or structure of your piece. By varying the length of your sentences and varying the length of your paragraphs you will determine its pace and tension. Short, sharp sentences are most commonly used for dramatic effect or emphasis, whilst other methods such as persuasive language, facts, statistics, or opinions can be used to sway your reader, as will the 'voice' of the piece.

Your writer's 'voice' is your individual writing style – the rhythm, pace and intonation of your written voice. It can also relate to the formal or informal 'tone' of your voice. For example, an email to a family member or a friend will be less formal than the one you might write to your boss, which will be different again to how you might respond to a solicitor or other professional.

And the voice you use, whether you write in the first, second or third person, will have an impact on how your reader connects with your writing.

- **First person**: I, me, my, mine or in the plural form, we

- **Second person**: you, your, yours, yourself, yourselves

- **Third person**: He, his, hers, she, they, theirs, it

The third person voice is the industry-preferred and most popular format for your writing;

It is thought that the Saxons were among the first to farm these lands.

Chapter 3

Writing about a personal account or experience would be written in the first person, this would be as a travelogue, memoir, or an autobiography.

I traced the path up through the mountains, high above the city, where my ancestors had made their pilgrimage.

The second voice is most frequently used in persuasive writing or advertisements.

You must try this tonic, it's the best on the market!

Our language is very powerful. We use it to communicate and connect with each other but – if handled incorrectly – we can just as easily alienate one another. The same goes for our reader. When we get it right, we can have our reader engrossed in our text but get it wrong and they won't give us (or our work) the time of day.

We all have favourite authors, or will favour the work of one writer over another, and that's because we resonate or relate to the voice, style, and tone the author uses. Even though their work may differ article by article, or book to book, we will subconsciously recognise similarities in each written piece.

Know your reader

You will have heard the term, 'write for your reader'.

It might sound strange at this early stage of writing, but what you have to do is write as if you are the reader. This means you have to understand who your reader is, what makes them tick, and what turns them off.

Gender, age, and ethnic, religious, or social background are basically inconsequential. Your reader can be anybody, from any walk of life – they will all have different outlooks, political views, or social or economic attitudes. Nevertheless, what they are all looking for is *information*.

How do you get to know your reader?

By *identifying* your audience.

Knowing your audience means appreciating what it is your readers want to know, and adapting the content of your writing to fulfil their needs.

Ask yourself, who do I want to read this?

Who else might read this?

And why might it appeal to them?

One way in which you can do this is to study your competition. I do this by analysing the content of my fellow writers' works, but I also consider the reviews and feedback they receive. *Amazon* has some very useful tools including reviews, star ratings, and rankings of books, and it will also suggest other titles similar to those you have selected.

Social media can be very useful here too. If you follow book clubs, organisations and societies, authors, literary agents, and other relevant industry professionals, on *Facebook* and *Twitter*, you will discover the books people are talking about and what they are saying about those books.

That's all very well, you might say, but what about writing articles instead of books?

Even reader's letters in magazines and newspaper reviews can give you clues as to the topics readers are interested in, and the information they want to know.

If your subject matter is perhaps less mainstream, you may struggle to identify your target audience. In this instance, there are some online tools which might help. You could join online forums or chat room discussions on your chosen topic, search for bloggers writing about your subject, and review the comments and responses they get.

Alternatively, you could invest in some online surveys (this is likely to cost you money). If you take this latter approach, you would have to carefully construct your questions to get the answers or responses you are searching for, and that isn't easy. Furthermore, you have to find ways of getting people to respond in the first place; again that is not so easy.

Essentially, what you are trying to discover is where gaps exist in the market that your knowledge or expertise could fill. Not only should you be looking for specific areas where there might be limited information available, but also openings in the marketplace.

What you are trying to uncover is the information your readers are searching for. What answers do they want, and to what questions?

Chapter 3

That might sound like a riddle but it is not. All the clues are out there.

For example, *Write From The Start* is a book aimed at people who would like to know how to be writers, but equally, writers with some knowledge might read it to brush up on their skills. Others will use it to generate new ideas. This book was written to inform, educate and encourage new, novice, and improving writers, but I would not necessarily expect a professional writer to read this.

However, *Nicola Morgan*, the author of *Write to be Published*, has targeted her book at authors asking for publication guidance, assuming the majority of her readers will be people who have some knowledge of writing practices, or who write regularly, and believe they are ready to take the next step.

While there are obvious differences in our content, the readers of both our books are likely to be a mix of male and female, primarily (but not exclusively) aged 35 to 65 years old, and will come from a variety of backgrounds and social classes.

In both instances, as authors, Nicola and I have to make assumptions about how much our readers might already know. For instance, how conversant they are at using a computer, do they know how to prepare a document for submission, and how familiar they are with publishing or writing terms such as: manuscript, copy-count, or by-lines. We also assume they are reading our books because they want to know more about writing and publication, by choice not by force.

Despite these similarities, our writing styles will be very different. We both have to write to inform and, at the same time, entertain our readers. Our voices need to be encouraging and informative, friendly, and yet conversational in tone. We want our readers to learn about writing craft, and put it into practice. We do not want to over-complicate our instructions, or use levels of language, or unfamiliar words that will alienate those readers.

If, on the other hand you were writing an instruction manual, the information you provide would be more formal and intrinsic. Your sentences would be shorter and more succinct. You wouldn't necessarily be concerned with entertaining your reader, but instead, provide them with detailed instructions to complete the task at hand. You might keep your language relatively simple to avoid confusing your reader, or equally, have to use specific terms which are only relevant to your subject matter.

However, what we all have in common is that the language we use has to *satisfy* all of our readers.

The language we use is referred to as 'standard English'. According to *Wikipedia*, the definition for Standard English means:

> *Whatever form of the English language is accepted as a national norm in any English-speaking country. It encompasses grammar, vocabulary and spelling.*

In real terms, your work should not be too formal and equally not too informal. It should not contain fancy language, verbose sentences, or words with an overwhelming number of syllables. You should also avoid colloquialisms or jargon.

Colloquialism – a word or phrase that is not formal or literary, and tends to be used in ordinary or familiar conversation. Be aware of regional dialect and pronunciations too, and avoid them. In Yorkshire, for example, it is common for people to say *'nay'* when they mean *'no'*. And, in the Southeast, *'alwight'* is often used for *'alright'* or *'all right'*.

Jargon – special words or expressions used by a profession or group that are difficult for others to understand (most commonly used in trade and industry publications or specialist titles. Examples: data-cube and pentapeptide). In some cases, *jargon* may be essential, but the author should define its meaning in layman's terms.

Understanding the different levels of language should become clearer in the following chapter: *Writing for Magazines*. By studying an assortment of publications, you will be able to distinguish the varying levels of 'standard English' and identify the target readership, just by its use of language.

Developing your style

Are you concerned about your writing style?

Many new writers worry unnecessarily about their writing style. Put simply, it is a reflection of your personality, your unique voice, and the way you address your readers.

Chapter 3

Many elements of writing contribute to an author's style, but three of the most important are word choice, sentence fluency, and voice.

Kathleen Cali, a doctoral student in the Early Childhood, Families, and Literacy program at the UNC-Chapel Hill School of Education

Your style should be attractive and easy to read. In other words, it should flow naturally, and when read aloud it should sound good to you. If you don't like how it reads, then the chances are your readers won't either.

> *Tip: Always read your work out loud. Reading aloud will sound very different to how you read in your head. If you stumble over a sentence, read it again in context, and if you stumble again, rewrite it.*

Your writing style will develop the more you write; spend time practising your writing craft, and editing your work. That does not automatically give you the free will to write as you please, you will be governed by other constraints such as your audience and the publication, and by the rules of grammar and punctuation.

Style is not a matter of right and wrong but of what is appropriate for a particular setting and audience.

Kathleen Cali

While it is important to understand the basic rules of grammar and punctuation, your writing can become very stilted if you insist on following every grammatical rule to the letter. Instead, focus on the flow, tone, and natural voice of your work.

All the faith he had had had had no effect on his life is grammatically correct but would sound much better, and would be easier to understand if you wrote;

For all his faith, it had no effect on his life or even *All his faith had not affected the outcome of his life.*

And, be aware that because our language continuously changes, as writers we have to adapt our work to suit our audience, which can mean breaking some of the rules of written English. Failing to do so can affect the readability and saleability of your work.

Other fundamental elements to consider include the 3 C's: Clarity, Coherence, Conciseness.

Clarity – Your writing needs to be clear. Your readers won't thank you if they have to read a sentence or paragraph more than once to understand its meaning. Clarity of thought must precede clarity in writing. If you are not sure of the message you want to deliver you will struggle to find the correct words. You should have a clear idea of what you want to convey at the beginning, in the middle, and at the end of your piece.

Coherence – Your ideas should be expressed in an orderly manner, and a logical way, so that your reader can follow your thinking and reasoning. Initially, you may have to work on the logical order of your work, but with time and practice this will become more habitual.

Conciseness – Be concise. Long-winded explanations will only bore your reader. Avoid irrelevant facts and unnecessary words, and don't overcook your work. If you try and spell out every detail, your reader could lose the concept of your original message. Often one word can replace many. Being concise does not necessarily mean writing with brevity. Your article can be long in length and written concisely.

Something else to be very conscious of is repetition. Not just in the multiple uses of the same word, (often, new writers will repeat the same word in one sentence, and time and time again in the same paragraph) but, also, saying the same thing twice but written in a different way. Writers will quite often repeat themselves without realising it; only realising what they have done during editing or, more commonly, when reading work aloud.

In the first instance, look at replacing one word with another. Using your Thesaurus, look for a similar word that best represents the word you chose initially, and which has the same meaning (a synonym). Avoid choosing obscure words as this could irritate your reader. In the paragraph above, the repeated use of *realising* should be exchanged for *recognising* or *appreciating*. And, yet, swapping it for *understanding* or *comprehending* would not work, even though the thesaurus lists them as comparable alternatives.

Chapter 3

In the second case, it is less obvious to see the repetition of a thought or an idea. As you become more adept at editing, or when you are way over your copy count (the word length of your piece), and forced to reduce its size, you will more easily spot those repetitious sections.

That said, repetition can be used for effect. Often, authors will use repetition to reinforce an important point, or to help lodge an idea or phrase in a reader's mind. Most commonly known as the rule of three:

> *The rule of three or power of three is a writing principle that suggests that things that come in threes are funnier, more satisfying, or more effective than other numbers of things. The reader or audience of this form of text is also thereby more likely to remember the information.*

Wikipedia

> *Blood, sweat and tears.*

General Patton

> *Stop, Look and Listen.*

THINK! Road Safety.

> *Government of the people, by the people, for the people.*

The Gettysburg Address

And one of my favourites.

> *See no evil, hear no evil, speak no evil.*

The Three Wise Monkeys

Throughout the editing process, and certainly in the earlier days of your writing practice, you might find yourself cutting, pasting, and deleting quite a lot, but as you progress, and your style becomes more intuitive, your work will evolve more naturally.

Tip: Always, always leave your work to rest. Never – I repeat, never – write an article then send it off without leaving it to rest. Coming back to it will allow you to see it with fresh eyes, enabling you to spot errors, repetitions, and weaknesses in your work that you previously overlooked. Also, reading a hardcopy (printed) version of your work often highlights errors you didn't see when reading on screen.

Step 1. Write, proofread, edit, read aloud, edit - rewrite, reread, leave to rest for at least a couple of days.

Step 2. Read a printed copy, edit, reread, rest.

Step 3. Reread, tweak, reread, submit.

Language

The English language is just beautiful, isn't it? But it can be equally frustrating. Having such a diverse language enables us to write more creatively, and when you have a passion for writing you will develop a passion for language, and appreciate its diversity.

With hundreds and hundreds of words to choose from, selecting the right one will alter your work considerably, and bring variety and depth. Different words can be used to create emphasis, emotion, and evoke reactions in your writing.

Examples:

Tomorrow will be hot.

Tomorrow will be scorching.

Tomorrow will be sweltering.

It is easy to get carried away with 'word swapping' so remember the words you choose should be selected to fit your audience and readership. Avoid tripping your reader with difficult words, and always err on the side of simplicity.

In the same vein, by changing the order of a sentence, we can change the emphasis of its meaning.

The rain stopped, and the sun came out.

The sun came out, when the rain stopped.

In the first example, the emphasis is on the 'rain', but in the following sentence, the 'sun' becomes the focus. We can also change the emphasis through punctuation and – love or hate punctuation – when you understand its power you'll appreciate its beauty.

Our use of language, however, is not just about words and their order, but the techniques we use to give them purpose.

There are essentially four elements of writing: persuasive, descriptive, expository, and narrative.

We see persuasive writing every day in opinion or editorial newspaper articles, in advertisements, other sales literature, and product reviews. Social media is littered with persuasive writing. Just scroll through *Facebook* and *Twitter* feeds and you will find hundreds of influential postings.

In persuasive language, the author expresses his point of view, and wants you to agree with it. His writing will contain argument, justification, and reasoning.

In descriptive writing, an author's purpose is to describe in detail such things as people, places, events, situations, or locations. Conveying what the author sees, hears, tastes, smells, and feels, enables the reader to paint a picture in his mind's eye. You may think that descriptive writing is more commonplace in fiction but equally it will be used in news bulletins, nature, and food writing, as well as journals or memoirs.

Expository writing is used to explain. The common uses in this form of writing are found in textbooks, 'how-to' articles, recipes, and journalistic news pieces (not editorial or opinion-based articles). You are likely to see this style of writing in business, technical, and scientific writing also. Expository writing is subject-oriented with the focus on the topic or subject, without author opinion, and explains a process. It is usually written in a logical order or sequence, and contains facts and figures.

Narrative writing tells a story and is mainly used in fiction to tell us about a character and what happens to them. However, we do sometimes see examples of narrative writing in non-fiction works such as biographies and autobiographies.

Irrespective of what type of writing you are doing, you should aim for fluency and flow. Fluency in your writing helps your reader move through your piece effortlessly, reading sentence after sentence without stumbling, and moving from one paragraph to another coherently. The flow is how your piece is composed, and the movement of your work that joins the beginning, the middle and the end together naturally.

You can improve the fluency and flow of your work by avoiding verbosity (long-winded explanations), repetition, and add to that, circumlocution. As grand as it may sound, circumlocution simply means 'the use of many words where few will do'. This technique can be used to great effect if you want to be vague or evasive, but if you have a tight copy count, replacing several words with fewer will help you cut back. Check your work for phrases such as: *due to the fact that, in order to, as well as, in the case of* - these expressions can all be replaced using: *because, to, and,* or with, *instead.* I know I'm guilty of using some of these phrases, and I work hard to avoid using too many, but sometimes the simplified version just doesn't express what I want it to. Again, it's about choice, voice, and flow - not just word economics.

Clichés are overused phrases or sayings. Because clichés have become so familiar, they are often used loosely and out of context, and for that reason, avoid using them in your written work.

Slang and obscenities should generally be avoided, especially in your non-fiction writing. Slang is regarded as informal, often used in everyday speech, and more often associated with writing dialogue and speech. However, as slang words change rapidly, you run the risk of outdating your work, so use with caution. The same is advised for obscenities. The use of obscene words in non-fiction work is rare, and not recommended, even if you want your writing to appear 'current'.

At this point, don't stress over the techniques. In these early stages of writing, focus on getting your thoughts and ideas onto paper or on the screen. Try and work logically and coherently. Once you have expressed yourself, read through your work looking for the obvious signs of repetition, circumlocution, clichés, and the use of inappropriate words or language.

Chapter 3

It is likely that you will have written way more content than is needed, or that meets your chosen publication's criteria, so now you have to cut and edit.

Work through your piece again, look for sentences that can be rewritten to tighten your writing. Also, look for superfluous words, and sentences, even whole paragraphs that if removed would not affect the outcome of your piece.

Grammar and spelling

I have to say that I am envious of those people whose grammar and spelling is exemplary. Mine is not. However, throughout my tutoring career, and the content of this book, I strongly maintain that your focus should always be on the readability of your work. That, however, is not an excuse to ignore the rules of grammar and punctuation because, when you understand the rules, you will appreciate which ones can be manipulated or broken to suit your needs.

Modern society influences our written content. It is important, therefore, to read regularly and across a broad spectrum of sources, to enable you to keep up with the evolution of our language.

For many, one of the most troublesome causes for concern is the correct use of the apostrophe. There are legitimate campaigns to rid the English language of this blight. *www.killtheapostrophe.com* is just one of the many websites supporting its abolition, claiming that:

> *On the basis that it [the apostrophe] serves only to annoy those who know how it is supposed to be used and to confuse those who dont.*

And, not so long ago, I might have agreed. Although, the urge to put back the apostrophe in the word 'dont' above is almost too much to bear. However, now that I better understand its use, I would certainly be in the remain camp, largely thanks to Lynn Truss and her revolutionary book: *Eats, Shoots and Leaves.*

I have read countless books and articles on grammar and punctuation that often left my brain in a blur. However, Lynn's explanations, her eloquence, and the simplicity with which she explains its use, and that of other punctuation marks, is a true case of filling a gap in the market, and understanding her audience's needs. And, one of the reasons why, in seven years since publication, this book is still ranked in the top 2,000 of the *Amazon* bestsellers list. (Should there be an apostrophe in bestsellers?)

If you believe grammar and spelling is a weakness, then I highly recommend that you do your best to learn the basic rules. It doesn't have to be all at once, because, as you develop (writing more and reading more) you will learn more. Equally, there are so many online tools and resources to help you improve your skills, there really is no excuse.

Be warned, although your work won't get rejected because of a few grammatical errors, editors and publishers will NOT accept sloppy writing and poor grammar. You should always aim to write the very best piece you can. Check for errors, misspellings, and (un)readability. Use online tools and resources (remember *Grammarly*) and, if in doubt – leave it out!

If on the other hand, you know the rules of the English language inside and out, be careful not to get so caught up in the rights and wrongs that your creativity is stifled. Writing well is about using the English language to communicate your meaning, your ideas, and your thoughts, in a manner that others will understand. Remember the three C's: clarity, coherence, conciseness.

Spelling on the other hand, don't groan, can also have an impact on the quality of your work. Essentially there are three types of misspellings: incorrectly spelt words, using the wrong version of a word (e.g. *there* instead of *their*), and the American spelling of words (e.g. *color* instead of *colour*).

A word processor's 'spell checker' is, in my opinion, a gift sent from heaven! It can help you identify words you have spelt incorrectly and find those annoying typos, so use it! However, it should not be totally relied upon to find all misspellings, as it won't necessarily pick up when you have typed *peace* instead of *piece*. But, if you have trouble with your *i's* before *e's*, and your *ing's*, it will certainly help. As will the book *Troublesome Words* by an American-born author, *Bill Bryson*. Yes, I know, an American telling the British how to write English, whatever next?

To overcome Americanisms in your work, it's just a matter of changing the language setting on your computer. Nevertheless, you would do well to familiarise yourself with some of their rules; using

Chapter 3

z's instead of *s's* in words such as *organization* – *organisation*, and the elimination of *u's* in words such as *color*.

What your spellchecker may not do, is flag up words which sound the same as the word you meant to use (so-called homophones; compare *steal* with *steel*), as I found out to my dismay when I used the spelling of the word *yew* when writing an article on livestock and not trees. You can imagine my mortification and embarrassment when my editor sent me a very cross email about *ewes!*

Oh, it can happen. You can suffer from word blindness, and it's simply another reason why I reiterate that you should leave your work to rest. Allow yourself enough time to prepare, plan, and write your work to meet your deadlines, and avoid putting yourself under the pressure of sending your work off shortly after it's been finished. No excuses.

Tip: If you want to improve your spelling, and not exclusively rely on your spell checker, especially for more complex words, try correcting the spelling yourself when it is underscored in red. In other words, don't automatically use that right-hand button on your mouse!

Chapter 4
Writing for Magazines

If you are serious about getting your work published, and looking for kudos or perhaps earnings from your writing, then writing for magazines is a good place to start.

Even with the upsurge of online news, social news and e-zines (online magazines), resulting in the exodus of many printed copy newspapers and magazines, there is still a huge market for your articles and opinion pieces. In fact, with an ever-increasing number of e-zines, one could say the market opportunities have never been greater.

The publishing industry has experienced dramatic changes over the last decade, resulting in the biggest shakeup of working practices in its history. Primarily, the meteoritic increase in internet usage, across the globe, led to the demise of publishing jobs, and at the same time caused a drastic drop in advertising revenue.

While you may be inclined to think it is the news and articles in publications that keeps them alive, you would be sadly mistaken. The cover price paid by subscribers barely covers the cost of the paper let alone the wages of journalists and editors. Advertising, or rather advertising revenue, is the back-bone to the success of a magazine, whether it is in printed format or online. As advertisers have embraced the internet and experimented with online advertising (including the use of email marketing and social media) the impact of losing this income stream has had a major effect on the continued success of almost every publication, and a catastrophic impact on the livelihood of thousands of people.

Adding further fuel to the fire, with the introduction of word processing, desktop publishing and emails, thousands of technical jobs suddenly ceased to exist. Where one article or news item used to be handled by several people, from commissioning editors, sub-editors through to editors-in-chief, proofreaders, typesetters, and the printers, suddenly work could be submitted, pages set, and printed pretty much in one fell swoop. And, with more people choosing to work from home, or working freelance, editors also saw ways to cut costs by paying per article rather than through salaries. In doing so, they also reduced their obligation to provide desks and computer equipment.

However, it's not all bad news. With all the tools at your fingertips that we have already discovered, and with a little more know-how, opportunities for freelance writers are still very much in demand.

The market still requires content on just about every conceivable topic you can imagine, from model making, crafts and hobbies to homes and gardens or specialist interests such as the military and ancestry, and that is even before we look at trade and industry or travel publications.

As trends and fashions change, some magazines will cease publication but these are often succeeded by alternatives, launched in their place. Just look at all the food, cooking and baking titles now available: *Baking Heaven Magazine, BBC Easy Cooking, Cakes & Sugarcraft, and Bake & Decorate*, to name a few, but not so many years ago very few people seemed interested in home cooking or baking.

In many respects, the job of a writer has also become so much easier, with the advantage of being able to do much of your research online and in the comfort of your home or workspace. Even interviews are almost always carried out over the telephone. However, not everything you write about should be done at your desk. A writer's life can be lonely enough without becoming a complete recluse! Moreover, your work will, without a doubt, have greater depth, and in many cases, will be easier to write if you have experienced the situation first-hand.

You will gain far more from visiting a place you intend to write about. You will get a better feel for your subject, and will be able to write more honestly, having had that face-to-face encounter. Everything you see, feel, hear, touch and taste can be written about more accurately when it is real. How could you honestly relay the heartbreak and devastation of living in a country where conflict is rife and your life hangs in the balance day after day, if you have never been in that situation? How can you explain in detail what it is like to feel the sand between your toes and taste the salt on your lips if you have never been to the seaside?

Contributor fees, and out of pocket expenses such as travel costs and hotel rooms, do play a huge part in the viability of first-hand experiences. If you are only being paid £60 to write a 500-word feature on a town event that is 100 miles away, your travel time and costs alone would outweigh your earnings, and that is before you have even put pen to paper. If, however, you could write a variety of differently angled articles about that town, and sell your work to several publications, your trip would become more feasible.

For example, while covering the town event you might find that a person of interest lives in the vicinity and you could arrange an interview. Perhaps the town was home to someone infamous or of historical importance? Maybe there is a 'bizarre' angle as the town is renowned for its annual raft race.

As part of a much larger research project on the medieval wool towns of Essex and Suffolk, I wrote several articles using some of the material I had uncovered. *A Good Yarn about Suffolk* (published in *Suffolk & Norfolk Life*), was followed by *At the Heart of Hadleigh* six months later, in the same publication, plus various other pieces for the supplement *Summer in Suffolk* and for *Essex Life Magazine*.

Equally, an editorial piece I wrote about a Suffolk-based company who handcrafted and restored traditional wooden rocking horses, could have been rewritten for a variety of different periodicals including regional magazines, a woodworking title, or even a country homes style publication.

Think creatively. Inevitably you may gather more notes and information than you can include in just one article, and you don't want to cram everything you know into one piece. Review the information you have collated and jot down as many permutations as you can imagine. Alternatively, flick through your *W&A Yearbook* to identify magazine titles and this might help you generate multiple ideas.

Research is time-consuming and can be costly, so ensure you benefit as much as possible from each of your endeavours.

What you cannot do, however, is regurgitate the same copy or sell the same article to two different publications at the same time. Most publications will require an exclusive article. Every piece you write needs to be written for a specific publication, and must meet the style, content and length of similarly-based articles in the magazine.

For example, one travel magazine may run several regular features: *My Holiday Hell, A Natural Beauty Spot* and *Beautiful Beaches Abroad.*

Chapter 4

My Holiday Hell is likely to be written in the first person, be 400-500 words long with a couple of holiday snaps. *A Natural Beauty Spot,* written in the third person voice, is 1500 words long, and covers several pages with at least six amazing images. *Beautiful Beaches Abroad* is a double page spread of 150 words dedicated to each beach along with one (photo-library provided) photograph – the whole article covers half-a-dozen locations from across the world.

In a different travel magazine, they might also cover beaches but dedicate 300 words to each beach, spreading the article over numerous pages. They might also do a piece on real-life holiday blogs of 350 words highlighting the highs or lows of a reader's trip. The point is, although they are both travel magazines (that might even cover similar topics and even the same locations) the way the articles are written, styled and published will vary enormously, and it's your job to do your research and write your pieces accordingly.

Editor's Advice

Just before we get into the nitty-gritty of writing for magazines, Richard Young, Editor of *Hertfordshire Life Magazine* very kindly shared this advice:

> *My first advice would be read the magazine you are pitching to and get a feel for the kind of content it publishes. Sounds obvious - but if you don't understand what it does, then how can you pitch an idea that is likely to be given consideration?*
>
> *Editors are very busy – the idea that there are dozens of people at all kinds of 'desks' is an anachronism. Much of journalism today is done by overstretched, dedicated people juggling all kinds of content, often wearing several different journalistic hats. A result of this is that a flood of emails reach editors every day – a big chunk of it from PR companies, as well as individuals wanting to get coverage of some kind or another, plus internal mail. Decisions about whether to read, flag-up, file, delete or respond to an email are made in seconds, sometimes milliseconds. Freelancers pitching an idea need to cut through that chatter.*
>
> *So make it easy for editors. Don't make them work hard to understand what it is you are offering. If you do, they will simply delete your email. Good journalists are clear, concise and engaging. Get that right, with an*

idea that fits what the magazine offers its readers, and you have a fighting chance.

Don't be misled by 'fits what the magazine offers' to mean the same old thing though. Editors don't want to tread the same old ground. They are always looking for original ideas or new ways to tackle a theme. Having a good sense of what is 'newsy' is also crucial. Why should the magazine publish this story/article/feature now? Why is it relevant? Editors always look for 'hooks' to hang a story on. Do bear in mind too that what is 'timely' is often being commissioned months in advance.

Head up your article pitch email with a clear statement: Freelance feature idea about XXX or similar – there's no need to be fancy. Then lay out your pitch clearly in the email. Don't go overboard – two or three paragraphs is fine. If you've already written it, then attach it in a Word document.

You may get a response back asking some questions about the idea – the editor trying to work out if the idea stands up. This may lead on to a discussion about commissioning the piece. On the other hand, you may not. This doesn't mean the idea is dead in the water - it may be filed or flagged for later attention.

If you've not heard anything back, say in a week or so, don't be afraid to follow up with a call direct to the editor you sent the article idea to, and resend the initial email if necessary. It will jog the editor's memory and is a chance to talk to them direct about your idea.

If you get a rejection, don't be downhearted. Keep coming up with ideas. Keep pitching. No editor is going to hold it against you – they need your ideas.

Richard Young, Editor, Hertfordshire Life

Readers' letters

If you are very new to writing, or looking to be published for the first time, then a reader's letter is an excellent place to begin.

For a start, readers' letters should be short and succinct, and as we have already discovered this is a key element to developing your writing skills. Every magazine that has a readers' letters page will have different requirements, and there is a trend or theme to the content of all the letters published.

Chapter 4

Weekly tabloid magazines such as *Chat* and *Take a Break* pay well for anecdotal pieces, true life mishaps and funny photo snaps. They pay between £25 and £100 if they publish your letter or photo, and more for the Star letter.

Monthly glossy magazines, including regional titles such as *Hertfordshire Life*, often prefer to give away prizes such as quality pens or bottles of champagne for one 'star letter'. The readers' letters in these magazines are often selected because they connect to an article, in a previous issue of the magazine, or relate to the content it typically covers. In this context, it could mention a Hertfordshire-based person or place.

Chat or *Take a Break* have pages and pages of letters and photo snaps but they also receive thousands of letters each week. Monthly glossies usually print three of four at most. Readers' questions pages in something like *Grow Your Own* might publish a few more.

In all cases, it is about doing your homework and research.

1. You will need to evaluate several copies or back issues to study the types of article the magazine covers and compare the information to the published readers' letters.

2. Count the number of words in each printed letter so that you can find the average. This will help you to write yours to the required length.

Why is the length important? Surely the editor will cut what he doesn't want?

Editors are very busy people. The more accurate your piece, the higher your chances of publication. This advice applies to articles, features, and editorials, as much as for readers' letters.

If you meet the editor's criteria of word count, language style, and topic (meaning the editor has minimal alterations to do to your piece) it is more likely to get published. An editor's inbox is going to be full of email submissions, with contributions and letters from people just like you. If two people send letters on similar topics but the other person sends a 300-word letter and you've sent one at 80 words, and the magazine tends to publish letters of around 50 to 100 words, whose are they likely to use?

Tip: Buying lots of magazines can be costly. Waiting rooms at doctors or dentist surgeries often have magazines for patients to read while they are waiting for an appointment – make use of these. Alternatively, contact the magazines and enquire about back issues (previously printed editions) some will happily send you some, others might make a small charge. Often, if you mention you are studying creative writing, they may send them for free, or ask for a contribution to cover the postage. Either way, you have nothing to lose, and it will cost you less than buying lots of issues of different magazines.

3. Read the submission guidelines carefully. If the magazine tells you to email: letters@chat.co.uk then do not address it to the editor. If, however, there are no direct instructions, address your email to the editor, whose email address is usually found on the publication's information or index page, generally located near the front or at the back of the magazine, or sometimes at the foot of the contents page.

Don't discount a magazine just because it doesn't pay for readers' letters. If it is a specialist interest title or covers a topic about which you are very knowledgeable, then it is worth submitting... and regularly. If the editor sees you writing and submitting worthy comments and information, and frequently, he might need another expert writer or he might have an opening for a regular contributor, and that could be you.

Also, be aware that everything you write that gets published adds to your writing portfolio, and could be just what you need to open the door to another publication. Being able to say you have been published in *OK, Hello* and *Vogue* magazine is not a lie if it is true, and could offer you a strategic advantage. If you are asked to show examples of your work, sending copies of your reader's letters is perfectly acceptable but may not land you a 3000-word editorial slot just yet.

Articles and features

What do you know?

Throughout this chapter, and the following chapters, we will explore in more detail how to write for *specialist* magazines, including craft and hobbyist publications, and travel writing. In the meantime, what else do you know?

Chapter 4

General interest magazines are everywhere, and are almost certainly the publications many writers cut their teeth on. You only have to scan the shelves of *WHSmith* or your local newsagent to appreciate how many periodicals are non-specialist, and therefore, present you, as a new writer, with an abundance of opportunities.

General interest titles are aimed at a cross-section of people, of different age groups. The content encompasses a broad spectrum of subjects, and of varying copy lengths. Often, the articles are supplied by contributing authors, and while studying several issues, you may frequently spot the same contributor's name. These writers may be in-house or staff writers, or commissioned to provide an article on a particular theme for every issue. For example, for about ten years, consecutively, I wrote the monthly Art page feature for a number of *Archant Life* magazines. For some months, I would also provide additional articles on other subjects.

Regional publications are also categorised as 'general interest' because the magazine topics vary enormously; however, the angle of each article will relate to the region in which the magazine is dedicated: Somerset, Devon, Norfolk etc.

You don't have to travel far to find something of interest to write about, unless of course, you choose to.

I reside near Hadleigh in Suffolk, a town whose eminence and fortune was founded during the medieval years. Since moving to the area, I discovered that, by comparison, Hadleigh has nearly as many listed buildings as the nearby town of Lavenham. While hundreds of tourists flock to Lavenham each year to admire its oak-beamed and ancient properties, Hadleigh's Tudor buildings are less visible. For several hundred years, after the booming wool trade of the 14th and 15th centuries, Hadleigh remained a significantly richer town, enabling wealthy residents to disguise their medieval properties with much grander Georgian facades.

Hadleigh also boasts of three rather notable structures, built within touching distance of each other, and erected within 100 years of one another. The difference between them is their construction, each one was erected using different materials and methods of the time. The flint and stone structured St Mary's Church was extended in the 1450s, although its tower is dated to the 1250s. The Guildhall, formally the Market Hall, was built in 1438, using wattle and daub, the most traditional method of the time, and the Deanery Tower, finished in 1495, is constructed of red brick, the most lavish and expensive material of the period.

The point I am trying to make is that when I moved to Suffolk I knew nothing about Hadleigh but when I went looking for topics to write about, I uncovered numerous facts about the town. I went to a couple of town talks, I took part in a guided tour of the town, and I spoke to local historians. From the information I gathered, I have published numerous articles about Hadleigh, in a variety of magazines.

If you step outside with an open mind, and explore the opportunities on your doorstep, you never know what you might discover. Every place you visit, everything you do, and every person you meet, provides potential material for your work. At the very least, it should help you generate ideas, for more than one article, and aimed at more than one publication.

Even if you have *specialist knowledge* on a given subject or are a keen hobbyist, explore ways to use your expertise and experience to contribute to general interest titles.

But, if I have *specialist knowledge* why can't I submit to specialist titles?

You can. However, you may find it more difficult, in the first instance, for editors to take a chance on you as a new writer. They may be more willing to review your ideas if you have a portfolio of other published work. Specialist titles do command specialist knowledge, and editors must be confident that you can deliver the facts and details that meet their readers' needs. If you write blogs on a particular topic, and have a good number of readers or followers this can be very useful to build your credibility.

> *Tip: As a writer, it is not essential to have a blog. However, many writers do, as they can showcase examples of their work and their expertise, and this can be useful for editors to get a feel for your writing style and abilities.*

Another way to generate ideas is to read your local or national newspaper. Look for snippets, or a small article on something that interests you. By doing further research, or following up a story, you could uncover enough information to write a longer article or two.

One of my former students was researching her family history when she discovered that one of her 'well to do' great-aunts had eloped to India with her fiancé. Unfortunately, for the love-struck couple, their ship sank and they never made it to shore, but their tragic and scandalous story did headline the society pages of a national newspaper.

Now imagine what you could do with that sort of snippet. You could research the couple involved and their direct families, but also think laterally. How many British citizens emigrated to the country during the period of British governance in India? What was it like living in India during the time of British rule?

Once you have a topic in mind, then you should decide 1) What publication(s) you might offer it to, and 2) Give the editor a reason to publish.

Every article needs a 'hook'. Editors receive numerous 'unsolicited' articles and ideas every day, and therefore, give them a reason to publish yours, and a reason to publish it sooner rather than later.

Unsolicited means an article or idea sent on spec. It is something the editor hadn't asked for, but you are hoping to convince him to publish.

Use the anniversaries of deaths, births, marriages and historical dates of importance to help you find your all-important hook. Equally, an annual event or celebration, an auction, a regeneration project or local discovery – anything that gives your piece immediate prominence.

For example, let's say my student's great-aunt was born in Shropshire in 1895, and died in April 1917. Her pitch to the editor of *Shropshire Life* Magazine for the April 2017 issue, may have said something like:

100 years ago, this month, Agnes Young of Much Wenlock, died tragically in a quest to start a new life in India.

Agnes and her fiancé, George Harper, had planned to elope to India, during the country's time in the British Empire…

While the article would contain a little more information about Agnes and George, and should include a little more about her upbringing in Much Wenlock, ultimately, it is likely to deviate into a much more interesting piece about the British occupation of India. Unless, of course, Agnes was infamous before her hasty and ill-fated departure.

Alternatively, if you can write something fresh on a seasonal topic, editors will be interested to hear from you, as they are always looking for something original, especially for the festive season. Bear in mind, however, that ideas aimed at Christmas publications need to be submitted at least six months beforehand.

In general, article deadlines for monthly magazines are at least two months ahead of the issue. E.g. the deadline for the May edition could be early March, which means you should be submitting your outline at least a couple of months before that (say January). There is absolutely no point in sending an article for the January issue in December, it will be far too late. Weekly magazines will have a much shorter lead-time but you should be submitting your query letter or concept at least four to six weeks ahead of publication. Some magazines have their main content or feature's list compiled up to a year before. While some publications will not disclose this information, others do publish their features lists. It is useful to find out what is on the features list as you could provide the content, or find comparable topics to pitch. Likewise, if you send your proposal early enough and your idea gets rejected, you still have the time to submit to another title.

Your query letter

Very few editors will want to see your completed article. In the first instance, most would prefer you to submit a query letter or email.

1. Editors are very busy; they do not have the time to read in full and respond to every article offered to them.

2. If you submit an idea, not only can they decide if the idea is viable, but they will also get a feel for your writing style and can make a judgement about how they would like you to proceed.

3. They may like your idea but want you to write it from a different angle or in a different format or style. For example, you send in an 800-word article on caring for geese and the editor would prefer it written as a questions and answers-style piece, or even, *Ten Reasons to Keep Geese*.

4. If your first submission gets rejected, it is typically not viable to completely rewrite your article to suit the style of the next publication on your list, or the next, before resubmitting.

Your email should outline your article idea. Include this as part of the body of your email or as an attached document. It is very rare these days to be asked to submit by post. Either way, refer to your *W&A Yearbook* for submission guidelines or check the publication's website for clarification.

Always write your query email/letter in a professional manner, addressing the editor by name when provided. Where possible, do your best to find out the name of the person you should be submitting to. In larger organisations, they will have commissioning editors for each of the different sections of a magazine, such as, *the interiors editor* or the *food editor*. Do as much research as you can; laziness in this area could indicate a lack of effort, and that could reflect poorly on the thoroughness of your proposed work. Only use *Dear Editor*, as a worst-case scenario. Never use terms such as *Hiya*, or *Cheers*, even in a bid to appear friendly. Keep your submission brief and spend as much time checking for grammatical errors, typos and misspellings as you would for your finished article.

Do not try to be clever or funny, unless of course you are submitting humorous articles, and don't even think about including Emojis or other symbols.

Always sign off with your full name or pseudonym (pen name) and include a contact phone number, in case the editor needs to contact you directly.

Your outline should include the title of your article (although the editor may change this), a strong opening line and first paragraph, possibly even the one you intend to use for your piece, followed by a brief summary of the facts, details, and any other evidence you intend to include in your work. Mention if you have images available, or if you plan to source them elsewhere.

Tip: Sourcing publishable quality images can be a major headache for editors; if you can, always provide 'copyright free' good quality photographs to accompany your work, but if you can't, then make the editor aware from the outset. Do not send images you have downloaded from Google images or the internet unless you have the correct permissions to reproduce them for commercial use.

Remember, to include the *hook* to entice the editor to bite, and always give them a viable reason to publish.

Do include a line or two about your published work and/or the reason the editor should accept the article from you (e.g. *because of your expertise or specialist knowledge* etc.,) but only send copies of your previously published work if asked to do so. It is not necessary to send a complete biography of all your published work, only send the details of relevant publications. E.g. if you are submitting to *Gardener's World*, you should mention if you were published in *Garden News* and *Garden Answers*, but your article in *The Woodworker* would not be relevant, unless perhaps it was an instructional piece on *How to build a vegetable Trug*!

NB: Readers' letters should always be sent as a complete piece!

Ultimately, what editors want is good stories and particularly, fresh ideas. For themed magazines, or those that cover annual events year in year out, editors need to provide their readers with original stories to bring the same topics to life, year after year. There is no point submitting a proposal to an editor on a subject that has already been covered many times before unless, of course, you have something new to voice. For instance, *The Twelve Days of Christmas* is a popular theme during the festive season, and has been covered countless times in many different magazines, but *'12 things you might not know about The Twelve Days of Christmas'* would surely grab an editor's attention. (And, yes, that has been published.) Equally, contacting an editor and suggesting an interview with Colin Firth is not going to raise an eyebrow, unless you have riveting new information about the actor that he has not previously revealed. Even if you are a close family member or friend, do not offer what you cannot deliver. Unless Colin Firth has given you permission to do an interview with him, and has agreed to shed some light on his personal life that he has not previously exposed, do not say you can do it, unless you absolutely can – lack of delivery will certainly ruin your credibility. In this particular case, it would be better to do the interview, get the information and then offer the piece, once you have the facts.

Chapter 4

Tip: Always use a recording device when interviewing people, and keep the recorded information safely stored until you are sure you won't need it again.

1. Recorded interviews can help you clarify a point you might have forgotten to note correctly.

2. You can use the information as direct quotes.

3. Your recordings could be used as supporting evidence in the defence of a defamation claim from the interviewee.

Interview-style articles and profiles

Interview-style articles come in many guises and it is worth knowing the different techniques you can use to add variety to your written work.

You might be inclined to think that interviewees are just celebrities or famous people but that is just not the case. Anyone who has a 'real-life' experience, an interesting story to tell, or even a fascinating job or hobby can be a potential interviewee. Even people you know including family, friends and work colleagues can prove viable.

Once you have found your interviewee, it is just a matter of planning your article type and deciding on the publications to approach.

Despite misconceptions, interview-style articles are not always told in the first-person voice, or from the interviewee's perspective. There are a few different ways you can present your article, but always remember that it should fit the style and format of your chosen outlet.

In the first person – Many interview or profile articles are written by someone else, even those written in the first person voice, but they give the impression they have been written by the owner of the story. Of course, if you have an 'interesting' or 'topical' personal experience that you wish to share with a wider audience, by all means write your own story as an autobiographical piece.

Although your article is to be written in the first person, don't assume that you must begin with 'I'. Your work will be far more interesting to your reader if you can pull them in with an action, statement or a quote:

It is a great privilege to be able to step, for a brief time, into the lives of others. To share stories with them, appreciate life from their point of view and put the world to rights is always fascinating. Many sitters have remained good friends.

Richard Stone, Royal Portrait Painter

The best moment came when I was on the way home from the hospital; I looked down and couldn't believe I looked like that. It was great, I was really pleased but it wasn't until my friends told me how good I looked - I knew I'd done the right thing.

Interview with Megan Davis for Shine Magazine

Third person voice with quotes – Personal experience stories, told in the third person, are desired by general interest publications and specialist titles. The writer keeps himself and his opinions out of the story but writes the piece as if he is looking in. Quotes and pull quotes are extremely important here, as they add another dimension to the article, and give it 'real time' appeal.

A quote is when the author writes word for word the actual speech spoken by a person.

Alison admits drawing has always been her passion and she labours long and hard at it. 'I am always trying to improve my technique,' says Alison, 'I learn by making mistakes and I constantly experiment with my equipment and materials looking for other ways to improve.'

Essex Life

A pull quote is a publishing term used to draw attention to a particular quote. Often the text will be in a larger font and sits somewhere else on the page from where the quote has actually been used. It is a technique used to attract the reader's attention to a specific part of the story.

Chapter 4

As our little pioneer column trotted away from Fort Jameson stables, I realized that for the next few days I would probably be the easiest meal-ticket in the entire Limpopo Valley.

Global

Expert opinion – writers will often use an expert's opinion to give credence and credibility to the topic they are writing about. The expert's opinion could be written as a quote or part of the narrative.

Hillary Clinton sparked a controversy Friday night after suggesting half of Donald Trump's supporters belonged in "a basket of deplorables" which she described as consisting of "the racist, sexist, homophobic, xenophobic, Islamaphobic – you name it."

The Guardian

Men are notoriously bad at looking after their health. "Men spend more time, cash and effort maintaining their cars than looking after themselves," says men's health expert Dr Sarah Brewer. The results of this male reticence can be serious. "The diagnosis and treatment of male cancers, lag behind high-profile female ones, in part because men are less comfortable with 'embarrassing' problems and reluctant to take ownership of their health," says leading cancer researcher Dr Clare Turnbull.

Woman & Home

Q&A (Questions and Answers) – the article is written in a simple style and includes only the interviewer's questions and the interviewee's responses. There is no other content included in the piece.

Q: So, John, tell me – how many films have you directed now?

A: This is my third film as sole director but I have also co-directed six more.

Q: Didn't you also direct 'A Shining Light' an amateur production when you were at school?

A: Yes, yes I did, but we shan't talk about that one. It's not the sort of work one tends to put on one's CV.

When writing dialogue, or quoting a person, you must always use speech or quote marks. Check your publication's house-style to see if they use single or double quotation marks for direct speech. The only exception here is when your article is a Q&A - very few publications will use speech marks in this instance, because it is obvious to the reader that the contents are direct speech, given the style of the article.

Whether you conduct your interview face to face or over the telephone, it is advisable to plan your questions in advance. Your preparation and research will help you prepare relevant questions to ask but can also help the interview stay on track.

There are a few additional things to bear in mind on this point:

1. To be a good interviewer you should also be a good listener. Although - in my experience - writers and journalists can often talk for England, it is essential that you learn when to be quiet and listen, and when to talk.

2. Your interviewee may be very confident when it comes to being interviewed and will happily answer your questions but he may also take you on a different tangent. Having your questions pre-prepared can help you bring the interview back in the direction you want to take it. Be aware, however, if your interviewee does reveal something unexpected you may want to follow his lead, as this may help you write a more interesting piece.

3. If your interviewee is less confident, shy, or gives one word or closed answers, your pre-prepared questions can help keep the interview going, and avoid those awkward moments of silence.

4. Some interviewees like to be prepared and may ask to see your questions prior to the interview taking place.

5. Some interviewees will ask to see the draft copy of your article before submission. It is entirely up to you whether you agree or not. On the one hand, it can be useful as your interviewee can point out any misquotes or perhaps where you have misunderstood his meaning, or even where you may have made a mistake about something important like dates or places. On the other hand, your interviewee may not like your piece at all and completely rewrite it. This obviously causes problems as it is no longer your work, and may not fit the style of the publication or editor's requirements. Alternatively, the interviewee may insist on

adding information that he felt should be included, that perhaps you did not - the difficulty here can be that the revised version is longer than your desired word count.

During the interview try to stay calm and relaxed, as this will also put your interviewee at ease. Be polite and do not try and trip your interviewee up or draw him onto uncomfortable subjects or taboo topics – you're not a tabloid journalist.

It is customary to seek permission to record the interview but if your interviewee is reluctant, politely point out that it is in his best interests to agree – as nobody likes to be misquoted. Don't rely on your memory. It is advisable to make written notes too, as you cannot and should not totally rely on your recording device – technology does have a way of screwing things up, and usually at the most inconvenient moment.

Always thank your interviewee after the event, and whenever possible send a copy of the published article or, even better, the complete magazine issue or newspaper it has been published in.

Online magazines and e-zines

The only obvious differences between printed copy publications, online magazines, and e-zines is the published format and layout. (An e-zine is a magazine published only in an electronic format.)

Exactly the same approach is required when writing for e-zines as for printed versions. Editors want and need fresh, original content that is well-written and publishable. It must be written to meet the language, style and tone of the magazine and word counts will still apply. You may find dedicated e-zines have slightly lower copy-counts than their printed counterparts, because, onscreen, we read differently compared to how we read hard-copy. However, online magazines that replicate the content of their printed versions will often use the same copy but with a different layout. Article contents are often shown as headlines with a standfirst, and followed by 'clickable links', through to the main body of the article.

Standfirst - (Journalism & Publishing term) an introductory paragraph in an article, printed in larger or bolder type or in capitals, that summarizes the article.

www.thefreedictionary.com

Some publishers have opted for e-zines which are displayed in the same format as their traditional magazines; in other words, a digital copy of the printed version that uses page-turning technology so reading is done page by page, in a conventional way.

Your query email, outlining your idea, should also be the same, irrespective of the magazine's format, unless you are asked to use an electronic form. Your images will be of equal importance too. And so will the deadlines.

The deadline is the date your final copy should be submitted. Deadlines are VERY important. Lots of things happen between when you submit your copy and when it makes it to the page. Editors have to double check your facts and query anything that might not be clear. They check your article for its readability, proofread it, and ensure the inclusion of any necessary acknowledgements. They may be able to use the images you supplied or they may have to source alternatives.

One of the most frustrating parts of an editor's job is when writers miss deadlines. Do not, without very good reason, miss a deadline. Wherever possible, submit your copy early... editor's will thank you for it. The easier you can make your editor's job, the more likely he is to give you more work.

Tip: It is in your best interests to do as your editor asks. Do not be too precious about your title or, in fact, your copy. The editor knows what she needs to satisfy her readers, so if she asks you to clarify a fact or source, or asks you to rewrite your article, or even tells you to cut your copy – there is no point in questioning her unless it is absolutely necessary.

Article structure

Now you know how to generate ideas, find suitable markets, conduct an interview, and submit a query letter to an editor - it is time to understand how to compose your article.

Titles – Do not get too hung up on your title. You could waste a lot of time trying to come up with the perfect title and yet, when your article is published, the editor changes it anyway! Start with a working title if something more imaginative doesn't spring to mind immediately, you can always change it later. Try and pick something that helps you stay focused on the article's theme or topic.

Titles are important. They need to catch the attention of your reader, and they should always be relevant to the article topic. Titles don't have to be masterpieces or the work of a genius. A plain title can create as much impact as an imaginative one. However, your title should always fit the general title style of your publication. Titles can be: a play on words, a trigger, a straightforward message, humorous, controversial, ask a question, persuasive, or a promise. In these early days, practice writing titles in other ways.

A good yarn about Suffolk

Woolly words from Suffolk

The 10 best Wool Towns in Suffolk

A Suffolk Wool Town Trail

Discover Suffolk the Wool Way

5 things you didn't know about Suffolk

Headline or Standfirst – Some publications use titles followed by a standfirst, others use a headline instead of a title. The concept is the same – headlines are used to grab the reader's attention but where a title might only be one or a few words long, a standfirst is like a summary sentence:

Headline: "Every Internet Entrepreneur Regrets Not Doing This Sooner"

Title: Iconic Pop that Rocks

Standfirst: Essex Photographer, Bill Orchard was a major part of the 1960s and 70s Pop scene and a collection of his iconic photographs will be on display at Hayletts Gallery in Maldon this month in aid of the Helen Rollason Cancer Charity. Caroline Foster reports...

Opening paragraph – This is your showcase! Your opening paragraph is without a doubt the most important part of your article. It has to do many things – it must hold the editor's and reader's attention, it should be relevant to the rest of the article, and it should lead the reader through the first paragraph and on to the remainder of the article.

Your opening paragraph should not be dull, obscure, be too involved or lose touch with the theme of your piece. It won't matter how good the rest of your article is if you fail to impress the editor or your reader here… they won't bother with the remaining paragraphs.

Try to keep your opening paragraph brief and to the point. Your sentences should be short and succinct. Do not try to cram too many ideas into your opening but give your reader enough to get them interested.

Example opening:

Photographer Bill Orchard hasn't strayed far from his Essex roots and yet his iconic pop images have brought him world-wide recognition. Hayletts Gallery in Maldon, is delighted to be given the opportunity to show his celebrity photographs, in what is only the second exhibition of his collection.

Middle / The rest of your article – the article body – should be written in the same style as your opening paragraph, but this is where you pack in the facts and the detail. Many new writers fail to include enough facts to give their article substance. Try and include as much relevant information as possible but stay on track. It is very easy to wander off on a different tangent and lose focus. Pre-plan what information you want to include and leave out irrelevancies or material that could be better used in another feature.

It is always better to overfill your piece as you can cut superfluous material during the editing process – but it's much harder to pad an article out if you have failed to include enough data in the first instance.

Another easy mistake to make is to cram everything into your first three of four paragraphs and have nothing left for the remaining piece. Aim for balance.

Example of main body:

In 1957, after winning first prize in a photography magazine competition, Bill was fortunate enough to be taken on by Bishops Studio in Fleet Street as an assistant. At the tender age of 17, he began to take cover pictures for women's magazines and was reckoned to be the youngest person to do this at the time. The 1958 printer's strike had a profound effect on the city and Fleet Street, and Bill, like many other workers in the printing industry found himself without a job. But this was all the encouragement Bill needed to start freelancing. He also managed to get a part-time job working nights, for the aristocrat photographer Anthony Armstrong-Jones in Shaftsbury Avenue.

Chapter 4

Bill got a lucky break shortly afterwards and started working with the photographer Brian Worth. In 1960, he worked with Brian on the very first publicity pictures for Coronation Street for Granada Television. Bill's career began to flourish as new bands and pop singers emerged wanting to be photographed out on the town. The Beatles, Rolling Stones, Cliff Richard, David Bowie and many other musicians and pop artists were more than happy to have their pictures taken and Bill's collection encapsulates the very essence of the music scene during the swinging 60s, as well as the personalities of these artists at the time. Bill worked for major publications such as Today, The Telegraph, The Mail, The Mirror and had the privilege of touring alongside many A-list bands. Bill also worked for TV companies and was a weekly photographer for Ready Steady Go.

End – Endings can often be the most troublesome part of writing your article. When you have put a lot of time and effort into your opening paragraph, and worked through your sequence of facts and detail to create the body of your piece, how are you going to bring it to a conclusion?

There are a couple of techniques you can use to help write an ending that is worthy of your piece. You can summarise your article, you can end at the beginning, or you can leave your readers with a question or quandary.

Reiterating some of the facts and bringing your piece to a natural conclusion is one of the most traditional methods used to end an article. Using terms such as 'in retrospect, in conclusion, or the time has come' may help you achieve this.

If you choose to end at the beginning, your aim is to bring your article full circle. You might start with a present-day quote from your subject, the main content is a reflection of his journey up to now, and then you end with a comment or quotation that links to the very first line – in this case, the opening quote. This type of ending is effective and not easy to master, but if you plan your piece carefully from the start, this type of ending can be used to great effect.

A great ending is to leave your reader wanting to know more. If you can end your article with a question, or leave your subject in a quandary, your readers may not thank you for it – but it will give them food for thought.

What you must not do is leave your readers confused, angry, or agitated. They can feel slightly miffed by your outcome, but anger and confusion may result in heated letters to your editor, and she may or may not be very happy about that.

Example ending:

The collection includes around 40 different photographs, some in colour and some black and white. Each one is a hand-signed limited edition photograph, on sale at an affordable price as Bill is giving the proceeds to the Helen Rollason Cancer Charity. Hayletts Gallery is also giving a percentage of their commission to the same charity.

Sally from Hayletts said she is delighted to have Bill's iconic collection of British rock and pop photographs at Hayletts and that it should not be missed, especially as it is being done to raise funds for such a worthy cause.

Remuneration

So, what can you earn as a writer?

We have established that readers' letters can pay anything up to £100, or the chance to win a very nice prize, and they can also help you build a portfolio of published work.

However, in respect to pounds and pence for articles, features and editorials – the sky's the limit.

As vague as that may sound it is very true. Publication rates vary considerably from one magazine to another, and the pay can vary due to the style of the magazine, the type of article, its length, and the experience of the writer. Some editors offer a fixed rate per article, others pay by the word or per 1,000 words. Many publications adhere to NUJ guidelines or at least offer the minimum NUJ recommended rate.

As an example, monthly glossy titles such as *Cosmopolitan* or *Grazia* pay somewhere between £300 and £500 for a feature, whereas a regional magazine such as *Dalesman* may only pay around £70. Some will also pay extra for photographs and illustrations.

Check the newspaper and magazine listings in your *W&A Yearbook*, some rates have been shown where publications have provided the details, others will say 'by arrangement' or 'by negotiation'.

Chapter 4

The above, however, is also subject to the rights you sell. You may be asked to assign *'all rights'* or you might just be assigning *'First British Serial Rights'*.

> *When you sell 'first serial rights' to a newspaper, magazine or periodical for a piece of work you've written, that media outlet has the right to be the first to publish the article. After the piece runs, you're free to resell it [as second rights] to another medium or to package a collection of your work into a book.*
>
> *When a magazine buys 'all rights' to your work, they own that particular piece and the specific way the article is written. [All rights includes print, online, digital and other media]. By writing another article on the same topic and giving it a new twist, you will have created a new piece of work that has its own copyrights.*

www.writersdigest.com

Rates vary considerably depending on the type of publication, the advertising revenue it generates, and its circulation figures.

Is there anything I can do if I'm not happy with the rate offered?

Any negotiations in respect of rates will be between you and the editor. If you are not happy with the rate offered, you can go back to the editor and state your claim, giving valid reasons why you think your rate should be higher. However, you will stand very little chance of negotiating a better rate if you have little or no publishing experience. If you are not happy with the result, you can decide not to write for that publication and offer your piece to another title, providing you haven't already signed a contract or committed yourself to providing the piece before fee negotiations.

Contracts

Most publications will offer proper, legally binding contracts which set out your obligations and the agreed fee, others will not. In some cases, you may just agree on the rate via email. Some publications will send a remittance, and this is nearly always the case for readers' letters. Others will ask you to provide an invoice. Payment details are usually set out in the contract but if they are not, ensure you state your payment terms on your invoice.

It is quite normal for publications to pay up to 30 days after the month of publication issue, so bear that in mind when submitting your piece in March for May publication – it is likely you will not get paid until at least June. And, if the publication of your article gets delayed, which can happen, you may have to wait even longer. Although it took one magazine 18 months to publish a feature I submitted, this is very rare. Content can date and quite quickly. Delays can happen, but do not hassle the editor if the article you expected to appear in a particular issue does not. By all means, politely enquire or ask for an explanation. In most instances, your article is likely to be rescheduled for another issue but if the agreed article is accepted by the editor but does not make it into the publication, you should receive a *kill fee*. This fee will vary, again publication to publication, but it is usually an agreed rate between you and the editor.

The NUJ recommends that any work commissioned and delivered on time and to specification should be paid for in full, whatever happens to it after that.

However, in many cases a kill fee may typically only be half the agreed fee. If you are very lucky there may still be time for you to offer your work to another publication.

Coping with rejection

Rejection is part and parcel of a writer's life. It comes with the job – get over it!

We writers may have sensitive souls but we have to face the reality that our feelings and pride may get bruised each and every time our work gets rejected. When you have ploughed hours and hours of time, research, and energy into preparing the best piece of work you can, and you are positive the editor is going to love it – but it comes back with a swift 'no' – you will want to know why.

Do NOT hastily send an email to the editor demanding to know why your suggestion to write *The Ten Best Tips to Grooming Persian Cats* was rejected.

There are many valid reasons your piece could be refused, and it may have very little to do with the writing. However, that's the first thing you should check.

Chapter 4

1. When you receive a rejection, review with a critical eye what you sent in the first place – and ask yourself if it can be improved. Try and be objective.

2. Don't waste time feeling sorry for yourself or scrutinising the rejection letter. Start afresh – not all your work will be rejected. As your experience grows and your writing improves, the number of rejections should progressively reduce, assuming of course, that you are adhering to the guidelines and have done your publication research thoroughly.

3. Just because it was unwanted by one editor does not mean another will also reject it. Once you have looked at your idea objectively, find another publication to submit it to. Do your magazine research to ensure it fits the magazine's criteria – and when it does – send it off again.

Other reasons for rejection include: the editor did not like your concept or it does not suit his readership, he may have covered a similar topic recently, or he has already commissioned a similar piece from another writer. Editors, often receive many great ideas but they just can't print them all – they haven't got the page space.

Do not despair, put it down to experience and move on.

> *Tip: Very occasionally you may see an article, similar to the one you suggested, in the magazine that rejected yours. Don't instantly assume they stole your idea. The chances are it is purely coincidental; that someone else submitted a similar idea to yours, or that it was already commissioned. There is no copyright on ideas and you would have a very hard job proving the publication stole yours.*

Columns

One thing we have yet to touch on is your opinion.

In the majority of your writing, your opinion is irrelevant and should be kept out of your work. Unless you are someone of notable importance – a celebrity, a politician perhaps, or a highly-respected journalist – sadly no one is interested in who you are, or what you have to say.

There are, of course, exceptions to the rules. Unless you are writing a first-hand experience piece, *'My heart surgery'* or a travel piece such as *'Travels Across India'* or a blog perhaps, then your articles should only contain relevant information and the facts, and your opinions should be kept to yourself. If, instead, you have managed to secure yourself a magazine column, then your opinion may be just what the editor and his readers seek.

> *Columns, like features, come in many forms. They are defined by ownership; the column "belongs" to its author who has that ultimate journalistic luxury, a slot, guaranteed space over which he or she presides and has, in some cases, near total control over content. The assumption is that readers seek out the writer first rather than the subject matter, because they are interested in that writer's opinion, whether or not they agree with it.*

www.theguardian.com

Columns come in a variety of forms. Celebrity columns often cover a multitude of topics with the celebrity commenting on other celebrity news or current affairs. Then you have fashion columnists, gardening, financial and banking, current affairs or political correspondents. These columnists are *specialist* writers, and they write knowledgeably, informatively, in a lively way, and sometimes humorously on their chosen subject, and are eager to share their opinions.

Columns are not always written in the first-person voice, it is about the columnist's ability to get a reaction from his readers, whether that is in agreement, disagreement or for amusement.

> *The good column will have a clear identity, so that the readers will feel they know the writer, his or her prejudices, enthusiasms and obsessions. The best columns inform the opinions of the readers; the best "me" columns are retold by their readers as though they are gossiping about friends.*

www.theguardian.com

Editors love reader interaction, even when expressed in anger, frustration or disbelief. Often, they desire these types of reactions over readers who wholeheartedly agree with the author.

Chapter 4

Being a columnist requires a more dedicated approach to writing than perhaps any other form. For a start, no editor is just going to grant you a column, irrespective of how persuasive your case may be. You should demonstrate a level of consistency, dedication and a thorough knowledge of your subject before they will even consider you. In some cases, you may be lucky enough to spot an opening or opportunity but, still, the editor will want to see some credentials or writing experience relevant to the column subject.

You stand more chance of becoming a columnist if you have been regularly contributing to the publication. Once the editor has a feel for your commitment and writing style, he is more likely to consider you as a regular columnist.

With the popularity of blogs and blogging, some bloggers, who have shown real potential and commitment to sharing their knowledge and experience, and more importantly, have a wide audience or loyal readership, have been offered the opportunity to write a regular magazine column.

Most columns are shorter in length than newspaper and magazine articles, usually around 350 to 1000 words. The writing is tight and yet engaging, and the format is often predictable. Column content, however, is less predictable and original. Readers should feel the information and author's insight is new and refreshing; it's what keeps them coming back for more.

Although readers will identify with the style and theme of your column, especially over longer periods of time – this is what keeps them engaged – your job is to keep your column interesting and appealing. Being able to write fresh, original and engaging copy on such a regular basis, and in the format your readers yearn for, will take all the writing skills you can muster.

Plan your work carefully. Keep up to date with the current trends in your field, and stay connected to your readers. If writing satire or humour doesn't come naturally then find another style, one you are comfortable with, and one you can maintain. Readers will always spot a fake, and readers are very quick to let you know when you have got something wrong or are misinformed.

Being a columnist does come with a certain prestige, not to mention a stream of regular payments, and who knows to what else it might lead?

Women's magazines

Writing for women's magazines is probably one of the most competitive sectors to break into (alongside travel writing). However, women's magazines are dominant in the market, presenting many opportunities to find an opening. Pages dedicated to women's issues in national newspapers and in their weekend supplements are also worth reviewing.

One of the reasons why women's magazines are so widespread is that publications for women have to provide material for such a diverse group, from single teenage girls to the elderly lady, young mothers and the professional career woman. Magazines like *The Lady* and *Woman Magazine* have dominated the shelves for decades because they've got the formula right, while other titles have tried and failed.

Do not assume that hobbyist titles, home, lifestyle or cooking and baking magazines are just read by women, it wouldn't be politically correct to do so, and research suggests that today's men are just as keen to learn more about domestic activities such as cooking, gardening, and parenting, as their sisters, wives, and mothers.

In turn, men's health matters including beauty treatments and maintenance, skin care products, cosmetic surgery, and relationship issues are also 'hot topics' with an ever-increasing audience.

One area where gender may impact success is the Feminist Press where articles are primarily written for women by women. Male writers who really want to contribute to these types of magazines might consider using a female pseudonym.

Topics for feminist magazines tend to have a greater bias towards hard news than articles aimed at women's mainstream publications. If you do want to write feminist-style articles, make sure your content is current. *Working Mothers' versus Stay at Home Mums* is old news while *Female CEO's* is still relevant. Nevertheless, you would have to find something fresh and original on this topic as new stories about *'not enough women in top boardroom positions'* is already wearing thin.

Chapter 4

Tip: When writing these types of articles, consider using 'expert opinions'. Contact organisations or governing bodies relevant to your topic, or use statistics from surveys or public opinion polls to help substantiate your story.

Women's titles embrace just about every conceivable subject that affects the lives of today's women including: fashion, health, beauty, relationships, money, careers, education, parenting, homes, lifestyle, and hobbies. Within each of these genres, the articles are written in many different formats: *real-life stories, triumph over tragedy, issue-based, product reviews, Q&As, ask the expert,* and *celebrity interviews.* And, while women's magazines are definitely not all the same, they can be roughly categorised into three different types of publication:

1. Weekly tabloid (or sensationalist style) such as *Chat, Take a Break, That's Life.*

2. Mainstream or glossy, such as *Woman & Home, Glamour,* and *The Lady.*

3. Specialist such as *InStyle, Mother & Baby,* and *Families First.*

The *weeklies,* as they are often called, are (in the main) printed on thin paper, they are extremely colourful and the cover-page is a jigsaw of big headlines and lots of images of women. The cover is designed to draw you in, and get you excited about the magazine's contents with strong headlines, shocking news or celebrity gossip. This format is carried throughout the magazine. Some pages have lots of snippets, photos and captions; even the feature and article pages have colourful *pull quotes,* lots of images, and *sensationalist headings.*

Do not be mistaken that the articles inside the publication are just gossip or about people seeking their 'five minutes of fame', some of the issues covered often have very serious undertones and consequences, or have been shared by heartbroken individuals. Some carry a message of hope and forgiveness, others, perhaps, are a warning to readers about the scandalous behaviour of love cheats or fraudsters. These types of stories are often written by in-house or staff writers, or sourced through specialist agencies, but that does not mean to say that if you have a real-life case study (your own or someone else's) the magazine won't be interested. However, the owner of the story must be willing to be named and photographed or they will not run the article. The publication may also want exclusive rights and will not be interested if the piece, as a whole or in part, has been published before in another magazine.

It is absolutely essential that you study several copies of the magazine you want to pitch your article to. You must familiarise yourself with the content and style in which the copy is written, the word count, and what topics are covered.

During your research, you may also spot an opening for an idea about something that does not appear to have been covered recently.

Women's *mainstream* or *glossy magazines* overall, tend to be monthly. The high-end finish, heavier weight paper, general content, and product advertising smacks of 'expensive', not to mention the cover price ranging from £3 to £6 per issue. The content style, language, layout and format will be subtler and less 'in your face'. Most of the covers will have one central image with perhaps a few article headlines and one or two offers to grab your attention, but these won't be screaming at you. The articles and features will be a combination of personal stories, celebrity interviews, and lots of advice on health, relationships, money matters, etc., depending on the genre of the magazine.

Take a publication like *Homes & Lifestyle*. It may feature a celebrity's home or a reader's home makeover, and even though the magazine is targeted towards those interested in homemaking (and not just general women's topics) there are similarities to consider. These parallels can also help you pitch your idea(s) to more than one publication.

An appropriate example here is *Good Housekeeping*. Covering topics such as baking, healthy eating guides, relationship tips, fashion, hair and beauty, gadgets for the home, toys for the kids, breakaways and family day's out, this magazine uses various different formats to cover everyday topics and concerns. One issue, for example, included *'Posh' products contain more sugar than their budget counterparts, 5 things you should never say to someone with autism*, and *how to declutter your bedroom*.

Specialist titles are similar in design to mainstream/glossy magazines in terms of the layout, style and format. The difference between the mainstream and specialist titles for women is that the latter will predominantly focus on just one or two topics or themes. For example, *Mother & Baby* primarily covers matters relating to… ahem… mothers and babies, but the articles comprise of anything from concerns expressed by new mothers to baby-friendly holiday destinations. The subjects covered will vary every month so use your creative skills here. Child-friendly vehicles, best baby buys, health issues for mother or baby, exercising with your baby, finding love as a single parent – in effect, anything and everything(!) that women care about could be covered or discussed from a new mother's perspective.

In turn, something like *Women's Fitness* is described as *'an upbeat magazine focusing on exercise, healthy eating and wellbeing'*. These topics could also include *eating less sugar, how decluttering your home can help clear your mind* or *exercising with your family*. In fact, all these ideas could be highly suitable for *Good Housekeeping* magazine too.

Writing for women's magazines is perhaps one of the genres where you could write from personal experiences, irrespective of whether you are a male or female writer. Has anything happened to you, a family member or a friend, people you have met whilst travelling, an emotional story, a health issue, some family trauma, an amusing or sad incident – any situation that can be turned into an article or story for a women's publication?

If you are an expert in your field, if you have an interesting job or hobby (or know someone who does) see if you can come up with a creative angle to suit one of the many women's titles.

You do not have to sensationalise your story, it could be that you are a fitness instructor and you have just taken a course in a new 'dance style' exercise class – after all, *Zumba* was new once!

The articles and features in the glossies tend to have much longer word counts than their tabloid counterparts, and will cover subjects in more depth, often over several pages. Expert opinions or other specialist advice will be more welcome here too, as the editors will be looking for lots of facts and less sensationalism. Editors will be looking for ideas that link to current subjects, including the latest television series or celebrity news. Anything to do with new trends, fads and fashions, 'hot news' or latest must-haves, will be door openers for you, but you really have to offer something fresh or write it from a new angle.

In doing your research, you will also discover that some subjects or article themes are covered month in month out, or are more frequently reported than others. Scrutinise several issues, see who is writing about what topics (and how often), keep an eye on new trends and fads, and get your ideas in early. Your timing can be as crucial as the idea itself.

Specialist magazines

Where do we start on specialist titles?

Think of a topic, any topic, and you are likely to find a specialist magazine that covers it. Embracing just about every imaginable subject, specialist titles can be found that cover religion and politics, sport, exercise and health, art and music, history and ancestry, pets and stock animals, equestrianism and horseracing, cars, bikes and aeroplanes, technology and gaming, science and nature, and so much more. Just browse the magazine section of the *W&A Yearbook* and you will be blown away by the diversity of subjects covered. Better still, scan the shelves of *WHSmith* or your local newsagents and your mind will boggle at the vast array of titles available.

That is your marketplace, your prospects, and endless possibilities. However, before you get too excited, regardless of what special interests you have, to pitch work to any of these titles you ought to know your stuff. Here, more than anywhere, editors will only consider work from you if, and when, you can prove you can deliver what readers want. Many readers may well have more knowledge and experience than you, irrespective of the field you are writing about, and make no mistake, they WILL contact an editor if the information you include in your article is out of date or misinformed. The editor himself will, of course, know his subject matter inside and out, but it is guaranteed that many readers will know even more than him.

That said, not everyone has the inclination to be an author. Not everyone has the time to do the study and research required to write about their favourite topic, and many would not even know where to start.

Chapter 4

A lot of people believe you have to be an expert in that field to write for a specialist magazine. While knowing a decent amount about the subject helps, it isn't the be all and end all. More important is the drive to find the information you need to produce the best copy you can. You've got to be bold and not be afraid to ask questions, especially if the person you are interviewing/speaking to isn't giving you the information you need.

Gemma Padley, www.wannabehacks.co.uk

If you have a special interest or two, chances are that you are already keeping up-to-date with the latest developments in that industry or arena, and aware of what is happening in the world of your chosen subject. You may subscribe to one or more publications covering your interest or specialism and, if you are, this will help you appreciate what is already being written about, and where there are gaps that you could fill. And, if you're not, and you intend to write about your specialist interest, then it would be advantageous to subscribe to either hard-copy or online issues, and access other information relating to your topic of interest, such as blogs.

Let's look at fitness and exercise. This is now a massive industry, and there are countless magazines dedicated to general sports and fitness. Equally there are many committed to specialist sports, some written just for women, and some specifically aimed at men. You might be keen on triathlons, and may have even competed in a few. You do not consider yourself an expert triathlete but you may be able to put together an interesting article, using your own experiences: *Triathlete Training for Beginners, the Diary of a Novice Triathlete,* or *Eating to Compete* – of course, your magazine research will tell you if these have been done before (and they probably all have) and by which magazines.

But it is *how* you write it, *how* you submit your ideas, and *how* relevant your story is, that will secure you the commission.

Instead of tackling the whole theme in one go, why not look at just one element of the sport? Something along the lines of: *Taking care of those triathlete Legs, Building Stamina to Tackle those Hills,* or *Swim to Win.*

And, ensure you also include facts and statistics from other relevant sources and organisations. You are bound to be able to find out how many triathlons are held in the UK each year, and how often. Equally, you could think globally. *Where is the most difficult course, the coldest water,* or *the hardest course to cycle?*

Be creative. Use questions to help build an article of relevance. Asking *Who, What, Why, Where* and *When* is the perfect place to start. Irrespective of what subject you are writing about, the *5Ws* will help you come up with an idea and help you to develop it.

You might be interested in steam railways, and have religiously read every issue of the *Heritage Railway Magazine*, which covers all aspects of Britain's network of preserved railways. Now, before you ask the question what could I possibly write about that has not already been written about – do not be defeatist. The UK has a massive network of historic railways and railway enthusiasts, and something new or newsworthy is happening all the time. It could be a railway line extension, a station house restoration project, a rusty shell of a steam engine brought back to life, a carriage refit – yes, these things happen and happen almost every day.

The magazine cannot possibly report on everything, the editor would not have the time or the resources to do so, and he relies on his sources and his writers to help keep his readers informed – one of which could be you.

Although some more media- or PR-savvy organisations will regularly send articles and press releases to these magazines in the hope of some free exposure, many do not. The majority of historic railways are run by volunteers, those interested in preserving the steam trains and railway network, but those people, dealing with the everyday jobs of maintenance and upkeep, may not have the wherewithal or know-how to keep these railway enthusiast magazines informed of their latest developments.

Put yourself in that place. Use social media to like their sites, sign-up to their newsletters, or become a member to access information the public cannot. Stay informed of the latest news and developments, or even become a volunteer, and offer to provide media support, as this will enable you to put yourself between the organisation and the media, and stand as an invaluable link.

However, *Heritage Railways* is not the only magazine for steam and railway enthusiasts: *The Railway, Steam Railway, Steam World, Steam Days, Old Glory, Rail, Rail Gazette, Railway Herald,* and *Trains,* all cover various aspects of the rail industry – so broaden your horizons, collect back issues, and do your research. Discover which magazines cover which topics and how, and see what and where you could fill some pages. Remember to use the content you gather in numerous ways, and submit to more than one publication.

Then use the information you have gathered, or articles you have written, and submit different ideas to the general interest titles too. *The Bluebell Railway* in Sussex, for example, may have an annual open day or special event days; you could go along this year, gather information and take photographs and use what you have learned for an article aimed at *Sussex Life*, in time for next year's event, coupled with lots of photographs showing the crowds of enthusiasts that attended. Alternatively, they may have a special engine for the day or the launch of a recently restored train which – with a bit more *'insider'* information – could be offered to one of the specialist titles.

You could even interview one of the volunteers and write a piece on *How to Be a Volunteer* – explaining what is involved, and the difference it can make to the survival of a small enthusiasts' steam railway.

Irrespective of the topic or theme that appeals to you, applying these techniques to specialist interest titles will help you get a foothold and see your work published.

Overseas markets

It is worth noting, here, the potential of overseas markets. There are many preserved railways or railway networks across the world which could make interesting topics for articles and features in UK-based magazines. Furthermore, it is the same the other way around. There are railway enthusiasts across the world who would love to know more about the British railway and steam networks. Visitors from America, Europe, China, and beyond, love to visit the UK's steam railways, meaning you could be pitching to those overseas magazines too. Also, consider in-flight and tour operator magazines, these markets are specialists in their own right but also cover a wide variety of general interest material for tourists, travellers, and globetrotters.

Of course, for everything you write about for the UK market there is likely to be an overseas market equivalent. Referring back to triathlons, many people across the world are triathletes who may be interested in competing in UK-based events. Variety is the spice of life, so while you might get excited about an event in the Netherlands, the Dutch may want to compete against you in Scotland.

Primarily, unless you are fluent in another language, you might want to stick with countries where English is widely spoken and printed, including Canada, Malaysia, Africa, and much of Europe these days.

If you are interested in writing for American magazines in particular, and it's an obvious choice, the annual *Writer's Market Guide* is the *W&A Yearbook's* US equivalent.

Your approach, your submissions, and your content for overseas markets are primarily the same as they are for the UK, and your research here is equally as important. If you are not a frequent traveller, you may have to find other ways to review these magazines. You should also check what currency you will be paid in, and what charges your UK bank may apply for receiving foreign currency and currency exchange, as this may have an impact on the viability of writing for an overseas publication.

Trade and industry publications

The opportunities to write for trade and industry publications are gargantuan. For a start, what jobs have you done? For every conceivable job, industry, profession, trade, market (whatever you want to call it) there is at least one publication dedicated to it whether that is banking or investments, building trades, technical, IT or computing, domestic services, public services, grocery, retail clothing, manufacturing, mining, utility services... the list goes on and on.

It may be hard to believe, but despite the number of these types of publications, many freelance writers do not even consider submitting to trade and industry publications.

Why, you may ask.

Chapter 4

Breaking into trade magazines as a freelance writer can be tricky. Many editors of trade magazines choose not to list their writer's guidelines. Editors of trade magazines are extremely busy and short-staffed. These editors avoid having an open call for submissions to avoid a ceaseless cycle of reviewing, critiquing and rejecting unsolicited articles and query letters sent in by writers, non-writers and their moms.

Many freelance writers break into trade magazines by pitching an idea to the editor or contacting the editor directly. These freelance writers pitch brilliant article ideas, they've reviewed the magazine in advance, and they aggressively market themselves and their work with confidence.

www.freelancewriting.com

Although newsagents do stock some magazines dedicated towards certain trades such as farming and horticulture, commercial vehicles and haulage, and writing, and you can pick up grocery titles while doing your supermarket shop, trade and industry publications are generally sold on a subscription- or members-only basis. This means they are not that easy to get hold of, and as your first task is always to review several copies before submitting an idea, writers who are 'less inclined' to make the effort don't bother. Needless to say, there are other ways and means to get hold of magazine copies. Ask family and friends what publications they read in connection with their business. What about your car mechanic, hairdresser, dentist, accountant, your local pub landlord or restaurant owner? These people will have access to magazines relating to their industry or will know of titles you can pursue.

Think of an industry and do an online search using simple keywords. Not only will you find various titles relating to the industry but you will be able to access their websites, obtain back copies, and identify whether they are e-zine or published in printed format. If it is an industry for which you already have some knowledge, and for which you may be able to write, consider subscribing to the publication, at least until you are published with them, then you may receive a free copy containing your work as well.

You can also get a comprehensive list of publications from the *Willings Press Guide*, an annual publication containing details of the world's media in two volumes: UK & Ireland and *World News Media*, but it's not cheap; at over £300 for one volume, make sure you are committed to earning from your freelance writing in order to claw back this expense.

While the above shows you the markets available, what about the content?

Much of the content for trade and industry publications comes from two main sources (1) In-house writers and staff (2) PR and marketing departments and companies.

In-house or staff writers cannot, however, cover everything to do with their industry. They may have access to several CEOs or industry professionals who feed them valuable information, but they may only be able to include larger organisations or those in city locations, which limits the stories they can report on.

Good PR and marketing companies will keep the industry titles fuelled with the latest acquisitions and mergers, technological advances, expansions, key staff promotions and product launches, and this material is invaluable to help fill magazines. Featured companies are often advertisers within the publication but the PR company's job also means securing as much 'free space' as possible.

The downside to the numerous press releases that editors of trade and industry magazines receive is that the copy is obviously biased towards the company the story relates to, and is often over-worded and unsuitable for publication in its original form. Editors either spend considerable time cutting and rewriting the content or pick out the headline information to use as short snippets, fillers, and news pieces.

Now, this is where you come in. Is there a new shop or business opening in your neighbourhood? Whether it is a boutique clothing store or an artisan bakery, there is a publication or two interested in that – try either a general retail publication like *Retail Week* or an industry-specific title such as *Baker Magazine*. Has a large company just moved into vacant offices or had one purpose-built? It could be a solicitors or accountancy firm, in which case, you might pitch to the *Solicitors Journal* or *The Accountant*. Is your high street thriving with a hub of new retail outlets or is it standing the test of time with family businesses that have been in the same shop for decades? A jewellery store perhaps? Try *Professional Jeweller* or a florist – *The Florist Magazine*. Is there an influx of similar style outlets? If so, you might want to write a piece on the trend and why there are so many

Chapter 4

similar shops opening. Is there a new betting shop opening? Then *Betting and iGaming News* or *Betting Business* magazine could be worth a try.

Writing for trade and industry titles may not seem very glamorous. I know from experience that writing about some industries, which even the business owners themselves declared to be 'boring', was a challenge, but when needs must it is surprising how much you can write about re-sealable plastic bags, commercial contract cleaning, and the haulage industry. Equally, I have provided content for a bridal store, a floral designer, and numerous restaurants and hotels, so it has not been so bad – especially when I have eaten in some very nice restaurants, and stayed in quite a few 5-star boutique and spa hotels. Just some of the perks of the job!

Finding the content for trade and industry media may be challenging for you, especially at an early stage of your writing career. Nonetheless, you have all the tools and resources at your fingertips. Search for the latest statistics, comments from an authoritative body, other news stories, competitor information, and overseas comparisons, relative to your topic. It is surprising what you can find. Then look for a way to use the facts to write your piece. Often, these details can help you create a strong headline or provide the elements you need to write a counter-argument, and using quotes from relevant organisations or spokespeople will help substantiate your piece.

Here is your chance to be creative. Are you going to write an interview-style piece with a local business owner? Do you think there is enough mileage on an industry trend? Or has a news story about a dying or resurgent business got your creative juices flowing?

Whether you come up with your idea first and then seek out a suitable publication, or the other way around, it doesn't really matter, but writing for trade and industry publications can be lucrative. Payment is often very good for the length of the article provided, the marketplace is awash with possibilities, and it appears that fewer writers are vying for copy space. This means, if you pitch things right, you could be onto a winner.

> *Tip: The writing style for trade and industry publications is often very tight and precise. Avoid word wastage and stick to the facts. What you write must be accurate. In the same vein as the specialist titles, readers of trade and industry magazines know their stuff.*

Quizzes, puzzles and crosswords

The obvious way to earn from your writing is to put together letters and articles and then sell your work to publications, right?

But writing is about words – and how those words are put together – so isn't writing quizzes, puzzles, and crosswords just another form of writing? Yet, many writers would not even consider compiling a word quiz or crossword puzzle, let alone selling it to the media.

When we refer to puzzles, these can be crossword puzzles, word searches, or word association games and quizzes.

Crossword puzzles are still one of the most popular elements found in many newspapers, and a reason people still buy one – meaning there is a healthy demand for those who can write and sell them.

I think it would be fair to assume that you will enjoy compiling these games if you enjoy doing them. It is very difficult to be enthusiastic about something that does not really interest you but if you think you can attack it with gusto and enjoy the challenge, then I would encourage you to do so.

The large newspaper and magazine publishers tend to use in-house crossword compilers, or buy from specialist puzzle agencies, but don't be put off by this. If you are new to producing crosswords and puzzles, then you might want to pitch to smaller publications initially. That said, it is always worth a punt to any publisher who prints them, as you never know when they are looking for fresh blood or looking to introduce something different. It could be simply a matter of timing that gets you through the door. Consider selling your puzzles to puzzle book publishers too, they often have a need for additional suppliers.

Chapter 4

You should approach these projects in exactly the same way as all your other writing endeavours – research your market. Some publications will stick to specific themes and formats. Some will publish crosswords or puzzles of a particular grid size, for others even the grid pattern is the same for every crossword, just rotated in a different way or a mirror image.

There are computer programs available that can help you create and/or solve crossword puzzles, and although some are free, the better ones tend to be expensive. However, it may be a requirement that your puzzle has not been created by computer, so do check first.

Alternatively, you could use a crossword dictionary, or use your thesaurus to help you write the clues by compiling a list of words which mean something similar to the word you have chosen.

Word games have become increasingly popular as publications try to find other ways to engage with their readers. Some word games or quizzes might be relevant to the topic or theme of the publication, or relate to its articles, while others will be more general.

A common but less obvious quiz is the questionnaire-style piece you generally find in women's titles, TV listing and teen magazines, and many Sunday supplements. The type that asks you: *How well do you know your spouse? What does your favourite colour say about you? Can you find your perfect love match?* etc. These multiple-choice-style questionnaires usually only contain 5 to 10 questions and the answer is revealed by a number or letter scoring system. These quizzes are often light-hearted and frivolous, other times more serious.

The market for questionnaires is huge because they are used in a variety of different publications and they can be targeted at a very wide audience. Some are designed for partners, husbands and wives (or friends) to do together.

> *Tip: Don't forget to try your specialist titles too. Themed puzzles and quizzes about pets, trains, or TV and film offer you even more markets.*

Of course, if compiling these games is not for you then you can just play them instead – send them off – and win yourself a lot of money! Magazines like *Take a Break* and *Chat* offer one lucky winner or sometimes a few winners, prizes and cash worth hundreds and thousands of pounds. Other types of publication also offer cash and prizes, so if you enjoy puzzles and mind games, then keep a look out, as you could be their next winner!

Chapter 5
Freelance Journalism

The first thing you need to appreciate about journalism is that it is a very different beast to writing creatively, and journalists are an unusual species.

To be a journalist you need a particular skill set, and you must be prepared to 'put yourself out there'. If you prefer the life of a reclusive writer, then forget about journalism; this is not a job for a shrinking violet – you need to be made of tougher stuff than that.

Journalists, ignoring for a moment tabloid journalists, must seek out the facts and report on issues, timely events, and current trends that are of interest to the public. The job entails speaking to lots of people, following leads, and putting oneself on the frontline. Accordingly, confidence is a must.

The definition of journalism is 'the occupation of reporting, writing, editing, photographing, or broadcasting news or of conducting any news organization as a business.

dictionary.com

Creative writing is any writing that goes outside the bounds of normal professional, journalistic, academic, or technical forms of literature, typically identified by an emphasis on narrative craft. Due to the looseness of the definition, it is possible for writing such as feature stories to be considered creative writing, even though they fall under journalism, because the content of features is specifically focused on narrative.

Wikipedia

There are also very distinct differences between journalism and freelance journalism.

Journalists are usually employed full-time or part-time, and work for one (or several) publication(s) within a group of publications as a paid employee. Some journalists may choose to report on specific topics such as politics or sport, while others prefer to deal with the day-to-day news, or find relevant stories to report on. They are, however, governed by the editor, meaning they typically have to write about the stories they are given to report on, or they have to seek permission before following a story.

Freelance journalists have the freedom to write about the stories they choose. They are self-employed and can supply copy to many different publications. They can choose the hours they work and where they work from.

To be a freelance journalist, you need to find your markets, contact editors, and negotiate fees. Self-motivation is a prerequisite, as is building your contact database, including press contacts and the sources behind reliable stories. You will also be responsible for your own tax and National Insurance contributions.

Journalists don't have the luxury of time to labour intensely and slavishly over every word; they need to gather the facts, write their story, and get it to the editor before the story goes cold. Journalists must be FAB (fast, accurate, brilliant), and a freelance journalist even more so.

How the media works

Let's start by defining the key roles of editorial staff.

Journalists research, write, edit, proofread and file news stories, features and articles. These stories are used in magazines, journals and newspapers but equally for television and radio. A journalist typically reads and rewrites press releases, researches articles, establishes and maintains contacts, interviews sources, attends events, and writes, edits, and submits copy. He will also liaise with editors, sub-editors, and photographers. A journalist must keep up to date with privacy, contempt, and defamation law.

Editorial Assistants, in general, support the editorial staff in the production process and the publishing of magazines, newspapers, and journals. Editorial assistants can also work for publishing houses, press agencies, and professional associations. The job of an editorial assistant normally includes writing and editing copy, proofreading and checking facts, interviewing contributors, researching and sourcing images, researching and commissioning features and articles, and liaising with authors, marketing staff, designers, and printers. Editorial assistants may also be responsible for planning and organising projects, plus budgeting and calculating expenditure. Many editorial assistants aspire to become editors.

Sub-editors for the press are mainly responsible for overseeing the content, accuracy, layout and design of newspaper and magazine articles. A sub-editor's tasks usually consist of corresponding with journalists, reporters and editors, as well as writing, rewriting, editing and proofreading copy, writing headlines, picture captions, and story summaries. They also rework reports and press releases, and gather and prepare information such as sports results. More importantly, they are responsible for ensuring that the stories are to the correct length, and that the 'house-style' is adhered to.

House-style is a company's preferred manner of presentation and layout of written material.

Google

Page layouts and designs, correctly inserting copy on the page, sizing photographs and placing them within features, are also the responsibility of a sub-editor – as is ensuring the stories are accurate and not legally compromised. Sub-editors have a very different role to assistant editors; they carry out technical tasks, are less involved with the generating of editorial content, and do not naturally progress to being editors.

The news

Have you ever wondered where journalists find their stories?

The main sources for news, stories and press releases come from press agencies and newswires.

A news agency is an organization that gathers news reports and sells them to subscribing news organizations, such as newspapers, magazines and radio and television broadcasters. A news agency may also be referred to as a wire service, newswire, or news service.

Wikipedia

The *Press Association* (PA) is the leading national news agency for the UK and Ireland, and describes itself as "a leading multimedia content provider across web, mobile, broadcast and print." The PA has news reporters filing hundreds of news stories every day including *'breaking news'*, *'showbiz gossip'* and other *'human interest'* stories.

The PA is not the only provider of news stories. The SWNS is the biggest independent newswire in the UK – providing news, pictures, PR and features to media organisations around the world. The SWNS specialises in hard-hitting content including news, real-life human-interest stories, photography, video, PR and market research, and has editorial offices across the country.

The *Associated Press* (AP) is, on the other hand, a global news network. With reporters sending in stories from across the world, the AP considers itself a leader in the field of journalism.

There are, of course, many other news agencies and newswire organisations where newspapers, magazines and other media outlets can 'buy' news, reports and other information.

So how does it work?

The vast majority of newspaper and magazine content comes from independent press agencies and freelance journalists. Many staff journalists working for a publication actually act as buyers and purchase content from the agencies and other journalists. In some cases, the story may be used in full or in part, or the journalist will pick up the bones of the piece and carry out their own research or further investigations to fit the story to their publication's style. This is the reason you might read the same story from conflicting sides, or see how one newspaper will carry a more in-depth article and another may just run a snippet.

Tips or tip-offs might sound like a crooked deal but, in fact, this is where most news stories start. A tip-off is not just about disclosing a secret piece of information, although *Talk to the Press, SellUsYourStory.com, Famous Features* and other similar organisations will happily pay for material relating to anyone in the public eye. A tip-off can equally relate to a local story, a controversial issue, or insider information given anonymously. If you offer a tip, the buyer will require a certain amount of evidence to back up your story, and will pay according to what is revealed. This is dependent on how much supporting evidence you have, such as documents or photographs, etc.

The rates for tip-offs and stories vary considerably but typically you could earn £50 for providing a comment on a topical issue or appearing as a small case study and up to £10,000 for an extreme or sensitive story, a rare or unusual story involving a celebrity or public figure.

The details you provide will be taken by a staff journalist and the story sold on. If you sell through one of these agencies, you are likely to be paid more for your story, depending on who they can sell it onto, and whether it is an 'exclusive' to one publication or sold to several.

If your story is sold through a newswire service that sends lots of content to every publication daily, you will be paid for the column inches your story takes up. This is a bit like receiving *royalty* payments.

Exclusive stories tend to pay more but the newswire service might be more appropriate if the story is more of a news piece than a real-life feature or tip-off.

You can sell your story direct to one newspaper or magazine, or contact a few and see who will pay you the most, but unless you are a fantastic negotiator you would be better off contacting the professionals and letting them do it for you. Do not, however, try to play one news agency off against another; they are unlikely to bite and you could lose out completely.

If you prefer to write and sell your own work, there is still a strong market for news, articles and features from individuals. Pitch your idea directly to the editor of the publication you have selected and researched, but only do so if you are confident you can supply the copy to meet their criteria and readership.

Understanding the differences between newspaper types

Newspapers come in different types, shapes and sizes but essentially, they are categorised as a *broadsheet* (for instance *The Times* or *The Guardian*), or a *tabloid* (such as the *Daily Express* or *The Sun*). These papers are classed as national dailies as they cover the whole of the UK, and most have a Sunday equivalent: *The Sunday Times*, *The Sunday Telegraph*, *Sunday Express*, and the *Sunday People*.

Chapter 5

There are regional dailies like the *East Anglian Daily Times* or the *Yorkshire Post*, and morning/evening papers such as *The Metro* or *The Birmingham Evening Mail*. Additionally, there are numerous local weekly and bi-weekly newspapers.

Then there are the *Free-sheets* – newspapers that are distributed for free, usually in relatively high numbers, to attract local advertisers. These publications depend on advertising fees to cover the cost of printing and distribution, and may allocate between 70% and 90% of their pages to advertisements. *Free-sheets* will endeavour to keep their running costs to a minimum and rely heavily on freelancers to provide copy. However, very few pay for contributions, or will only pay a token amount. So, check with the editor before committing to sending in material. That said, *Free-sheets* are worth considering as a place to start building your confidence and your portfolio of published work.

> *Tip: If you are trying to promote a local event or a local business, free-sheets are almost certainly worth sending your press releases to.*

But, let us take a step back, as it is vitally important to understand the differences between broadsheet and tabloid newspapers. It is not just the size of these publications that differ, everything about them could not be more contradictory. Not only is the size and layout at odds with each other, but the language, the content, the headlines, and the journalistic style are also completely different.

You will find the tabloid papers assign more pages to celebrity gossip, the scandalous behaviours of public figures, and real-life stories that they can sensationalise. It is not all gossip, of course, as the tabloids will cover much of the same material as the broadsheets, but their reporting style will be very different. You will find stories on education, health and money as well as '*What's on*' guides to TV and film, plus movie and book reviews. The broadsheets may well report on celebrity behaviour too, and have society pages, but more column inches will be allocated to current affairs, world news, politics and financial reports. Both will cover sports news and scores but, again, these will be presented in very different formats.

If you plan to write for the newspapers, it is worth taking the time to understand the different styles and types, and you MUST write accordingly. You may already be conversant with one type over another, for example you may read *The Telegraph* on a regular basis, so you should familiarise yourself with *The Sun* or *The Mirror*, and vice-versa.

1. Does the paper have a political slant?
2. Is the language style easy to read or more formal?
3. Are the headlines strong, bold and sensationalist or to the point?
4. Does the front-page lead with a celebrity gossip piece or current affairs?
5. What size images do they use? Is it one large photo of a public figure and several others, or many smaller ones?

Each of these points gives a paper its identity. Its style and format is familiar to its readers and, in turn, helps the reader identify with the paper. Each newspaper is in competition with another to gain readership, and its editors and journalists know what stories its readers are interested in, and *how* they want to read them. The target audience has been carefully analysed over time and by understanding their readers, the newspaper endeavours to feed them 'more of the same' to keep them interested and, more importantly, to sell the paper.

Examples of a story published in both a tabloid and a broadsheet newspaper:

'I'M SORRY' Missing Arthur Heeler-Frood found TEN MILES from home after revealing he has been sleeping rough in London, Birmingham and Manchester

The 15-year-old was spotted at a train station yesterday afternoon apparently 'on his way home'

By Kathryn Cain and Ellie Flynn THE SUN, 16th November 2016

A SCHOOLBOY who vanished two months ago after telling his parents he was "bored of life" has been living rough in cities across the UK.

Arthur Heeler-Frood, 15, has apologised to his family and police after turning up "tired, grubby and rather smelly" yesterday.

Chapter 5

Schoolboy who ran away 'because he was bored' reveals he has spent 10 weeks sleeping rough across Britain

By Patrick Sawer, Senior Reporter, THE TELEGRAPH, 16th November 2016

His head full of George Orwell's adventures as a vagrant and itinerant dishwasher, 15-year-old Arthur Heeler-Frood appeared to be determined to follow in the writer's footsteps.

Shortly after reading his seminal 1933 work 'Down and Out in Paris and London' on his Kindle, the teenager disappeared from home, leaving behind a note declaring "I have run away because I am bored of my life".

Ten weeks later the schoolboy has been found safe and well, revealing that he spent his time sleeping rough while exploring England's three largest cities.

Notice the differences in the headlines in the two examples, but more so the opening of the stories – *The Sun's* headline is more personalised, and the intro is much shorter and sharper taking the reader straight into the story. *The Telegraph* tells us immediately why the boy ran away; however, the intro is much more laboured, painting a picture of the lad's longing to follow in the footsteps of the author George Orwell. Later in the story, *The Sun* also refers to Orwell's book but barely gives it a passing reference; in contrast *The Telegraph* pins the theme of the report to contents in the book.

In both instances, the remainder of the reports include quotes from Arthur and his parents, and both include details of the note Arthur left on the day of his disappearance.

The other stories highlighted in *The Sun* on the same day included: *Mother from Hell [mum filmed brutally punching baby], Don't Mess with Me Argentina [Jeremy Clarkson slams 'ignorant little worm' who kicked stars off flight],* and *EU-ER Missus! [outrage over nude photos of Ukraine's 24-year old minister of European integration].* The Telegraph reported on: *West Virginia official who called Michelle Obama an 'ape in heels', Theresa May attacks Deloitte and BBC over leaked Brexit memo,* and *Rome in Shock as Bernini elephant statue vandalised.*

Tip: When writing your copy for newspapers do not waste time writing a headline. Sub-editors write headlines, reporters do not. Give your work a catchline; a single-word based on the theme of your story. E.G. Schoolboyreturned or Elephantvandal etc.

Stories are just a small part of a newspaper's identity – everything from features and travel destinations to the advertisers and their products will give you clues as to whom the publication is targeted. The tabloid newspapers are likely to run holiday pieces about Spain, Portugal and Croatia, with flights from *EasyJet, Ryanair* or *Monarch*. These destinations will be considered more affordable for the everyday person who is looking for a cheaper packaged holiday via budget airlines. The broadsheets are more likely to cover Mauritius, the Caribbean and Dubai with *British Airways, Emirates* or *Virgin*. The broadsheets' advertisers will be the likes of *Rolex, Jaguar* and Regent Street retailers, whereas the tabloids will be *Aldi* and *Lidl, Primark* or *TK Maxx*. The property pages of the tabloids will cover terraced and semi-detached houses in outer London and the East End suburbs, whereas the broadsheets are more likely to showcase detached properties in Surrey, Sussex and Hertfordshire. Already, you should see a pattern developing here, and you should be able to ascertain the lifestyles, aspirations, and social classes of the readers of each publication.

Furthermore, study the language of each publication. How persuasive is the copy, or is it more informative? Does the journalist want you to accept what he is writing is the truth, the only truth, or does he allow you to make up your own mind by revealing both sides of the argument? Do the articles include lots of facts and statistics or just quotes and hearsay? Can you distinguish between the two? Often, we can be led to believe what we are being told. Think back to the *Brexit* campaign, and how the media supporting each side of the campaign would tailor stories to back up their positions.

As a journalist, you have an ethical responsibility to present an accurate, well-balanced explanation of the stories you write about, and an obligation to present all sides of an issue. However, the reality is that a journalist can pick what information he wants to include and what he chooses to leave out, depending on the angle of his story.

> *Tip: If you want to write for newspapers, read and study as many different ones as you can and keep well-documented notes on all the above areas. Prepare a template, as this will help you gather the same notes to compare one against another and help you decide which one(s) you may prefer to write for.*

Writing for newspapers

As we have already discovered, there are two routes into journalism – as a staff journalist or a freelance journalist.

To become a staff journalist, you must have obtained certain qualifications. Very few publications will even consider you without either a journalism degree or graduation from an accredited course with the *National Council for the Training of Journalists* (NCTJ), (the most recognised in the industry). The NCTJ provides full and part-time training courses including distance learning and bespoke courses, across a variety of different journalistic genres. They can also help with trainee vacancies.

The PPA (the voice of professional publishers) also runs accredited courses in journalism and publishing. Other independent companies and organisations advertise their courses too, so it is worth doing your research to see which ones best suit your goals and aspirations and, more importantly, will give you an accredited certificate that the industry recognises. Further to this, internships, apprenticeships, and trainee positions are available through a variety of different institutions and associations. If you have studied journalism at degree level, your university will be able to advise the next best route.

If, however, you are looking to improve your skills for a career in freelance journalism, the NCTJ also offers one-day courses for freelancers, whilst the *National Union of Journalists* (NUJ) provides comprehensive and affordable courses for member and non-member freelancers looking to start a career in journalism, or those who need to renew their existing skills.

Another option for the freelancer is to offer yourself for some work experience. With many publications incredibly understaffed, an extra pair of hands from an eager recruit could offer you just the experience you need to get your foot in the door. If you already have some writing or journalistic experience, you might consider taking some shifts on a news desk – to build your confidence and portfolio.

Never has there been so much support, help, and advice to aid you in building your freelance journalism career. Websites such as *www.journalism.co.uk* are full of useful articles, links, and contacts in the world of journalism. Sites such as this can put you in touch with an online community and lead you to forums of freelance journalists, giving you the tools and access you need to link up with other journalists, editors and publishers. Doing so will help you find out what is happening in the world of journalism, and better enable you seek out those all-important opportunities.

Facebook, *LinkedIn* and *Twitter* all have groups (although some are closed groups) dedicated to freelance writing and journalism. It is worth associating yourself with these groups. Being able to stay abreast of the latest trends and topics could help you spot openings, or provide opportunities to assist other journalists with a project. These groups will also discuss topical issues including changes in the laws relating to journalism and publishing, copyright issues, and (frequently discussed) fees and payments.

I cannot emphasise enough how invaluable these contacts and groups can be. You may be thinking that these other people are your competition, so why would they be so willing to share information and opportunities? Think of it as a community where someone can help you, or offer you advice or an opportunity and you – in turn – can share what you know with others too. Not only that, it's a very big world out there and there is plenty of work for everyone if you are willing to put in the effort.

Breaking into journalism

If you are just starting out as a journalist, I would recommend that you start small and local. Many of today's highest paid editors started their journalistic careers on a 'local rag' before moving on to the nationals.

Look for local stories that might fit your regional paper but which staff journalists are unlikely to cover. Interesting people in your neighbourhood, those doing good or charitable things in the community, and other human-interest stories are incredibly popular. What is happening at the local school, the church, or some other organisation that could be spotlighted? If the item you are reporting on spreads across several regions, such as a sponsored walk by a man and his rescue dog looking to raise money for The Dog's Trust (for example), then use the information you have gathered and offer it to several papers across each of the regions he is walking. Keep them abreast of his progress.

Sport is an area that is ripe for a new writer. Local papers, in particular, do not have enough reporters to thoroughly cover all the sporting events in their area, especially when many events are held on weekends and in the evenings when staff reporters may be less inclined to cover less prevalent fixtures. Being a novice sports correspondent may not pay particularly well but it is good initial experience, and could help you gain confidence, build your cuttings portfolio, and enable you to write for other sports titles and the nationals. Equally, if you love sport generally or are passionate about just one sport – you get to enjoy watching the event as well!

You are more likely to succeed if you can report on a less popular sport and, perhaps, even find an opening to write a column. If you are interested in clay target shooting, for example, and can provide details relating to a local club and its competition results, plus regular information about changes to the rules or equipment, or other relevant details – it is worth pitching this idea to an editor.

Tip: Becoming a member of the NUJ or other journalism or freelance writing organisation often comes with a press or members card, which can have many benefits such as discounts or reduced entry fees, and in some cases, if you are reporting on an event, you may be able to gain free entry.

Do not discount theatre, film, and book reviews either. Although your local paper is likely to have an *Arts Correspondent*, that person cannot be everywhere at the same time. If you have a passion for amateur dramatics or cult films it is worth writing and submitting some copy.

Book reviews are slightly different. Most nationals and Sunday papers have professional reviewers and most local or regional titles will only cover books relevant to the circulation area, be that a local author or a book that is set in the circulation area. If, however, you happen to know an author, or have specialist knowledge on the subject covered in the book, by all means, offer to review it.

Other significant points to note:

Accuracy is one of the most important factors of journalism. Names, dates, times and places must be accurately recorded and correctly spelt. Pay particular attention to names; is it Shaun or Sean, Pete or Peter or James 'Shaggy' Jones? Is it Wood or Woods, Walker or Wallaker? – people hate it when their name is incorrectly spelt. Get into the habit of asking for a person's FIRST name(s) not their CHRISTIAN name; if they are not of a Christian faith then they do not have Christian names and may be offended by your question.

Newspapers also like to report on the age of subjects, as this can quantify experience, or lack of experience. A 12-year-old boy with cancer may get more support than a 50-year-old single man, but a 30-year-old mum, equally so. I'm not saying it is right, it is just how it is.

Journalists generally, however, avoid mentioning race, religion, sexual or gender identity, unless it is pertinent to the story.

House-style

Earlier, I briefly mentioned *house-style*. It is important for you as a freelance writer or journalist to understand the relevance of house-style and the devices to look out for. You will save the editor or sub-editor a huge amount of editing time if you can offer your copy as 'page-ready', especially in the day and age when copy can be lifted from a *Word* document, and cut and pasted directly onto the layout or page template of the publication.

House-style is an additional method publications use to differentiate themselves from another newspaper or magazine, and when you discover some of the layouts they use, you may wonder why they bother. But it is about consistency and uniformity. Take *McDonalds* by way of comparison. Everyone who eats a *Big Mac* knows what it should look and taste like, no matter where in the world they buy one. This formula is what gives *McDonalds*, and other companies like it, their brand identities (as well as the most obvious elements of their brand like colour schemes, logos, and straplines).

Chapter 5

When we refer to publications (including online ones), some of the more recognisable traits to look out for are the font size and type that the publication uses; this includes the size of headings, sub-headings and by-lines. If you are unsure of the font size and type used, always pick something traditional or simple like *Times New Roman 12, Ariel* or *Garamond.* Do not use any *Script* style or fancy fonts, as this could cause translation problems when the editor is formatting from the font you chose to the one he uses and it is potentially not in his font library.

Typically, the most obvious style to spot and address is whether the publication uses single ' or double " marks for speech and quotes. Less obvious is a single or double space after full stops (a double space after a full stop has become far less common since the introduction of word-processors), or indeed, a double line space between paragraphs.

I am sure you can appreciate how long it takes for the sub-editor to go through every journalist's submitted copy just to change these simple little things, and how much time you could save them by sending your copy 'page-ready' in the first place.

Further techniques include an oversized first letter or CAPITALISING the whole of the first word, or IN SOME CASES, the first three words. Indentations of the first word or the start of a new paragraph are still sometimes used, (again this is a method we see less of since the digitalisation of printing).

Some publications will use the subject's name in full the first time they are mentioned, then only refer to them by surname thereafter, others by their first name. Some will capitalise the first letters of a person's job title (Managing Director) others will choose not to (managing director). Many will put a caption under each photograph or image that has been used and, if this is the case, you should provide a caption too, even though the sub-editor may change it.

We previously looked at *pull quotes*, and if a publication uses pull quotes, then you can enhance your copy by picking the ones you think are best and include them in a separate list with your captions at the end of your copy. But, don't overdo it. Some publications may only use one or two pull-quotes and you should do the same.

Fact boxes. More commonly used in magazines than newspapers (with the exception of travel articles), fact boxes are where a summary of additional information can be supplied, such as entry costs, opening times, other things to see, or additional information the writer feels will benefit the reader. These details are placed in fact boxes because they would be cumbersome if they were included as part of the copy.

Example fact box:

London Zoo is open 9am to 5pm all year except Christmas Day
Entry prices: Adult £18, Children £12, Concessions £12
Animal feeding times are advertised daily at the zoo or on the website.
Online booking available at www.londonzoo.co.uk/bookings

Presenting your work correctly and meeting the publication's house style can be time-consuming. However, the more effort you put in, and the less the editor has to do, will ultimately work in your favour.

Laziness and journalism do not go together. You must do everything you can to ensure what you write is factually correct and not libellous, is without typing errors or misspellings, and written to the best of your ability. Wherever possible, go the extra mile. Send your copy to meet the publication's house style and provide captions, pull quotes and fact-boxes where relevant. In some cases, you may also have to provide reference notes to show your research sources but also remember, if you cannot validate the information from more than one independent source be wary of including it, and memorise the phrase: IF IN DOUBT – LEAVE IT OUT!

Chapter 6
Food, Crafts and Hobbies

There is a very good reason I decided to dedicate an entire chapter to food, crafts and hobbies – away from the general chapters of writing for magazines. Even though everything you have learnt so far about studying your target publications, preparing your query submissions, and developing your copy still applies, the upsurge of interest in these topics warrants specific consideration.

In addition to the renewed popularity of growing your own fruit and vegetables (and keeping chickens), sewing, crochet, quilting and many of the other handicrafts and skills that were prevalent in the 1950s and 1960s (but which died a death by the 1980s and 1990s) have become increasingly popular once again. In my opinion, surprisingly so, given our general obsessions with the television, smartphones and tablets.

In turn, no one can deny the power of *YouTube* and 'how to' videos or the popularity of shows such as *The Great British Sewing Bee, The Great British Bake Off* and *MasterChef*; shows which have ignited a passion in generations who thought darning socks and baking cakes was archaic.

However, another reason for pulling aside these subjects is that writing recipes, cookbooks, 'how tos', and instructional articles, is unlike all the other types of writing you might undertake.

Food

The topic of food is astronomically big (or should that be gastronomically?) and it's global.

And, writing about food is equally a colossal business. From *WHSmith* alone, it is possible to purchase more than 30 different magazines dedicated to food and drink, not including women's titles, general interest, and other newspapers and magazines that carry food-based supplements, articles or recipes.

One way or another, there is a global obsession with food, and the marketplace is saturated with food writers, bloggers and vloggers (video bloggers). Despite the competition, there are still a million things we can write about food because we think about it every single day, whilst shopping, cooking or eating it. We may want to eat healthily and therefore hold an interest in nutrition, we may suffer from food allergies, or we are (always) dieting and making choices about whether to eat in or eat out.

During my career writing for magazines, I wrote a number of restaurant reviews; I even met and interviewed a few celebrity foodies (Jean-Christophe Novelli, Gordon Ramsay and Jimmy Doherty) and attended Food Fairs and Food Festivals. I also wrote features about specialist growers of mushrooms, asparagus and strawberries, and I had a delightful encounter with a herd of goats whose milk was used to produce a superb collection of cheeses. However, what I have since come to realise is that writing about food goes way beyond what I first envisaged, and if it is a subject that interests you, the world truly is your oyster (no pun intended).

One could argue that much of the modern trend for food writing started way back in the 1860s when Mrs Isabella Mary Beeton published a book about Household Management. This was followed by several more including *Cookery and Household Management, Mrs Beeton's Every Day Cookery,* and *Beeton's Book of Needlework.* A hundred years later, another female cook, *Mary Berry* also become a household name, as did a certain Delia Smith. But did you know that both women were food writers for the media before they were TV cooks? Mary Berry was the cookery editor for *Housewife Magazine,* whilst Delia Smith was the cookery writer for the *Daily Mail,* the *Evening Standard* and the *Radio Times.*

This is a key point, as almost every food writer I have come across has had some knowledge of the industry before they began writing about it. *Rose Prince,* author and journalist (*www.roseprince.co.uk*) learned to cook at home with her mother and French Grandmother, then when she left school she worked in a food shop and bakery. A lucky break, a lot of research, and a lot more cooking, gave Rose the resources and confidence she needed to write about food and cooking with authority.

It's no longer enough to be a good writer. There are lots of good writers in the world, so succeeding in this business means that you have additional skills – ideally many. Those skills might include a deep knowledge of food that you acquired while working in a specialty food shop. A job at a farm or a grocery store might not seem as though it has all that much to do with food writing, but by enriching your base of experience, you're gaining relatable, real world experience that – if nothing else – will give you something to write about. If you want to write about restaurants, for example, it never hurts to work in them first. If you think you want to develop recipes, get some hands-on food experience in a kitchen.

Jessica Battilana, Senior Editor for Tasting Table

Dianne Jacob, author of *Will Write for Food* suggests that the route to being a food writer requires three steps.

1. *Knowing how to write, how to develop and write a story, how to interview, research and report.*

2. *Experience in a restaurant or food service industry be that a chef, TV chef, a dietician, a nutritionist, home economics or food tech teacher, a food retailer or producer, farming or food production.*

3. *Blogging.*

Becoming a good food writer requires you to immerse yourself in the subject. At risk of repeating myself, read and study lots of books (including cookbooks), do your research (work in restaurants, watch television programmes about food and cooking), practise cooking from recipes and develop your own, grow your own food, follow food bloggers and other food writers, celebrity chefs, and food critics on social media.

What to write about food

At the start of this chapter, I referred to the size of the writing market on food and so far, we have barely scratched the surface. In addition to food magazines and cookbooks, *Foodies100*, an index of UK food blogs, boasts a membership of almost 5,000 and eight million readers a year, so let us have a closer look at some of the opportunities that are out there.

Restaurant reviews are an obvious choice. Most of us enjoy the experience of eating out and many of us are equally eager to share our experiences on online sites like *TripAdvisor*, but if you are able to expand your thoughts and observations, writing restaurant reviews could be a good place to start. Another obvious avenue is foreign food pieces, whether that is discovering local gems or traditional flavours in a region or a country. How many articles have you read about Italian cooking and the Mediterranean diet, Asian spices, or a big Texan barbeque?

As I found out personally, farming, food production and specialty growers always make great subjects for food-based features, as do articles that include statistics about food or food-related themes, such as food waste or new products. Food retailers including bakers, greengrocers, farm shops and chocolate shops can be a great source of food-related stories, too. Then there are articles about special diets: vegan, vegetarian, pescatarian, gluten-free, nut allergies, seafood allergies, and other life-threatening conditions associated with food or eating, such as anorexia and bulimia. Let us not forget about healthy eating, dieting, calorie counting, carbs, sugar and fats.

Moving on, there are writing opportunities as menu consultants, recipe developers and food testers.

Food writing can also include anything and everything to do with the storage, packaging and the distribution of food, and the people or companies that do it.

What about your kitchen? Every cooking utensil, pot, pan and machine can be the subject of a blog, a feature, or article. You could be testing the latest kitchen gadgets, writing about your favourite kitchen tool, or even how to lay the perfect dinner table, complete with candelabras and floral displays. *The Top Ten Best Kitchen Buys, The Five Top Kitchen Gadgets*, or a feature about the purpose of each kitchen knife all have their place. Author Tim Hayward managed to write a whole book on the topic of the different uses of a cook's knife.

Oh, and then we come on to recipes and cookbooks. Cookbooks come in all flavour types and styles – quick cook recipes to family favourites, cooking for one or entertaining at home. Some contain simple recipes with a list of ingredients and a photograph of what the dish should look like when complete, others have detailed step-by-step instructions and an image to go with each step. Some cookbooks read like a travelogue as the author takes you on a mouth-watering tour complete with recipe guides and best buys.

Lastly, there are general interest books about food. These are not cookbooks but an assortment of books which might cover the history of a specific food type or food group, cooking examples from another era, or even food myths or fads.

And we can list the whole cycle again for beverages including coffee, wine, beer, water, and soft drinks… whew! The list really is endless, and it is your job as a food writer to find the gaps or seek out the next food-related trend.

Food blogging

With the explosion of social media and online sites such as *Facebook*, *Twitter*, *Instagram* and *YouTube* – other than clips of cats and kittens (I'm guilty) and people doing stupid things (not guilty), and perhaps music, food is one of the most popular topics people interact with, and food blogging and vlogging is increasingly popular. In 2013, *Business Insider* reported that of the six most frequently posted and shared topics on social media, 'food, drink and travel' was second only behind technology and social media.

I am no cook, and I'm not that interested in cooking, other than having to do it, but even I've succumbed to following a recipe or two from Facebook for Maltesers Pie (an amazing no cooking chocolate indulgence) and a pastry wrapped brie and caramelised onion parcel – delicious!

If you are interested in writing about food, consider starting with a food blog first. Most food bloggers start one as a hobby and most don't blog on a full-time basis. For many, it may be the first time they have blogged. However, hundreds of food bloggers and vloggers now have publishable cookbooks, and editors and literary agents read blogs when on the lookout for the next talented author. Equally, many established food writers and cookbook authors now blog too, as it increases audiences, which in turn sells more cookbooks and food-related merchandise.

Chapter 6

When I posted my first ever #Leanin15 video on Instagram in early 2014, I never imagined it would lead to me writing this book. It all started as a bit of fun in my kitchen, with the idea of sharing simple recipes to help people get lean.

Joe Wicks, author of Lean in 15: 15 Minute Meals and Workouts

By the end of 2016. Joe had three *Lean in 15* books on sale.

Many blog pages have evolved into more extensive websites, where the blog is just a small part of the food writer's activities. A website can also be sales portal for selling books, promoting cookery courses, and other kitchen merchandise or celebrity-endorsed products.

But let us stay with the theme of food blogs for the moment. One of the reasons food blogging is such a phenomenon is that we all love a personal experience story. Being able to share the highs and lows of someone else's cooking achievements, and disasters, is what makes us human. Add to that a bit of family life, and domestic chat, and it appears blog fans can't get enough of it.

Spontaneous events in the kitchen, a strong personal voice and message, coupled with quality photography or video seems to be the key to achieving blogging success. A good blogger should engage with his audience and develop a loyal following of readers.

Blogging is the most exciting area of food writing today. Food bloggers are pushing boundaries, writing about food in ways that print can't. They write about their own loves, about current events and cooking, and about new restaurants and travel. There's immediacy to their writing, a kinship among fellow bloggers, and exhilaration in saying whatever they want, unfettered by editors.

Dianne Jacob, Will Write for Food, Third Edition

And that is true. Very few people – celebrity chefs or otherwise – can publish their work unedited, and there is no room for being able to express your frustrations with a kitchen gadget or tool, in your cookbook, unless it is autobiographical. *Although Fanny Cradock frequently expressed her dislike of electric cookers.*

Okay, so writing a blog is not necessarily going to bring you an immediate income, but it's a good place to start if you want to develop your skills as a food writer. I am not saying don't put together some well-researched feature ideas and pitch them to your favourite foody magazines, or that compilation of Grandma's favourite recipes would not make the perfect cookbook. What I am suggesting is that writing a food blog could give your writing kudos for when you do so, especially if you have grown your audience to a sizeable number.

Tip: Writing blogs will be covered in more depth in the chapter Writing Online. Alternatively, there are several books dedicated to blogging available (including how to set them up).

How to write about food

Nitty-gritty time. Firstly, food writers, editors and publishers have a general dislike for adjectives in food writing. Describing something as *'simply delicious'* or *'truly scrumptious'* just won't cut it. If you are going to write about a *steam-baked apple, drizzled with hot sultanas and raisins in a sugary syrup, and finished with a plum-sized dollop of Chantilly cream or vanilla bean ice cream* – then your description must be vivid enough for your readers to taste it.

Restaurant or food reviews are where your food writing skills will be most tested and one of the few chances you get to describe the look, smell, and taste of food. However, there is more to restaurant reviews than just the food. Think about the ambience of the restaurant, the lighting, the seating, the staff and the efficiency of the kitchen. These are important factors to note and provide useable material for your article.

Be honest but not scathing. Reputable food critics may get away with tearing apart the culinary skills of a top London hotel, but your opinion as a newbie on the food scene is unlikely to bear credence. Even though you may not like an aspect of a dish or ingredient, others might – so give it a fair assessment. Bear in mind the eatery's intentions as well, not just your personal preferences. If you don't like seafood, can you give an honest review of a recently opened seafood restaurant? A review is not a platform to express your likes and dislikes. If you hate salmon and go on about the fact that your fish pie was swimming in it – literally – you could alienate your reader. It could lead them to question why, with such a dislike for it, you would even consider ordering a fish dish in the first place.

It is advisable to comment on no more than three to five dishes – no one wants to read a shopping list – so pick the dishes that made the biggest impression; good or bad. Think about the presentation of each dish, the taste obviously, and remark on whether the taste reflected the chef's vision (or in fact, the menu's description) and if it lived up to, or exceeded, your expectations. Where possible, name ingredients, use descriptive language including metaphors and similes and let your readers imagine how it tastes.

Pay attention to the texture – how well was it cooked, was it hot enough, juicy and tender or overcooked? Always look for contrasts: something hot something cold, hard or soft, solid or liquid, etc.

Tip: Contrasts work well in all descriptive writing.

Think of your review as a story of your experience, and do your research. Find out what you can about the restaurant before you go, or after you have been. The order doesn't matter, but the details do. I would advise that you do not read other reviews or *TripAdvisor* before you go, as you need to visit with an open mind and an unbiased view. It could be useful to know, however, who the owner is, and the chef or wine waiter's background and experience. The more information you can gather will add substance to your article, or may provide a new angle. You may be able to glean a little more information from the waiting staff during your visit but be aware of being too conspicuous and asking too many questions. Try not to be too obvious about writing your review by keeping a notepad and pen at your side and scribbling away with every mouthful. Just make a few necessary notes and save the rest to memory. *Write up your observations as soon as possible so you do not forget anything important.*

As a reviewer, be conscious of the ethics of accepting free products or restaurant meals; be aware of the PR element and an obligation to give a good review because it was free. Readers won't thank you for singing the praises of a local restaurant when customers, following your article, do not have a good experience – remember, *your* credibility is at stake.

Writing recipes

Although there are gazillions of recipes in circulation, in print and online, writing recipes is not as easy as you might think. Like everything else, there is a formula.

Table of ingredients – most recipes itemise the list of ingredients first, and usually in a simple format, and in the order they will be used. Try not to use too many ingredients as this puts people off. Quick-cook recipes generally have fewer ingredients, as this saves on preparation time. It is no good promoting a bolognese that cooks in 15 minutes if it takes you 30 minutes to soak and peel the skins from your tomatoes.

Also, try and use ingredients that are easy enough to source from local supermarkets and shops. Seasonal produce should always be considered if you are writing for a specific issue of a magazine or (obviously) putting together a season-by-season cookbook. Try combining the use of multiple types of produce available during the same season, enabling your readers to source their produce locally and not having to rely on imports. No other strawberry tastes quite like an English strawberry in July – does it?

Avoid waste! Where possible, consider using the quantities in which people buy products such as a 400g tin, a whole pepper or courgette. People are very conscious of food and money waste.

Balance the flavours – Your readers will want to see a good balance of flavours in your recipe preparation. While testing your recipe formula, consider flavours that work well together as a foundation, and then experiment to see if you can enhance the flavour. Do not try and be too adventurous; seek out flavours that complement each other and which do not overpower one another. A touch of cinnamon can spice up an apple pie but too much and it will ruin it.

Personalise your recipe – even though there is no copyright on recipes, always try to add or change an ingredient or two – to put your own mark on it. I never make a Macaroni Cheese without a pinch of mustard powder in my sauce, and finish it with a sprinkling of paprika, or if I'm really daring – smoked paprika!

Chapter 6

Copyright law does not protect recipes that are mere listings of ingredients... Copyright protection may, however, extend to substantial literary expression – a description, explanation, or illustration, for example – that accompanies a recipe or formula or to a combination of recipes, as in a cookbook.

Paleomagazine.com

Method – Although many chefs are happy to throw in a dash of this or a splash of that, unless you know what you are doing when it comes to tasting and testing – and know how to get your seasoning right – this approach is not recommended. It also makes inexperienced cooks nervous. Too much salt or not enough liquid can ruin a recipe and destroy confidence. Always try to list exact measurements, using the correct measuring tools. Be precise with your timings, oven temperatures, and equipment sizes, especially for cake tins or flan cases. Use either imperial or metric as your preferred measurement of choice and be consistent. Do provide the conversion but do not swap from one to the other during the recipe. Clearly describe how the ingredients should be prepared; finely sliced, chopped or crushed foods (like garlic) cook differently depending on how they have been prepared.

Once you have prepared your list of ingredients, and written out your instructions – test the recipe thoroughly. Look for any ambiguity, have you missed out any important steps, and does it taste like it should? Make your amendments and test it again. This is an iterative process. Did you get the results you were expecting, can the recipe be improved, or could you simplify it at all? Give your reader tips or shortcuts if there are any, or options to replace one ingredient with an alternative. Be mindful of food allergies. Then ask someone else to follow your recipe step-by-step; their advice is often invaluable, and could mean the difference between a reader loving your dish or hating its complexity.

Write for your audience! If you are writing for a specific magazine or publication you should have a good idea of who your audience is, but if not, think carefully about who your reader might be. Consider your readers' budget or time constraints, the equipment they may have or need, and how easy it is for them to source the ingredients in your recipe. Are your readers likely to be beginners or more experienced cooks? Make allowances for both. Your jargon is important here too. Where possible, keep your instructions clear and to the point and use universal language in your methodology. Do not overcook your instructions but write enthusiastically; it will come across in your copy.

Crafts and hobbies

As a nation, we love our crafts and hobbies. From woodworking, model making, and cross-stitching to stamp collecting, horse riding, and photography – we have hundreds of choices to ignite our creative passions. We are also fortunate in that we have at least one craft or hobbyist magazine for every topic. For some of the more popular subjects, there are multiple publications to choose between.

This is good news for writers who have creative pursuits. Ultimately, if you can write well about your craft or hobby, editors will want to see your ideas!

Writing for craft and hobbyist titles should be approached in the same way as writing for specialist titles (see Chapter 4), especially if we consider magazines such as *Gun* or *Fast Car*, which may require more specialist information. Others may require extensive knowledge or expert opinion, and often include instructional or 'how to' articles and features. These types of articles require a different structure of writing to all other forms.

> *There is absolutely no way you will make the grade as a sustainable hobby writer unless you know your 'stuff'. If you have a plethora of knowledge about your subject matter, you will make money writing about it. If you are able to share tricks, tips, shortcuts, wisdom and lore you will be seen as 'sensei' by newcomers to your hobby.*

Ian Barnett, Hobby Writing: How to Make your Play, Pay!

So, what do magazine editors for craft and hobby titles want?

Read the submission guidelines! Most craft, hobbyist and specialist magazines provide guidelines for authors. If you want to stand any chance of success, follow these to the letter or face rejection – it is as simple as that.

Let's take *Tropical Fish Hobbyist Magazine* as an example, here. It has a very detailed submission guidelines page on its website *www.tfhmagazine.com.* I have picked out a few of the important ones for illustration but do have a look at the full article if you get the chance.

> *Be accurate. Research your topic fully. Do not repeat hearsay or opinions; report facts. When drawing conclusions from personal experiences, be sure not to over generalize.*
>
> *Proofread your material! Check spelling and punctuation.*
>
> *CHECK SCIENTIFIC NAMES! We often get manuscripts with misspelled or incorrect scientific names.*
>
> *The presentation of your material should be professional. We often receive articles that are formatted to look nice on the screen and all of it must be stripped from the text before we can send it to the Art Department. We want plain text without formatting.*
>
> *We prefer articles that are submitted with photos. Do not insert photos into the text. Photos must be submitted separately.*

It is true that publications such as *Tropical Fish Hobbyist Magazine* will already have a bank of experienced writers and industry professionals to call upon to provide good, newsworthy and up-to-date content. Indeed, they may also have a list of commissioned writers to provide fresh tutorials or to write the answers to readers' questions. However, just like pretty much every other magazine on the market, they will also be seeking fresh and original content, personal stories and experiences, and historical reference pieces to sit alongside the more traditional articles and features, and 'how to' tutorials.

New product reviews, new techniques, developments in (or changes to) rules and regulations within an industry all make for interesting readings. Take the publication *Drones*, for example. (Yes, there are already numerous magazines dedicated to drones and drone flying.) Due to the nature of the product, and the already controversial private ownership of drones, the rules and regulations as to where they can be flown is regularly being reviewed – and is therefore a constant topic of conversation within the industry and for enthusiasts.

Good hobbyist writers don't lecture readers, they provide engaging copy that helps readers learn. They do not patronise.

Your copy must meet the needs of newcomers to the hobby/craft, and even the magazine, as much as it does those who have been subscribing since the inaugural issue. Find a natural way to share your knowledge, use words and photographs or images to express your thoughts and meanings, and study many back issues and previous articles to get the tone of your voice right.

Writing truthfully often warms readers to your work and, as with blogging, people love to read about the successes *and failures* of your projects; give shortcuts and tips but also tell readers how to avoid mistakes. Asking readers for their advice and input encourages engagement and could lead to another article based on a frequently asked question, or a new time-saving technique or gadget.

Check your facts, and double check your facts, and if you are writing a 'how to article' always try to find a *guinea pig* to follow your instructions.

Tip: If you don't happen to know someone who has the same hobby as you, contact an appropriate club or group and ask for volunteers.

Writing 'how to' and instructional articles in this market should be approached in the same format as writing a recipe with a few additions:

1. Start with a fantastic photograph of the finished product positioned in an appropriate setting. If you have built something for the garden – photograph it in position outside. If you have made a necklace use a dummy bust or model friend to show it at its best. At worst, lay it flat on something white.

2. Sell it! Tell readers why it is such a wonderful item and how they can't possibly live without it.

3. Do not scare your readers off with an overly complex or detailed description when writing your intro.

4. Include a parts or materials list and provide an inventory of equipment that may be needed.

5. Write out clear, step-by-step instructions, providing (where possible) photographs of what the item should look like at each stage, so that your reader knows he is on the right track.

6. Try not to write too much for each step; keep your instructions concise. It is worth breaking up large sections of text with tips and hints, or providing fact boxes, depending on the format of the magazine you are writing for.

7. Not every enthusiast may be as geeky as you about your subject, so do not overcomplicate your instructions or, in fact, your product design.

8. Grade your project on difficulty; sometimes you should supply something relatively easy to construct and in another issue, aim for something harder.

9. Do not age discriminate – your readers may vary from teenagers to the retired – so write your article accordingly. Avoid out-of-date terms and references. Equally, avoid using overly modern expressions or phrases.

Photography

For many reasons, your photography skills may be as crucial as your writing skills when submitting to craft and hobbyist titles, especially with 'how to' articles. Foodie features, articles, and recipe guides also rely on good quality close-up shots of tempting and tasty food. Even with a celebrity cook in the picture, the focus is often on the food laid out before them.

Magazine editors do not have the budgets to provide photographers to take pictures for every article they publish, and given the quality of relatively inexpensive SLR cameras and even smartphone cameras, they do not need to. However, the quality of the photographs you submit with your query email, and then your finished piece, could influence your acceptance rates.

Take a photo of your project in good lighting on a plain, uncluttered background, and follow the magazine guidelines for preferred resolution and image format.

Michelle Mach, writing for Get Crafty

If you are not a confident photographer, I recommend you practice. Otherwise, find someone else to help you.

> *Tip: For step-by-step project photographs, you may find it easier to use a tripod, as the shots can be taken from the same angle. But, do not send numerous photos with your idea or query. Usually, one image of the completed project and one close-up will suffice.*

Whether you are submitting to online or hard-copy publications, photography has, and will always be, a very important part of article writing and publication. Many readers are visual and will be drawn to a magazine based on its front cover, and equally will be drawn to an article because of an image.

You never know, if your photograph is good enough it could even make the front cover!

Chapter 7
Travel Writing

So you say you want to be a travel writer? You want to wander the world, sending back tantalising tales of far-flung adventures to magazines, newspapers and websites. And get paid handsomely for it. Is that too much to ask?

Don George, Travel Writer for Lonely Planet

As glamorous as it might sound, travel writing is not about jetting off to exotic locations on an all-expenses paid holiday. Often, it's not a holiday at all.

Guidebook writers may only have a few days in which to cram in visits to attractions, restaurants and hotels in one place, and take enough notes, and perhaps snapshots, to help jog their memories when they come to type up their findings. And if they are extremely lucky, they might just about earn over and above what it cost them to get there in the first place.

Did you think they spent weeks staying in the 5-Star hotels they featured?

Given the above, travel writing is perhaps not quite the glamorous undertaking you may have initially thought – even if you do get the chance to stay in some beautiful locations around the world. It is incredibly hard work, expensive, and the returns can be negligible.

There is also a huge misconception that every traveller's tale will be of interest to editors and their readers. Ahem, the majority will not. Travel writing is one of the hardest writing genres to break. For every travel writing slot, there are probably 100 writers vying to fill it. Editors of travel publications have slush piles the size of Mount Everest from wannabe travel writers, reciting their holiday adventures from across the globe, and that is exactly what they *do not want or need.* No one is interested in your last holiday – it is not enough to tell them what a great time you had – you need to relate something new and interesting to your reader.

Chapter 7

Equally, telling an editor you are heading off to Timbuktu or somewhere similarly remote in the hope of an enthusiastic commission is just NOT going to happen. There is no shortage of people jetting away to remote places in the world waiting in readiness to share their stories. Travelling off the beaten track is not reason enough to be commissioned. What editors of travel magazines want is the same as what the editor of every publication wants – FRESH and ORIGINAL COPY – and then a little bit more!

You could be travelling to the most visited city in the world – and there will still be new things to be found, and new things to be said. In fact, a frequently visited place is no impediment as it means lots of people should be interested in the destination. It is the *rare find* you offer an editor – a new angle or a different aspect to a city – that might just grab his attention. In addition, of course, to the absolute most interesting, engaging and entertaining copy you can write.

Using your travel experiences both home and abroad as writing opportunities, between your other writing commitments, is a plausible way to start travel writing – and could be fun. It could even help pay towards the costs of your holiday, accommodation, or day trips.

Cast your mind back to Chapter 4 and general interest magazines and regional titles. Many of these carry travel-type features as well as town and village pieces, relevant to the region or county of the magazine. This is where your home town or somewhere you visit can be used as written material for a travel piece. Start with these and build up your cuttings portfolio ready to tackle the big boys.

> *Many inexperienced writers immediately think of lengthy destination pieces, but this is the area where competition is most fierce. Don't necessarily begin with big features. Scour publications for spots where you could supply something with a travel spin. It could be a news piece, a contribution to a regular column or a quirky filler.*
>
> Lyn Hughes, Wanderlust

Think laterally. Alongside the dedicated travel magazines, the newspapers' weekend supplements carry many travel features, as do many women's titles. You might even find a slot or two in your specialist magazine too – if you consider the likes of crocheting in Spain or fishing in Canada.

As we discovered in Chapter 6 (food), there are many ways in which you can tackle the subject, and the same applies to travel writing. Start with your personal experience or first-person features including practical articles such as travelling with babies or backpacking. Think touristy features such as pieces on monuments and architecture, pilgrimages or eating abroad. What about articles on fashion, foreign celebrities or living in another country? And, then there are travel books and guidebooks. The market is huge but so are the opportunities.

Breaking into the travel market

Initially, you will probably find it very hard to break directly into travel magazines as a bona fide travel writer. It takes years of experience and a real talent to write specialist travel features. Nobody is saying you can't do it – but the level and professionalism of the copy is probably, at this stage, tough to achieve until you have regularly been published, that is.

> *A basic error with travel writing is assuming everybody's interested. You have to work from exactly the opposite assumption: nobody is interested. Even your wife is not interested. You have to somehow make it so that they become interested.*

Bill Bryson, in an interview with Don George, Wanderlust

Nevertheless, some travel magazines do occasionally ask for reader's travel experiences so keep an eye out for these opportunities. Guy Everton, a former travel agent turned freelance writer, recently contributed to *Traveller* magazine recounting stories of his independent travels to Algeria, Zimbabwe and Ethiopia.

Chapter 7

It was pouring in Gondar when I arrived. Navy uniformed policemen and soldiers in fatigues were flanking the streets huddled together in doorways, rifle muzzles protruding from waterproof ponchos, faces etched with brooding menace. Windows around them bore the marks of strife, a polka dotting of punctures joined by jagged fractures. Lunchtime it may have been, but those people still outdoors moved in a wary hush like students in an exam hall. The city was on edge.

Guy Everton, Rain & Riots

The travel article

Although many travel publications still run features across five pages or more, during your magazine research you should also notice how many more pages are filled with shorter articles and small features, many less than 500 words. Travel blogs are equally short and punchy too.

Practice writing succinctly. Editors are mostly looking for short, informative stories that make a point and move on.

As mentioned above – the travel article is probably unlike any other you will come across. Your travel writing will probably have to be at its best if you are to stand a chance of getting it published. Just read some of the articles published in *Traveller* and *Wanderlust*, and you will understand precisely what I mean.

One top tip is to *'begin with a bang'*. Explode your idea at the editor and his readers.

For example:

Boston is a relatively small city and unlike other cities you might have travelled to, it's hard to get lost. It has 16 historic sites which are easily found if you follow the Freedom Trail, a line of red bricks set into the pavement.

* * *

A big city on a small scale – that's Boston in a nutshell. You can walk almost anywhere but if your sense of direction is poor, just follow the three-mile-long Freedom Trail. It links 16 historic sites with its line of red bricks set into the pavement, you can't go wrong.

I am sure you would agree that the second paragraph is far more dynamic and interesting than the first.

And what about this for an opening paragraph?

"Crabs. They're definitely crabs. Shit, I've got crabs." It was an early morning alarm call. Only my second day alone in the forest and here I was picking teeny creatures from my groin at six in the morning.*

Dominic Hamilton, Global

The above was illustrated in the *'Very Bad Things'* of a holiday guide but just goes to show how, with a little imagination and a great opening line, any aspect of your holiday – good, bad or indifferent – can be used as material for your travel piece.

Bill Bryson is the master travel writer when it comes to sharing his observations. In more cases than not, his excursions can encourage us to stay put in the cosiness of our armchairs rather than venture into the big wide world. And that takes formidable writing.

From the train, North Wales looked like holiday hell – endless ranks of prison-camp caravan parks standing in fields in the middle of a lonely, windbeaten nowhere, on the wrong side of the railway line and a merciless dual carriageway, with views over a boundless estuary or moist sand dotted with treacherous-looking sinkholes and, far off, a distant smear of sea. It seemed an odd type of holiday option to me, the idea of sleeping in a tin box in a lonesome field miles from anywhere in a climate like Britain's and emerging each morning with hundreds of other people from identical tin boxes, crossing the rail line and dual carriageway and hiking over a desert of sinkholes in order to dip your toes in a distant sea full of Liverpool turns. I can't put my finger on what exactly, but something about it didn't appeal to me.

Bill Bryson, Notes from a Small Island

Like Bill, you need to convey *atmosphere* in your piece through the sights, sounds and smells of the place you are writing about. Observe the native tongue, the national dress, and the comings and goings of the locals. What about the tourists? Are there lots of tourists or have you found some remote island yet to be discovered by the masses?

My impression of Ipswich was the first real impression of England. It was certainly not love at first sight. My first thoughts were that the houses were all so tiny after the tower blocks of Moscow, with such horrible colours, after the white washed walls of Greece. There seemed to be strange people everywhere wearing winter coats and sandals at the same time. A three-legged dog hopped past and a crazy Dutchman started talking to us. What was I doing here?'

Olga Hopper, Summer in Suffolk

Keep your copy lively and informative and don't drag it down with too many facts. Use side-panels or fact boxes, they show a touch of professionalism. Your side panels might offer *sights you must see*, *flight costs*, the *best places to stay or dine* or *what to avoid*. They can cover just about anything.

The ending

Your ending should be as striking as the beginning – leave your reader wanting to discover more; make them feel like they should go or, in fact, they have just been, through your creative narrative.

So, all the elements were in place – great local produce, a choice of alcohol, a fine kitchen to cook in, authoritative cookbooks and a shaded terrace near the pool to dine upon. How on earth did we manage to keep ourselves occupied? I am afraid only the bathroom scales know the full, gluttonous story.

Rob Ryan, Travel

The travel theme

Whatever type of travel feature you decide to write, whether it's a county town, your favourite holiday spot or the holiday of a lifetime – stick to a single theme. Don't clutter your work with different ideas all reaching out in several directions so the reader becomes confused.

Once you have decided on your theme or focus – *Museums in Moscow*, *Discovering the Dales* or *A Cuban Wedding*, perhaps – look to gain additional mileage from your excursion. If you are writing about *Museums in Moscow* for one magazine how about *Munching our way round Moscow* for another? While the first deals with history and architecture, the second is all about the food. And don't limit it to the local fare either. Might readers like to know what it's like to eat at *McDonald's* in Moscow? Are there unique local specials on the menu? (In Malaysia, for example, McDonalds offers chicken strips in porridge with chillies, ginger, and more. It's called *Bubur Ayam*.)

If you are writing about culinary topics, remember your food publications too!

> *Tip: Use every experience you encounter and write it down; make notes, keep a journal, or record it on a Dictaphone – just make a note of it because you are unlikely to remember all the details when you get home.*

Whether at home or abroad, visit the local *Tourist Information Centre* or wherever they give out information about local places of interest. Grab as many pamphlets and information leaflets as you can – everywhere you go – you might just need the details when you come to write about your travel experiences. And, one piece of information might spark an idea for another piece of writing, for the same or an alternative publication.

> *Tip: Accuracy is absolutely paramount. Irrespective of how beautifully you write your article, if your facts are wrong you will be in trouble. Double-check your copy for accuracy, especially the spellings of foreign words and names.*

Inflight magazines, aimed at airline passengers, are also another source of opportunity for your travel pieces. Here, you will find detailed features of varying types for the airline's destinations.

Inflight magazines for long-haul flights are sometimes more in-depth, to keep the reader entertained on a longer journey. Whereas, more concise articles will be found on short-haul flights. Bearing in mind that there are literally hundreds of airlines all over the world, there is a wide market of opportunity for the astute writer.

Copies of inflight magazines can often be obtained from the airlines directly. Their addresses can be found in the *Flight International's World Airline Directory* or the *Travel Trade Directory*.

Being a travel writer not only offers many opportunities for you to explore, it will bring a certain amount of excitement and exhilaration, and this should be evident in your travel writing copy.

Chapter 7

You've got to treat travel-writing like a business. I may only travel for a few months each year – the rest of the time I'm pitching proposals, negotiating free travel with airlines and tour operators, writing copy and generally plugging away at PR.

William Gray, Wanderlust

One more thing though – high-quality travel magazines want exceptional photography. So, before you pack for your hols, determined to write about your experiences, make sure you find out what they want in terms of copy and images, and make sure you can deliver what they need.

But if you are committed to being one, do it because you are already a curious and perceptive traveler who happens to be a good (if not great) writer, and do it the right way. Read a few good books on the subject and really do what the authors say to do. The advice is nearly always tried and true.

Tim Leffel, Transitions Abroad

Chapter 8
Writing Comedy and Humour

Did you hear about the tarot whiz who got hit by a truck? She didn't see it coming.

Jason Love

What is funny?

Good comedy writing is whatever makes us laugh.

Hopefully, you would have at least found the quip above amusing. Humour is, however, a very personal thing and writing comedy or adding humour to your work can be quite difficult – unless you already have a gift for it.

Writing comedy is one of the most difficult jobs in the world. Talent, patience, determination and perseverance are just some of the qualities needed to succeed in this tough business. Yet there is always a shortage of good comedy writers and people who can consistently churn out funny scripts are like gold dust.

Ken Rock, President, British Society of Comedy Writers

Good comedy writing can make us think. It can make us look at life from a different perspective, and can occasionally bring a tear to our eyes.

Read Miranda Hart's book, *Is It Just me?* and you could be forgiven for believing that writing comedy is easy. Miranda's comedy writing talent appears so natural that when she takes an everyday situation, shreds it to pieces, and then delivers it back as if it is all quite ordinary and normal; it shouldn't be that funny – but it is!

Maybe you're standing on a commuter train, using this book as a filter between you and a repellent armpit. If so, I'm terribly sorry. That's no way to start the day, is it? Face in pit. Commuter trains are the only place you'd not question standing what in any other social scenario would be freakishly and embarrassingly close to a friend, let alone a stranger.

Miranda Hart, Is It Just Me?

Consider the language here: *repellent* and *freakishly* – the words themselves are funny. Even *smelly* or *stinky* don't quite match up to *repellent* – do they?

Some of us may not be able to write as humorously as Miranda, and if you don't think you have a natural talent for writing comedy – don't panic just yet. With a little help and practice, it can be learned.

Since sense of humour is such a subjective thing how can you be sure that something you think is funny will get the same reaction from anyone else, whether it's the comedian or TV producer you are pitching your material to, or the audience which will eventually have to endure your efforts?

The simple answer is you can't be sure – comedy writing is a constant process of trial and error with most of the errors being done in public. However, you can increase your chances of producing usable work by studying as many examples of successful comedy as possible.

John Byrne, Writing Comedy

The good news, from a writer's point of view, is that humour is everywhere. Whether we enjoy reading, writing or listening to it – it's out there, and in a variety of forms. Television – where would be without the comedy sketches of *Laurel and Hardy*, the puns from *The Two Ronnies,* and even sitcoms like *Dinnerladies, Last of the Summer Wine,* and *Only Fools and Horses?* These comedy scripts are a good example of one of the comedic writing routes available to you, should you choose to pursue a comedy writing career.

What about cartoons?

Cartoon strips have been around longer than most of us will remember and are as popular today as they have always been. But what makes them so? Most cartoon strips use an everyday life example in a way that we can relate to, and this is what makes them funny.

Whether you are a complete beginner at writing comedy or you have dabbled in writing humour in the past, your main aim remains the same: *to stare at a blank sheet of paper and try to write something on it that will make others laugh.*

Wrong. Every comedy writer will tell you that is precisely what you don't do. To be a good (or great) writer of comedy, you need to experience life. Get out of your chair and away from your writing desk, and start studying people. Take notes of humorous things people say and do. Take a serious situation and see if you can put a humorous slant on it. Watch people's habits and idiosyncrasies and see how you can expand on them to make them funny.

Comedy situations are often an exaggeration of *behaviour*, in the same way as caricaturists over-accentuate the features of a person.

So how do you do it?

Like all professions, study the basic mechanics of it. If laughter is what you are trying to create, it makes sense to look at the human sense of humour and see how or why it works.

As you come to study, in depth, some of the magazines we have previously mentioned, you may come across a piece of writing that made you smile, chuckle or laugh. Ask yourself *why*? *Why* did you smile? *Why* did you find it amusing?

You may recall the extract from *Bill Bryson's Notes from a Small Island*, in the travel writing chapter. In terms of article writing, travel writing is the most likely place where writing humorously will be welcomed by editors and readers alike. Travellers' tales and amusing language, confusions or misunderstood meanings, give you the material to write amusing anecdotes or tales.

Remember *Dominic Hamilton's* encounter with crabs? Well, he went on to add:

> *You have to kill them too, otherwise they come straight back at you as fast as you can pick them off. You have to pinch them between your nails until you reckon you've extinguished their penchant for heights and warm places. Because, if not, with a hop, skip and a jump, they'll be back after the break.*

Jan Devey was 'the information lady' at the British Embassy in The Hague, The Netherlands, between 1991 and 2003. During her career at the embassy, Jan was bemused by all the weird and wonderful questions and enquiries she faced daily and had the foresight to jot them down. On her retirement, Jan produced a fantastic little book: *Can I take worms to Britain?*

Here is a little taster:

Chapter 8

I want to take photos of a hippy commune in Wales. Can you tell me where I can find one?

What is the weather like in Scotland?

My Chinese friend wants to return to Hong Kong. Is this a problem? He is dead.

Material like Jan collated is priceless, and given how much we all use the internet these days, it is unlikely that these sorts of questions will be voiced again. But, should you find yourself in a situation where the complexity of language affords you the opportunity, do not – for the sake of humour – miss it!

Spending time with young children will undoubtedly give you endless material. This is the sort of 'stuff' the tabloid weeklies like *Take a Break* and *Chat* pay for. The readers' letters pages of these and similar publications often contain amusing tales and mishaps, and the funny things kids say or do.

For example:

Recently, my eight-year-old son was telling us that Americans are odd because they think we all wear bowler hats and talk posh!

My five-year-old son then quipped, 'they're silly, we don't talk posh we talk English!'

This happened to me and made me laugh out loud, and because I found it funny, I remembered it, and then submitted it as a reader's letter.

It is not just the incidents themselves that are amusing. As writers, we need to be able to write in such a way that others will find amusement in our words. Children are a great source for providing humorous content because of their innocence, and in some ways so are the elderly, or perhaps it's just my 80-year-old Grandma.

'Don't play with the water in that bucket, Jonathan, it's static!' she said to my brother. We howled, 'I think you mean 'stagnant' Nan.'

The funniest things often come from people who are certainly not trying to be funny, like my Grandma, in the above situation. Watch the characters in sitcoms such as John Cleese as Basil Fawlty in *Fawlty Towers* or Kathy Staff as Nora Batty in *Last of the Summer Wine*;

these 'funny people' behave so innocently over what they've said or done. This is what funny is, and we love them for it.

One of my favourite television shows is *The Vicar of Dibley*. At the end of each episode, Geraldine Grainger (Dawn French) sits down with her willing assistant, Alice Tinker (Emma Chambers), and over a cup of tea tells Alice a joke – which she never seems to understand. Or, and here is the twist, if she does think she understands the joke, she has usually misunderstood it!

'Geraldine asks – what is brown and sticky?

Alice replies – 'I don't know- what is brown and sticky'

Geraldine says – 'A stick.'

Alice shakes her head and says – 'No! Sticks aren't sticky.'

Geraldine says – 'but they are, aren't they? Because they are sticks – they are stick-ee.'

Alice says, 'but that's not what sticky means, sticky means sticky. I mean some sticks are sticky because sap oozes out of them. But if you said what's brown and sometimes sticky that might work…'

You get the picture.

> *While you're watching, make notes. If you laugh at something, try and figure out why you're laughing. What was it that pushed the funny button in your brain? Something visual? Something to do with the way words were used? Or was it because the joke reminded you of something funny in your own life? Start to watch comedy in a different way. Take it apart and put it back together again. You'll soon start to notice that the same tricks are applied again and again and again.*
>
> Brian Luff, The Internet Writing Journal

Humour is around us all the time. Social media is absolutely full of humorous quotes and anecdotes. Besides Miranda Hart, read the works of other comedy writers such as David Walliams, Michael McIntyre and John Bishop. Watch the sketches of French & Saunders, Catherine Tate and Harry Enfield. Study the format of the successful sitcoms, including the American ones such as *Friends* and *The Big Bang Theory*. And if satire is your thing, *Yes, Prime Minister* or *Blackadder*, will, if nothing else, bring a smile to your face.

Chapter 8

How can humour help your writing?

Humour can be found in various forms: overheard conversations, misunderstandings, plays on words, and your understanding of these forms will help you write humorously.

Whether you are writing fiction or non-fiction, a touch of humour can make your work bright, attractive, and saleable. Think of humorous situations you have found yourself in, or experienced. Consider how you can use this in your work – especially if you can hit the editor with it in the first line!

It's not etiquette to eat peas with a knife. It is also very difficult.

John Cannon, Writers Bureau

What a great opening line and one an editor of a food magazine couldn't resist. The article itself went on to describe different eating habits around the world, interesting enough – but it was probably the opening line here that sold it. Although it was not an original observation, and it's not all that funny, the author managed to use a minimum number of words to amuse the reader, who was therefore, drawn to read on. And this is what you must try and do to capture the attention of the editor and subsequent readers.

We have, in previous chapters, looked at powerful opening paragraphs. We have even touched on the use of language. Consider why some words are funnier than others: *spider* or *creepy-crawly*, etc.

Categories of Humour

There are various categories of humorous writing. If you are interested in writing this type of work, it is probably best to find the category which comes easiest to you.

1. *Amusing event* – This type of writing is suitable for all general interest titles. It could be anything from seeing a funny name for something in the wrong setting to a peculiar event such as amusing accidents or a strange marriage proposal.

2. *Humorous piece* – probably the easiest and most natural for all of us. Again, suitable for general interest titles and particularly popular with readers' letter pages. It could be

something you've overheard, or it can be an amusing article based upon situations you've come across.

For example:

Group Therapy.

'It's bad enough,' said Eeyore, almost breaking down, 'being miserable myself, what with no presents and no cake and no candles, and no proper notice taken of me at all, but if everybody else is going to be miserable too–'

Ted Smart, Eeyore's Little Book of Gloom

3. *Satirical article* – These can be very funny. Essentially, they use ridicule, mockery, and sarcasm in the written form to expose follies, vices and the hypocrisies of others, particularly government, politicians and other people in the public eye – *The New Statesman* springs to mind. If this type of writing appeals to you, do be careful, to write successful satire you should know how far you can go.

4. *Nonsense farce* – these are funny because they touch on the ridiculous. For those who have enjoyed the works of *Spike Milligan,* you will understand the rewards for writing the nonsense farce article.

Besides writing your reader's letter quips and anecdotes, or the terrible tales of a lonesome traveller for a travel magazine, the market is eagerly awaiting the next comedy writer. The BBC are always on the lookout for good comedy writers and offer plenty of tips and advice for those willing to try their hand at writing TV sitcoms and comedy for radio.

The market also needs writers who can write jokes and one-liners. Whether you compile 100 jokes for a joke book, or provide the material for a stand-up comedian, if you have the skills to write comedy well, you *will* be in demand.

Subjects to avoid

As with most of the topics we have covered, there are always one or two do's or don'ts and I'm afraid, writing humour has a list too.

Chapter 8

Death, tragedy, disaster, unhappiness and human disabilities need to be avoided. You can argue that there are writers who touch on some of these subjects. Generally, editors will avoid them because their readers could be offended by them, or they could be considered 'sick'. Especially if it were a joke about a much-loved national treasure who had just died.

You might also point out that you have seen or heard comedians poking fun at people with disabilities or talking about death, but for some strange reason when this type of thing is performed, humans find it funny. It very rarely works in the same way in the written form. There are publications who like to cover these topics, but there are very few openings. Don't waste your time, if you can write humorously about non-offensive subjects spend your valuable writing time doing so!

Now go and write something funny – but if you can't – then read something funny. If nothing else, it will brighten up your day.

Chapter 9
Historical and Military Writing

Writing about historical or military subjects requires you to have yet another skill set. Not only must you have a passion for writing – a naturally inquisitive mind with a desire to seek out facts and an obsession for research are equally important. If you lack these elements, you may find it incredibly difficult to do justice to either of these topics.

Writers of historical and military content find that writing grammatically and stylistically is only one element of the writing skills required. The combination of structure and detailed factual assessment is what makes this type of writing more difficult – both for novices and experienced writers.

However, if you have a passion for history or military procedures, or the conflicts of war, and you are confident you can write well on these topics, you will always have an audience.

As a race, the documentary evidence we have already collated about the Romans, the Tudors, and the Victorians, is in abundance. We have compiled even greater knowledge of the First and Second World Wars, the Falklands and the Gulf Wars – and yet, every day, there are new discoveries, new evidence, and new tales to tell about each of these topics. Your job as a historical or military writer is to seek out those new discoveries, unearth any conspiracies, and even unveil contradictions. And then, put across your thoughts, theories, and conclusions in a readable, evidence-backed, and non-self-gratifying way.

Historical writing

The past is not the same as history – history is not about everything that happened in the past – just the important things. History is not simply a description of what happened in the past, but also our efforts to understand it, and writing about history requires evidence.

Chapter 9

As a writer of historical work, it is helpful to use three basic processes:

1. *Gather* the details and facts.

2. *Analyse* the information.

3. *Present* the circumstances including your interpretations and conclusions.

The gathering of information gives you the *evidence* you need to write your piece. While doing so, seek inferences from the evidence. Decide what is important and how you can interpret and make sense of it. Your next job is to find an appropriate way of presenting your interpretation.

Historical writing is not about patching together all the notes you have gathered from your various sources. Your finished copy should not be dull or uninteresting to your reader. It should flow well and without the interruption of different styles or irregular sentence structures – where the phrases of other authors have been slotted into yours – as this will almost certainly be evident to your readers.

In many cases, writing about historical subjects requires a similar approach to writing a novel. Your content should be written in an engaging style. The background, the scene, and the characters should be described in detail. Use sufficient historical evidence to create those descriptions. The only difference between novel writing and historical writing is that the first is a work of fiction, and historical writing is always based on facts!

On gathering your evidence, consider how you are going to broach the subject. You may only be taking a moment in time – a single event such as the Battle of Hastings. You might want to cover a longer period, perhaps the Life and Times of Elizabeth I, or even a much broader topic such as Living in 21st Century Britain.

You may decide to write one or a series of articles for a specialist magazine, for instance *History Today* or *Military Times*, or tackle writing a book. If the latter, what sort of book might you write?

It could be a historical biography – these are popular character-based accounts of the life of someone notable. Often written in a narrative style, the author's aim is to bring the character alive on the page, rather than just put together interesting facts about them or their place in history.

Diaries or journal-led books tend to be less narrative in style than historical biographies. Often, the author discloses information about a series of incidents or a timeline of events that relates to one thing.

Popular history deals with a theme or subject that is aimed at a wider readership, or takes a popular approach. This type of work is usually considered less scholarly than other historical works and often more narrative in style. For example, *Inside Vogue: My Diary Of Vogue's 100th Year* by Alexandra Shulman.

Official history – is usually sponsored, authorized or endorsed, and is most commonly commissioned for governments or commercial companies. Academic history, on the other hand, could be based on topics such as the history of medicine, ancient Egypt or the Russian Revolution.

Perhaps narrative history is more your area of expertise? Written in a story-based style, narrative history focuses on the chronological order of an event, driven by individuals, actions and intentions. The best example of this would be something like: *Narrative of Solomon Northup: Twelve Years a Slave: An African American Historical Narrative.*

You might choose to write about one element of history like flying a Spitfire during the war or collate a series of similar events such as *Crimes of Passion* (see below).

The presentation of your work might also take on one of three forms, or a combination of the forms, to cover different aspects of your work.

Argument – an argument-based piece is often written in the form of a thesis backed by the reasons for said thesis.

> *Ruth Ellis is assured of her small place in history, not only because she was the last woman to hang, but because her execution, considered barbarous by many, place her in that group of murderers, together with Derek Bentley and Timothy Evens, whose executions were constantly cited by those seeking the abolition of the death penalty.*

Howard Engel, Crimes of Passion

Chapter 9

Narrative – the narrative or story-like form is popular in historical writing. The author may want the reader to be engaged or inspired by the character or events, and therefore, he may want the reader to feel a connection with the person or incident.

> *Two armies faced each other on a battlefield. It was early morning on Sunday 29 March 1461 and the driving rain and snow almost blinded the men lined up in anticipation of hand-to-hand combat.*

Amy Licence, Elizabeth of York

Descriptive – use descriptive writing for the portrayal of a person, place, or object at a particular moment in time.

> *A dazzling blue sky, the early morning sun reflecting the innumerable shades of dainty flowers which covered the 'campo' like a thick carpet. Three galloping horsemen drew nearer to our 'puesto'.*

John Maxtone-Graham, Titanic Survivor: The Memoirs of Violet Jessop Stewardess

Irrespective of the type of historical writing you plan to tackle, your work must be *clear, precise, concise, organised, analytical* and *concrete*.

Writers of historical works are like detectives. They must seek out the facts, check and double check their sources for reliability, and present their works in such a way that they leave their reader satisfied with the outcome.

Wherever possible use *primary* sources:

A primary source is one produced by a participant in, or witness to, the events being written about. A primary source allows the historian to see the past through the eyes of direct participants. Some common primary sources are letters, diaries, memoirs, speeches, church records, newspaper articles, and government documents of all kinds.

Secondary sources are less reliable and often used by historians to see how other scholars have interpreted the past:

A secondary source is one written by a later person who had no part in the events of what he or she is writing about. (In the rare cases when the historian was a participant in the events, then the work – or at least part of it – is a primary source.)

Historians also warn of using the internet as viable primary or secondary sources.

Anyone with the right software can post something on the Web without having to get past trained editors, peer reviewers, or librarians. As a result, there is a great deal of garbage on the Web. If you use a primary source from the Web, make sure that a respected intellectual institution stands behind the site. Be especially wary of secondary articles on the Web, unless they appear in electronic versions of established print journals.

Hamilton Education, Writing a Good History Paper

Impartiality and detachment are essential aspects of historical writing. A writer's preconceptions, prejudices and partialities should not be evident in his historical writing. Writers must also avoid placing judgements on events of the past. It may not always be easy to do this, especially if your resources come from only one central source – say, perhaps, the police and the files for prosecution team, and nothing from the defendant or his lawyers. As a writer, your own personal experiences, the books you have read, or the countries you have travelled to, can also affect the objectivity of your work.

In all cases, it is advised to avoid the use of the first-person voice in your historical writing. Draw your reader's attention to the points you want to make, not to yourself, or the toil and trouble you may have gone to, in the processes of researching and writing your piece. Your focus should always be on what you want to say about your topic, not how you got there.

Because you are writing about past events, and in many cases not as a primary source, much of your work is going to be collated from your research. Here, more than anywhere, you must document EVERY quotation, paraphrase, or crucial idea that you borrow from a source. It is particularly important to document everything that cannot be considered as textbook knowledge. This is equally more important for any references to facts that could be considered controversial, or central to the foundation of your argument, analysis or indeed, your narrative.

While on the subject of quotes – use them sparingly. Quoting does not add authority, unless the source carries authority. The effective quotation is considered as a literary device – it is not a tool to be used to transfer information from your sources to your reader. You would be better advised to reword and rewrite. Aspire to write the content better than the original author. This is where your language skills come into play.

When writing historical works, consider how the words you use reflect the language of the period you are writing about (particularly pertinent when you are writing historical fiction); will you modernise your phrases to meet the needs of the contemporary reader? Obviously, if you are using a quotation in its true form, your quotation will be relevant to the period in which the quote was written (and not necessarily the period of history to which your work relates). If, however, you are paraphrasing, the words you choose will affect the overall content and style of your piece.

Tip: Don't forget about the etymology of words – use a good dictionary to help with this.

Be conscious of the *historical present.* You must be aware of the sense of time and context. Writing of past events in the present tense shouts novice, and a lack of the author's appreciation for the historical setting.

> *But even the author's act of writing a book took place in the past, even if only a year or two ago. Thus, Hofstadter ARGUED, not "argues", in his Age of Reform. Hofstadter is now dead, and presumably cannot argue (present tense). Even if he were still living, we do not know that he has not changed his mind; authors do change their minds.*

Geraldschlabach.net/historical-writing

One last thing to bear in mind on this subject is that historians have tackled almost every historic event in one form or another. Your ambition as a historical writer should be to write your piece as if no one else has ever written about the topic before.

Military writing

Much of the advice presented in the section about historical writing will apply to writing about the military and warfare. Especially the necessity to research and gather information and facts. Even if you are writing a personal account of a situation, your memory may not be as vivid as you would like to believe, and it is worth the time and effort to double-check your facts with other reliable sources.

Writing about the military is also not just about fighting wars and conflicts. Military procedures, hierarchy, weapons and military vehicles all make for thought-provoking reads – if you have an interest in these topics.

> *The first step to military history success then is to drop the military and instantly widen your appeal.*

Tim Newark, author and editor of Military Illustrated

The above quote was made during an interview with Clare Kingston at *Collins Popular Non-fiction* who said, *"You can start by taking out [the word] military. We are talking popular history, good people stories, strong narrative."*

In recent years, the market has seen a significant shift in the readership of military works. Even though the *tough-guy in a difficult situation* and details of combat to military precision are still high on the list of reads for men, good adventure stories by real people has led to an increase in female readership and an upsurge in the sale of military history books.

However, unlike general historical writing, much of the content for military works appears to come from primary sources including journalists and war correspondents such as Dexter Filkins (*The Forever War*) and Mark Bowden (*Black Hawk Down*). Furthermore, those with first-hand experience of combat or military forces also feature; people like Former Air Force Col. James Burton (*The Pentagon Wars*) and Marine Officer Nathaniel Fick (*One Bullet Away*). That said, several historians, with no personal experience of war, have paralleled the success of war veteran authors when writing about military history. They include Stephen Ambrose (*Band of Brothers*) and Pulitzer-prize winner Barbara Tuchman (*The Guns of August*).

It is fair to say, since the atrocities of 9/11 that the Iraq, Afghanistan and Syrian conflicts have been at the forefront of the media for some years now. Combined with the number of global terror attacks on civilians from various quarters, our thirst for first-hand military encounters and battle tactics has never been stronger.

Personal experience stories like those of bestselling writer and former U.S. Marine Anthony Swofford, author of *Jarhead* (his memoir of serving in Desert Storm) use military experience to land spots on bestseller lists. While book publications of this type are on the rise, the bad news is there are lots of other people with true stories too, and finding a new hook on which to hang *your* military experience hat could be more difficult than you envisage.

For memoirists, *Swofford* offers this piece of advice:

> *Very important to the memoir writer is killing the ego. When writing about oneself don't apply too much stage make-up. Let the wrinkles show.*

www.military.com

You could, however, apply another approach. Compile the true-life accounts of several war veterans, or choose to focus on the effects of those damaged by war: civilians, soldiers, or institutions. Equally, take a battle of the distant past. According to Michael Leventhal, publisher at *Greenhill Books*, battles or events on a small scale have dramatic appeal, and even new stories about the Second World War are currently in circulation.

Anniversaries are always a good hook but your research here is essential. What new twist or new evidence can you shed on a previously disclosed subject that will make editors and publishers fight for the rights to publish?

As with all your writing, the success of your article or your book is dependent on the research you do, the works of others you read, and more importantly the story you want to convey. You cannot emulate the style and narrative of other writers. You must find your own voice. Even if you intend to write a personal account of your time serving in Afghanistan, or as a medical nurse on the front line, the story you recall will be very different from those serving around you. That alone may not be enough to find a publisher ready to take your memoirs to the printer just yet.

You should ask yourself *what is different about your story?* Why would someone be interested in *your* recollection of an event? And, how might you make *your* story *appeal* to a wider readership?

It might be that you want to challenge the reasons for action (as in the case of Tony Blair over the Iraq War conflict). You might want to use the atrocities of war to raise awareness towards a demoralised nation. It could just be that you have a passion so strong for the subject – and a natural flair for writing – that it would be a travesty if you failed to put your thoughts down in words.

Whatever your reasons, military and historical writing still has a place on the pages of many general and specialist titles, as it does on the shelves of all good bookshops and e-tailers. Approach your subject with gusto. Delve into the depths of archives and wheedle out those little treasures of hidden gold – and you might just reward yourself with a very publishable piece of writing.

Chapter 10
Memoirs, Autobiographies, Biographies and Ghostwriting

A memoir is the recounting of a single event or a series of events written from personal knowledge.

An autobiography is the story of a person's life written by that person.

A biography is the story of someone's life written by another person.

There are a few misconceptions about writing a memoir and writing an autobiography. Many autobiographies are, in fact, memoirs because they only reveal some aspects or events of the writer's life. Someone please explain this to Katie Price who's fifth life instalment – *Love, Lipstick and Lies* – claimed it was *'My most sensational autobiography yet!'* Ms. Price, your books are not autobiographies – they are memoirs! In Ms. Price's defence, it could be argued that she could have two autobiographies; one of her life as *Jordan* and one as *Katie Price* – but five?

And the second misconception, (which further applies to Ms. Price, and Zayn, formally a member of the boy band, *One Direction*) you are never too young to write an autobiography.

Another slightly misleading autobiographical claim is when the autobiography is written by someone else – *a ghostwriter.*

A ghostwriter is a person who is hired to author books officially credited to another person. A ghostwriter may also write manuscripts, screenplays, speeches, articles, blog posts, stories, reports, whitepapers, or other texts.

A ghostwriter should not be confused with a co-writer. Some autobiographies are co-written, meaning another author has assisted the biographer with the writing of the book. The co-writer's name will appear as a co-author, whereas ghostwriters mostly remain anonymous.

In this chapter on writing memoirs, autobiographies and biographies, we will also explore the advantages and disadvantages of being a ghostwriter, and how to find work in this field.

Memoirs

Many writers choose to write about their own lives, and for any number of reasons. It is an obvious choice as it is something they know a lot about. Some people find it therapeutic to write about particular events; maybe a difficult childhood, or overcoming some adversity. For others, writing a memoir is about trying to make some sense of their existence or to find some meaning in the world. It could simply be that they want to leave behind memories for their descendants.

Memoir writing is handing over a piece of your life. It explains what you went through, who you are, and perhaps justifies why you behave the way you do. It is about sharing your experience *honestly*, and in the hope that someone else will benefit from your wisdom without having to live it.

However, there are many types of memoirs and you do not need to have gone through an awful experience to write your story. A considerable number of memoirs do include some sort of adversity, though.

A long way Home: A Memoir by Saroo Brierley, is a perfect example. Now republished under the movie title, *Lion: A Long Way Home*, Saroo reveals his heart-breaking and inspiring true story as a little boy who found his way home 25 years after he got lost on a train.

Other writers have a different kind of story they want to tell. In Michael Parkinson's *Muhammad Ali: A Memoir*, Michael revisits the interviews he conducted with the charismatic boxer. In Kenneth Clarke's *Kind of Blue: A Political Memoir*, he shares his progress from working-class scholarship boy to high political office.

Your memoir can be about anything, irrespective of how small or seemingly insignificant. Some people may find it difficult to pinpoint a specific event but if you can find worthy stories hidden in your subconscious – explore the opportunity.

I have.

Being a writer is only a small part of who I am, but my life as a writer – spanning 20 years or more – has been an amazing journey, thus far. It was not planned and it happened quite unexpectedly. I have experienced many highs and equally, many lows. I have met some truly inspiring people and some very colourful characters too. My memoir, as a writer and author, is written with the hope that despite the adversities I have encountered in the world of writing and publication – I can encourage other aspiring writers to keep writing.

If you already have an idea for a memoir that's great, I shall shortly reveal the methods required to develop your idea. If not, try this:

1. Write a list of six of the most significant moments in your life.

2. Write a brief but honest account of each moment.

3. One pivotal moment should stand out – it could be something intriguing or meaningful.

4. If not, go back to your list and include a difficult decision or where you faced a crossroads of choices. Include influential people, conflicts, lessons, mistakes, or beliefs.

Once you have identified a possible idea, your next challenge begins.

Writing your story in chronological order is a big mistake, and predictable. Your memoir is not a journal either. Focus on the lessons learned through experience and not the details of the event that matter only to you. If you are writing for publication, then you are writing for your audience. Think back on how to create your articles with an interesting opening – an unexpected event, some action – or a quote. Most books don't start the story at the beginning. Instead, they immerse you in a moment of action or intrigue. Tease your reader with your opening line and paragraph and – once hooked – flash back to reveal the chronological events and background information needed to flesh out your story.

Include compelling and emotional moments. Allow your reader to feel the tension and fear, or even the hope you experienced. Leave out meaningless time or events that take you away from the focus of the story. You are not writing a journal so allow yourself to skip irrelevant time.

Another good point to remember is not to make yourself the hero or, indeed, the victim of every situation. You must expose your weaknesses alongside your strengths, and sometimes make yourself the antihero. No one is innocent all the time. If you can demonstrate how and when you failed or misjudged a situation, your readers are more likely to respect your honesty.

Being honest and genuine is one of the best ways to write a powerful memoir. This is often very tricky, especially if you are revealing facts about other people. It is important to tell the truth, however painful or difficult it may be for you as an author. You can change the names of people or disguise their identities but you are writing non-fiction, and your readers are buying into your story because it is real and it happened. People may well recognise themselves in your work, irrespective of any claim you may make about *the real names of people and places being changed to protect their identities.* [Importantly, see the section on libel and defamation.] Remember too that most of your readers don't know who you are or who you are writing about. What they want is a truthful, unembellished account of your memoir – your story – the unique one.

One further point to note on honesty. Writing in a bitter tone, being judgemental, or whining about your experience, is not what readers want to read.

While it is important not to embellish your story, *good writers show – they don't tell.* Let your readers draw their own conclusions from the details you provide in your narrative.

It would be easy to write something like:

My dad was a bully and regularly hit my mum.

But it would create a more vivid picture if you wrote:

I heard raised voices for the third night in a row. The sound of breaking glass, yet again. Mum let out a scream and then I heard her sobbing as dad slammed the front door and left the house. The following morning, I could see the bruise on mum's face – despite her efforts to conceal it with heavy make-up and a half-hearted smile.

Do not be misguided into thinking that I am telling you how to write a fictional story – I am not. Good memoir writing must take your reader on a journey. It should have a focal point or theme – and be written in an engaging style and tone that has your reader gripped throughout. Just like a novel should.

Don't just aim to knock your readers' socks off! Intend to strip them naked. You want your readers to share your emotional journey. You want them to open their mouths in awe, have them laughing hysterically, or crying with you over spilt milk.

This emotional journey will be why your readers turn the next page and the next – as they move through your chapters yearning for more.

Be prepared to face the truths of your past – which may at times be painful. *Retrospection* is the key to successful memoir writing, and this means sharing what you learned from your experiences. It is no good wrapping everything in cellophane; the raw truth, however painful, however awful, should be revealed. If you are not prepared to do this, then do not write your story as a memoir – opt to write a fictional version instead.

Author, Alice Seabold did this. Her novel, *The Lovely Bones*, was conceived by her own experience of being raped. In her second published book, *Lucky*, Seabold reveals the real account of this harrowing incident as a memoir. If you read both books, you can see how her first story was influenced by the events revealed in the second.

Autobiography

Choosing to write your story as autobiography instead of a memoir enables you to combine lots of events from your life and bring them together in one place – the time and place you are at the time of writing your book. Often, this is done by people much later in life, such as Sir Tom Jones, who recently published *Over the Top and Back*, an account of his 60-year musical career.

For some writers, their autobiography is the book they have always wanted to write. For others, it is a cathartic way of leaving something of themselves behind, and for some, it is because they believe their life story is interesting enough that others would enjoy reading about it. These are all quite personal reasons for wanting to write an autobiography but what about commercial prospects?

It is true that many autobiographies exist because the author or a publisher wants to make money from it. Many bestselling autobiographies are written by professional sports people, celebrities or those in high office. And, there is nothing wrong with that. Indeed, those working in the media and publishing industry know this. They have the book sales to prove it.

My autobiographical collection includes books by Joanna Lumley, Richard Branson, Peter Jones, and Boy George to name a few. *Google* or *Amazon* search any professional athlete, musician, or actor and you will probably find their autobiography – from Jessica Ennis to Sam Allardyce to Dawn French. However, dig a bit deeper and you will find a collection of other very worthy and interesting autobiographical reads.

Commonly, there are autobiographies by seemingly ordinary people thrown into the media spotlight through a heart-breaking or dreadful incident, such as the parents of Madeleine McCann, Jamie Bulger, or Holly Wells. Equally, many individuals have written about being victims of child abuse, domestic violence or kidnapping. However, there is also a wide collection of more inspirational stories by previously unknown authors such as Shelly Wilson – *How I Changed my Life*, Paul Kalanithi – *When Breath Becomes Air*, and Treesa Middleton – *Treesa: The 12-year-old mum*.

For the layperson wanting to write their autobiography for mainstream publication you must find a way to cut through the chatter of the personality or celebrity author. Find a strong voice and make it loud enough to be heard. If you hope to succeed in this arena, your story should be *compelling, astonishing, extraordinary, emotional,* or better still – all these things.

If you think you have the voice, the ability, the determination, and the most interesting of life stories to share, then go ahead – *tell* your tale!

Memoirs, Autobiographies, Biographies and Ghostwriting

Structuring your autobiography

Whether you are writing for a mainstream publication or documenting your life for your grandchildren – a good story is what you are aiming for. It should have a protagonist (you), most importantly – a central conflict, and a cast of other interesting characters to keep your readers engaged.

Much of the information exposed in writing your memoir will also apply to writing your autobiography. However, it will help you compose a better autobiography if you prepare your life timeline first (although you are advised *not* to write your memoir or autobiography in chronological order; many biographers do). Nevertheless, this should not be confused with the preparation and planning stages of writing your autobiography that will benefit from the detail you include, while assembling your timeline.

1. Start from as early as you can remember.

2. Identify significant events and include important dates.

3. Identify significant people and those who will be the main characters of your story; include influential teachers, mentors, career advisors or even your bosses. Don't forget your siblings, your peers, aunts, uncles, boyfriends or girlfriends, ex-wives or husbands, and your children or step-children.

4. Consider the influences of your ancestors and, if relevant, gather information on your family history.

5. Do your research: check dates, events and the spellings of names and places. Appreciate that your memory may not be as good as you think it is.

6. What else was happening around you at the time of significant events in your life, and did these have an impact on your choices or decisions or of those around you?

I remember being fearful of working in London in the mid-1980s because of the IRA bombings at Hyde and Regent's Parks in 1982, and Harrods in 1983 – this had an impact on my career choices as I didn't want to commute to the city.

7. Music and fashion play an instrumental part in the time periods you reference, as do television programmes and influential people of the time.

8. Remember to include conflicts. These could be a school bully, a work colleague who was nasty or two-faced, or a dilemma you faced when being asked to do something you were not comfortable with, or which went against your moral high-ground. Take, for example, sexual harassment in the workplace: *Male colleagues thought nothing of making lewd comments or slapping women's bottoms at work, in the days before this was acknowledged as unacceptable behaviour.*

9. Remember to show your strengths and weaknesses, the *stupid, idiotic* and *careless* things you might have done – as well as your moments of greatness.

10. Consider the values or lessons you have learned – you can inspire others in this way.

11. Reveal your personality and don't try to write yourself as the person you are not. There is no shame in being honest about a disability or infirmity, especially as it may be the reason you are the person you have turned out to be. Would Alice Seabold have written *The Lovely Bones* if it were not because of what happened to her? If you are funny, write funny; if you are more reserved, show your reservations – it's who you are.

12. Find or create the theme or focal point to run throughout your story – remembering who your reader is, and why it might be of interest to them.

13. It is important to pick out anecdotal moments from the information gathered on your timeline. Your autobiography should not be a long-winded account of everything that has happened to you. Only include stories or events of importance and relevance to your central theme or focus.

When your timeline is complete, and your research concluded, it is time to prepare the structure of your autobiography.

Memoirs, Autobiographies, Biographies and Ghostwriting

1. Firstly, identify your audience. Your family and friends may just be interested in the more significant, tragic or humorous moments in your life, but a wider readership would be more drawn into the resonance or moral of your story.

2. Ensure that your story is strong enough to carry the central theme – this will help you develop your plot.

3. Decide on a title. Keep it short and memorable. If the title reflects the theme of your story, it not only tells your reader instantly what your story is about, it can help you stay focused and true to that central theme. *A Long Walk to Freedom* – Nelson Mandela, *Dear Fatty* – Dawn French, *What You See Is What You Get* – Alan Sugar.

4. Organise your notes, memories and anecdotes so they can be used to create the narrative arc in a logical and seemingly effortless way.

5. Consider the coincidences or sequence of repetitious events. People do make the same mistakes and, some, many times over. Perhaps you have had a series of failed relationships because you choose to date the same type of person time and time again? It could be that you are too hasty to fall in love because of your desire to be loved. It might be that you struggle to keep a job more than a few weeks because you have the inability to respect people in authority thus leading to conflict and arguments with your superiors.

6. Look for ways to build tension and create suspense. This is critical. You can do this by using a sequential number of stories that lead to the climax of each conflict or situation. *Take, for example, having and losing many jobs – each interview, each job offer, and each first day would be your high points – every subsequent job loss would be a low. How did you react to your first job loss in comparison to the last? At each loss, did you give yourself 'a talking' to, did you learn anything, or should you have learnt something?*

7. Find your resolution. Although many readers will want to know there is a happy ending – life just isn't like that. However, if your ending doesn't conclude on the happiest of notes - ensure it is satisfying and complete, in terms of resolution, instead.

Chapter 10

At the outset, each of those individual ventures was a step into the unknown for the company which I felt personally – like a loss of one's virginity – but, unlike really losing your virginity, in whatever world you make for yourself, you can keep embracing the new and the different over and over again. That's what I have always wanted for Virgin and, whether it's achieved by judgment or luck, I wouldn't have it any other way.

Richard Branson, Losing My Virginity

Ghostwriting

Ghostwriting offers an opportunity to write in the name of, or for the sake of, another person.

Who uses a ghostwriter and why?

As we have discovered above, autobiographies by celebrity and high profile personalities are very popular both for readers and publishers, but not everyone has the inclination, the skills, or the time to write a book, especially a full-length title.

Editors and publishers may also have concerns about the commitment of non-writer professionals to said book project, including the quality of the copy and the meeting of deadlines. Chasing an international sports personality around the globe, nagging an Academy Award winning actor, or a government minister, is not a comfortable place to be, and they would much rather have a ghostwriter do that!

Publishers are well aware of the difficulties in the promotion and marketing of an unknown author. Having *'a name'* – someone already known to the public – immediately gives them a head start. The media are more likely to interview a famous person, or publicise the fact this person has written a book, if they already have some media presence.

But, why don't ghostwriters write them as biographies instead – especially as they will be credited as the author?

For the same reasons as stated above. Publishers would have to try and market the work of an unknown author, even if the subject matter is a *'person of interest'*.

Andrew Crofts, sums this up nicely in his handbook, *Ghostwriting.*

Memoirs, Autobiographies, Biographies and Ghostwriting

I ghosted an autobiography of Gillian Taylforth, an excellent actress who was at the time enduring a high-profile persecution in the tabloid media while she was still appearing in EastEnders. At the time the book came out there wasn't a radio or television chat show or book programme that didn't want to have her on, and the publishers were able to keep her talking to the public about her book from the moment she woke up on the day of publication to the moment she went to bed. If I had written a biography of her under my own name, the publishers might have been able to lever me into one or two of these slots, but it's unlikely that anyone would have taken much notice, or rushed out to buy the book as a result of listening to me.

From the ghostwriter's perspective, publishers are also far more likely to pay a decent advance to the author if they are confident that the copy will arrive on time and be delivered to a *'publishable standard'*. Publishers have neither the time nor resources to re-write a submitted manuscript – but they can provide editorial and marketing resources for the right story.

If you were to write a biography (off your own bat), you would have to do your research – and a lot of it. Gain access to your subject, where possible, or other people known to the subject, and spend a considerable amount of time preparing speculative submissions in the hope that a publisher *might* take you on. If they do, the size of an advance (if you could secure one) would likely be nominal, and you would still have to complete the book before earning anything else. Being a ghostwriter puts you in a far better position both financially and, crucially, it grants you the *access* you need to your subject.

Being a ghostwriter does not mean you just write celebrity or high-profile autobiographies. Although these opportunities may arise, and can be sought after, there are many *'non-famous'* people who would also like to have their life-story told.

One site worth exploring in particular – *Storyterrace* – focuses on the writing and publishing of other people's *'life-stories'*.

I became a ghost writer quite by accident. An old family friend wanted to tell his life story and asked me if I'd write it.

Most people in this situation don't know what it is they want, or who their readership might be. Often, it is a shock to them that their life story is not as commercial as they thought, and as the writer, you are the one who must break the bad news.

Misconceptions surround the role of the ghost writer too. Most clients assume you can do everything, not just the writing but finding an agent and publisher, or managing the publishing if they just want to print a few copies for family and friends.

Be clear and concise about what you can deliver, and how much the project is going to cost, once you have ascertained, exactly what the client wants. Talking money can be difficult, and many people will have underestimated how much it is going to cost them, just to have it written, and that's before you begin to talk about printing costs. In some instances, they may assume you will write it for free and will get paid when the book is published.

Draw up a proper agreement, clearly stating your terms of business, this can help to prevent confusion or difficult situations arising in the future.

Work out a suitable and practical timescale for interviewing, writing, researching and completing the project. Don't underestimate how long this can take. Once people start to think about their life, they can unlock all manner of stories.

If you want to be a ghostwriter, one of the main attributes you'll need is being able to read people so you can communicate effectively. When clients are comfortable with you, they will tell you more. You also need to be intuitive. Good people skills will be needed to talk to people from all walks of life – without judgement.

Sharing their life story with you is a very intimate thing, and there are times when you need to have empathy and understanding but you must learn not to get too involved. There are going to be moments when your client will recollect a difficult memory, and you may have to allow them time to compose themselves, before they are able to carry on. They may also reveal personal information or bring skeletons from their closets, but they may not want the details included in the story. Be professional and respect their wishes.

Be flexible and make allowances for unexpected situations, or cancellations of appointments. Manage their expectations. While the project may be of the highest importance to you at the time, it may take a lower priority in your client's daily life and routine. Equally, you may have several different projects on the go, and this is just one of many, but to your client it may be the only pressing thing on their mind.

Most importantly, when writing as a ghost, you need to adapt your writing voice to replicate that of your client. Age, gender, social standing and where they were brought up will change the way a person speaks. Try and emulate their voice in your writing and use their language – which could be vastly different from your own. You don't have to write in accents but using their colloquialisms, dialect, and linguistics will add authenticity to their story.

Above all else be professional. Deliver what you say you will and do your best to stick to the schedule. Let your client review the copy at periodic times to ensure they are happy with how their story is developing, and remember it's their story not yours!

Sarah Banham, For the Love of Books

If you would like to understand the world of the ghostwriter (well, at least one in particular), take a look at Andrew Crofts' *Confessions of a Ghostwriter*. He has travelled the world and inhabited both the glamorous and shady worlds of the rich and famous as well as those of hitmen and hookers. He has asked the questions others have feared to ask, and he has delved into the skeleton-cupboards that others have found locked.

Biographies

As an unknown freelance writer, the likelihood of you being commissioned to write a biography is practically zero. Unless, of course, you can persuade a publisher that you are the best person to write it because you are an expert on the life of your chosen subject, and that you have something worth writing about that hasn't been printed a thousand times before. Who could write the biography of Billy Connolly better than his *wife*, Pamela Stephenson?

However, before you get too disheartened, as a writer, part of your job is to be an opportunist. Not only do you have a passion for writing, but research is also a massive part of your non-fiction life. We discovered very early on in this book that you must possess a certain amount of determination and persistence as a writer, and that is relevant here because you should not be put off from pursuing a line of enquiry (or from approaching publishers with your ideas) just because the journey may prove difficult.

Chapter 10

Our fascination with the eccentricities of people of historical importance, the rise and fall of a celebrity that once graced West End stages, or the adulterous affairs of a soap actor, means there is no shortage of biographical subjects. And, if you can find a way, that others perhaps cannot, to reveal a previously untold story, or evidence that your subject was not the person the public thought they were, then go ahead, and approach the right publisher with gusto.

There is no limit to how many times a person of interest can be the subject of a biography. How many books, films and publications have been written about Henry VIII and his wives? There are hundreds of books about Bob Dylan, alone.

Nevertheless, as a writer, what you need to do is demonstrate why you should write about Henry VIII again and why people would read your book.

Before you eagerly send off your idea – you need to plan the contents carefully, providing fresh information or evidence to suggest something that hasn't been said before, or which contradicts the theories of others. You must also have your facts together and be certain that your book will evoke not only the interest of the publisher but subsequent readers too.

In the first instance – *what interests you about this person?* Having some affinity for your subject will help you write more authentically.

Then consider – *what would interest your readers?* Your story may be of more interest to your readers if it covered less about what your subject did, and more about the obstacles or challenges he faced in getting there.

Find the story for your biography – avoid the chronological order and the 'what he did day-by-day' scenario. If you believe your biographical subject is interesting enough to write a book about – then there must be a story.

Look for the highs and lows of your subject's life. Include the chance meetings or influences of others if they had an impact on your subject's journey, and remember to include the mistakes or misguided judgements they made along the way. Don't forget to show your subject as the villain as much as the hero, when it matters, and avoid putting them on a pedestal, however much you *idolise* them for the person they are, or what they have achieved.

Your biography is not about you – it is about your subject – remain objective and stick to the facts.

Research and preparation

For these types of books, your research is an essential part of your preparation. You may need to contact relatives or descendants for information. You may have to consult many other reference books and titles on the subject, clawing your way through pages and pages of text to find what you are looking for. You may even have to search for official records, census material, parish records, and find other resource centres to uncover additional information. In most cases, you should find many people willing to assist you in this arduous mission or at least, point you in the right direction, particularly in libraries and Parish Record Offices.

> *Tip: Remember what I wrote about the information available on the Web? Ensure you check your information comes from primary sources or from a reputable organisation or society. Use the Web, by all means, but corroborate your information.*

Use your *W&A Yearbook* for information on *Resources for Writers*. But, before you go tearing off to your nearest library or resource centre, you need to plan your research carefully.

1. List the main topics you need to find out about and make helpful notes about where you might find this information.

2. List the research you might need to do including interviews, material collation, reference guides and evidence.

3. Then make a list of what you already know. This is important as you do not want to duplicate research; it is also useful in case you come across contradictory information.

4. Check your *W&A Yearbook* for resources for writers, picture agencies, libraries, and publishers of biographies.

5. Compile a list of people you might need to interview and where they are placed geographically. You could save yourself a considerable amount of time and cost if several

interviewees are in the same geographical area, and you can manage your diary to suit theirs.

6.   Contact relevant interviewees, and make your appointments.

7.   Prepare your research notes and file them in an easy-to-find format; this could be chapter relevant, by interviewee, or in date order. Find a way that works for you. The last thing you want to happen, when you are in the throes of putting your copy together, is to spend valuable time searching for one small piece of information. If you are judicious with your filing, it will make your life much easier when you come to write your synopsis and subsequent book.

8.   Familiarise yourself with the interview preparation techniques revealed in Chapter 4 *Writing for magazines - articles and features*. Pre-planning can save you the embarrassment of having to go back to your interviewee to clarify a point or to discuss a fact you missed in an earlier conversation.

Logical order

As with all your written work, you need to present your biography in a logical order. How many times have you read a biography that skips a few decades then brings you slap back into the middle of the subject's childhood? Again (and sorry for repeating myself), it is not about writing your biography in chronological order that is important but how the reader is moved from one period of your subject's life to another, without leaving your reader confused and lost. Prepare your chapter list in advance; plan a logical order and work with this.

Find a theme or central focal point as this will help you stick to the theme and avoid tangents.

Where possible, include significant dates or points of historical or political reference but avoid boring your reader.

Readers, if not already familiar with the subject, will be anxious to know not only who he or she was (and what they did and when), they will want to know the intricacies of the subject. What made them tick, and how emotive they were. Readers want to know about the subject's childhood, where they grew up, what their parents did and about the relationships they had – you need to give them as much information as you can but at the same time entertain them, enlighten them, and definitely avoid boring them!

Chapter 11
Writing for Children and Young Adults

Much of what we have covered so far has primarily been aimed at an adult audience. There is, however, a large marketplace for writing non-fiction for children and young adults. So much so that *Bloomsbury* even publishes an annual copy of the *Children's Writers' & Artists' Yearbook*.

The Children's W&A Yearbook is as equally packed as its adult counterpart – the W&A Yearbook – with detailed information and advice for writers aspiring to write for younger readers. It contains guidance from successfully published children's authors through to self-publishing instructions. There are listings for magazines, book publishers, literary agents and book clubs.

Writing for this age group is complex, and perhaps, more difficult than many writers envisage. The most fundamental aspect of writing for this category is *understanding* the age group of your readers. How you write for early readers is very different to how you would write for the 10 to 15-year bracket or indeed, the 12 to 20-year age range(s).

There is a huge difference in the *language, style,* and *interests* of each age group before we even consider any gender-specific activities or pursuits.

It is always essential, no matter what the genre is, to understand who you are writing for before you begin to write, and to know the reasons *why* you are putting together whatever it is you are planning to write. It is even more important to be clear about this before you embark on writing for the children's market because young readers can be very difficult to please. Children have a built-in *boredom beacon*; they know when they are being lectured or spoken down to, and they are very quickly turned off by the wrong use of language, old fashioned terms, or writers who are out of touch with today's trends.

Chapter 11

Ask yourself, *am I writing this:*

To inform them?

To entertain them?

To explain something?

To stimulate them?

It could be a combination of reasons, but be clear about your motivations before you start.

Then decide what age group you would like to write for. This could be children as young as one or two, who need an adult to read to them. You cannot simply aim your language at the adults though; your endeavour is to write to entertain your target audience – however young.

Pre-school children aged three to five are going to be looking for books with more than one syllable, even if they cannot read independently. These readers will want to be stimulated, as they start to recognise familiar words and rhymes. They will absorb and remember certain words and phrases, and if a story has been read to them, they may well remember interesting lines too.

One of the books my boys most enjoyed when they were younger was called 'Up and Around and Down'. It was the story of a farmer's hat that gets whisked off his head in the wind and blown around the farmyard. First it lands on a horse's head, then a cow's, and eventually it ends up caught in the reed beds of the river where a duck uses it as a nest. Throughout the book, the phrase 'up and around and down' is used every time the hat travels between one place and another. This repetition kept my boys' attention to the point that each time we came across the saying, they felt able to join in with the storytelling.

Then we have the age brackets – five to eight, eight to 12 and your teenage readers. Each of these markets is individual. The same topics or themes may be used for the content but the subject would be written to meet the reading needs of each age group explicitly.

The teenage or young adult market accommodates readers from ages 12 to 20, and there is a vast difference between a 12-year-old and 20-year-old. But it is not about the age of your reader that is important here, it is the *capability* of the reader that determines the level at which they read.

Subjects for teenagers are more likely to include friendships, school or college, clothing, music, leisure activities and more. Not forgetting, of course, that today's teenagers and young adults are also highly technology-driven and much of their social life is determined via social media. Their topics of conversation are often instigated by *WhatsApp*, *Snapchat*, *Facebook* and *Instagram* posts, including fashion, gadgets and relationships. The same goes for boys as much as girls. Self-image and celebrity or musical icons also have a much higher profile in the lives of today's young people than they did say 20 to 30 years ago. The same applies to online gaming, photography and videos. Smart phone apps also play a pivotal role in the interests and pursuits of today's youth – just cast your mind back to the 2016 *Pokémon Go* phenomenon.

Whatever age group or groups you decide to write for, you need to bear in mind that children progress at different rates – they come in all shapes, sizes, personality types, and have various stages of development. A child of say eight or nine could easily be reading material written for a 12-year-old, whereas another child of eight might like to read books aimed at a much younger market. Your aim, therefore, is to write for the broader age bracket.

To identify how to do this, it is vital to carry out market research by reading and analysing the books that youngsters read today (do not assume the books you read at their age remain relevant!). This will help you to recognise writing formulae.

For the young readers' markets, study a variety of written work aimed at the different age groups and identify which ones fit which groups. This can be easily achieved. Your local library or bookshop is the best place to find a wide variety of themed books. Pick a topic, for example, dinosaurs (children, particularly boys, love dinosaurs). Choose several books about dinosaurs from each age group. These are usually identified quite clearly in your library, either through a colour coding system or simply in age-appropriate sections. If in doubt, ask the librarian.

Now study the different *vocabulary levels*, the *sentence structures*, the *illustrations*, and note how the pages are laid out for each age group.

Compare the following:

Chapter 11

1. *Dinosaurs wandered the earth millions of years ago. Some ate only plants and leaves like the Sauropods, while the Tyrannosaurus Rex was a fierce meat eater.*

2. *Do you know what a dinosaur is? Is it soft and fluffy like a rabbit or is it big like an elephant?*

The first example would be aimed at a slightly older child as it uses a wider vocabulary range and a more complex sentence structure. The second would be more suitable for a young reader. Comparing a dinosaur to other animals the child may know will help the child relate to it in simple terms.

Start by analysing children's books in the first instance, then do the same for children's comics, periodicals, annuals, and other reading materials.

Once you have compared the language and style of children's books, and you have an idea for writing one, bear in mind the following: *to write for a child you need to think like a child.* This doesn't mean you should limit your imagination or enthusiasm – quite the opposite(!) – but understand the limitations of the child's experience. Your copy must be lively and vibrant to retain your reader's attention.

Children's built-in boredom sensor, mentioned above, is something which all children's editors are acutely aware of. This doesn't mean your copy needs to be quirky or unconventional to get published but it does mean that besides being obviously stimulating, your work should be thoroughly researched and comprehensible.

Children also have a sixth sense when it comes to *lectures* or being *written down to.* Avoid writing an essay. Children also have shorter attention spans – so use small blocks of text, with frequent breaks, and (where relevant) include illustrations if you can. This will give the reader something to pin the text to, and it will make it easier for them to understand.

For example:

The Normans

The Normans were originally Vikings who had settled in northwest France in the early 900s, by the River Seine. In 1066, an army of up to 7,000 men crossed the English Channel in hundreds of boats.

This invasion was led by William, who claimed that he was the rightful King of England.

Side box with illustration of William the Conqueror:

William I, The Conqueror (1066 – 1087) was the illegitimate son of Robert, Duke of Normandy. He defeated Harold, King of England, at the battle of Hastings in 1066 and was crowned king. He was a stern but efficient ruler.

Breaking up the text like this makes it easier for the reader to absorb.

Language matters

The most important thing about writing for children and young adults is getting the language right. This means choosing the right words for your audience, as well as paying attention to the way you structure your sentences.

We used dinosaurs earlier, so we'll continue with that for this example:

1. *Sharp teeth, long tail, long neck, big feet, big head – it's a dinosaur.*

2. *Do you know what a dinosaur is? Is it soft and fluffy like a rabbit or is it big like an elephant?*

3. *Dinosaurs were reptiles of many amazing shapes and sizes that lived a long time ago.*

4. *Dinosaurs wandered the earth millions of years ago. Some ate only plants and leaves like the Sauropods, while the Tyrannosaurus Rex was a fierce meat eater.*

5. *The first dinosaurs ruled the world around 225 million years ago, this was known as the Triassic period. The Jurassic and Cretaceous periods followed, this was when the dinosaurs became mainly land reptiles.*

Obviously, there are more permutations we could use to illustrate the different language levels, but you get the idea – pitch your language level as accurately as you possibly can.

Chapter 11

Avoid using words or phrases that are too long, meaningless, or old fashioned, and do not use slang. While you might find it amusing to use expressions such as *cool dude* because it's from an era you remember, an eight-year-old may not have a clue as to why you have written it, and it may just confuse them.

Aim for plain English not poor English – writing for young people needs to be easy-to-read and straightforward. Getting on with it is the clue to success. Say what you want to say then move on – and don't waffle.

Articles of general interest are usually informative, and contain well-researched material. Don't try and convince yourself that a smattering of knowledge will pass for an informative article just because it is written for children – it won't convince an editor.

If you choose to write about different breeds of cat, then do not just focus on the troublesome Siamese. Your work should include a variety of cat breeds, as you would for an adult audience.

Think about capturing your readers' attention. It would be very easy to write something like *The Battle of Hastings* but it would be far more attractive to a young reader if you wrote *Who won the battle of Hastings?* or even *A Medieval Battle*.

Furthermore, your copy needs to be exciting, especially if it is dealing with historical information with facts, figures and dates.

Example.

The Battle of Hastings

The Battle of Hastings was fought on October 14, 1066 between the Saxons and Normans. The Normans were led by William of Normandy and the Saxons, by King Harold.

***

A Medieval Battle

On October 14, 1066 two mighty armies came to fight at Hastings. The Saxons and the Normans were closely matched in strength and skill as the soldiers fought for eight hours, a long time for a medieval battle. King Harold led his Saxon troops, while William of Normandy commanded his Norman warriors.

Can you see the difference?

Which one do you think would more likely capture the imagination of a child?

Read some of the *Horrible Histories* books. What a clever way to capture children's attention. For a start, they are told that history is horrible, and secondly, the writers have used the horrible element to discuss topics such as The Great Plague of London, the beheading of two of Henry VIII's wives, and the trench warfare of World War I. In my opinion – genius!

What to write

What non-fiction material appeals to children?

Well, just about anything. You can tell them about the weather, the stars, the planets, animals, fossils, vehicles – basically just about anything you can think of.

First News is an excellent newspaper aimed at the younger audience, primarily for seven to 14-year-olds. While dealing with topical issues and current affairs, First News presents its news stories in a traditional, full-colour tabloid-style newspaper format. Its news coverage is world-wide, and its informative, entertaining and stimulating style encourages children to take an active interest in the world around them. Compare the way it covers one of its stories to a similar topic in say The Daily Mirror or The Sun.

The Week Junior is a new current affairs magazine also aimed at children aged between eight and 14. Filled with fascinating stories and information, written to engage young, curious minds – it looks to encourage them to explore and understand the world in which they live.

Choose your topic with care but do not be afraid to address current affairs, politics, or economics. Children are more exposed to these types of content because of media coverage and social media, and can be disturbed by certain events if they are not properly explained. Do not disregard them – find a way of writing about them so that children understand.

Of course, what you do not want to do is give children nightmares, or scare them unnecessarily, but be aware that some children are more sensitive to certain issues than others. That said, youngsters are always more resilient than we adults suppose. The publishers of the *National Geographic* magazine have a *Kids'* edition, and there is a magazine called *Eco Kids Planet* and *BBC Earth* – and the reason they exist is that young readers are interested in these topics.

Equally, there are magazines covering popular sports including football, wrestling, gaming, and how stuff works; they sit alongside educational topics like science and maths, plus factual guides on popular TV programmes and films, such as *Dr Who* and *Star Wars*.

Study as many different magazines as you can, and use the library to ascertain what types of books and other reading material children are interested in by the popularity of the loan record – it may also help you identify gaps in the market. There may be some mileage in looking for topics that do not appear to have been covered. It will also help if you talk to children. If you have contact with young children ask them what they like to read, or what their favourite book, comic, or magazine is.

Magazines and books for children are often bought by parents, teachers and other professionals – so remember to talk to them too about what is popular, the type of reading material they buy for their kids or protégés, and *why*.

'How to' articles

Despite the pull of television and smart devices, *'How to'* articles still remain very popular with children of all age groups. But, if you are going to write this type of article, you should think and plan your piece carefully. Don't take for granted that the child will automatically understand what you mean. It is also imperative to be safety-conscious. Always!

Say, for example, you were going to write a piece on *'How to press flowers'*, you would not write, *'The best places to pick wildflowers would be alongside a riverbank or canal. Go down to the riverside...'* What you could write instead is *'ask an adult to take you for a walk along the riverside and see if you can find some pretty wildflowers'*.

If you can, always include safety rules; an editor may decide to leave them out before publication but it is advisable to include them with your piece. *'It is not safe to pick flowers next to busy roads or near railway lines. It would be much safer if you have a countryside walk or visit your local country park'.* And don't forget about the law. If you are not allowed to pick wildflowers in certain places, you must let your reader know this.

With *'how to'* articles, you need to be concise with your instructions, providing clear *step-by-step* guides, and illustrations are a must. Illustrations or photographs will help the child relate to the piece as they are working through it, and can be used as a visual guide. They will need to know how something should look during the construction process as much as the final result.

A note about illustrations. If you are a good illustrator this could be an advantage but editors do have access to illustrators they know and trust, and may decide to use them instead. Equally, if you cannot draw, it should not affect the saleability of your work, as editors and publishers can provide any necessary illustrations. As an alternative to illustrations, use photographs. Again, if required, publishers will commission professional photographers but if you can provide them with clean, clear and professional looking photography, to accompany your text, even better.

The final step in your *'how to'* article should always be motivational, and as such should say something that means fun! This is the child's incentive to read through the instructions and carry them out. Ending with something like *'now your pressed flower is in its picture frame, why not wrap it up and give it to your Mum or Grandma – she will love it too!'*

Using your skills

Do you have an interesting hobby? Work out what interests you about your hobby and find a way to write about it so that it will motivate children to take it up too. In Chapter 6, *Food, Crafts, and Hobbies*, we learned how to structure the writing of *'how to'* articles. Follow the guidelines but bear in mind that you may have to simplify your project, revise the tools being used, and break down your step-by-step instructions to meet the needs of the younger reader. In some instances, your project may require the assistance of an adult. Stay conscious that not all parents or carers have the time or inclination to help their children.

Many topics that interest you as an adult will interest children. *Junior MasterChef* and *Junior Bake Off* illustrate this perfectly.

Chapter 11

Testing your market

If you can, test your material on a child or children of the age group you have written for. You can read it aloud to them but the best way is to let them read it for themselves. It is advisable not to tell them *you* have written it as they won't want to be unkind to you and may not give you an honest response. Listen to what they say and discuss their feedback with them. If they say it is too hard to read – ask them why? Is it the words or the way it has been laid out? Or is it the content?

If the response is '*it's okay,*' ask them if it could be improved; often they will be able to add another dimension to it, and one you may not have thought of. If they say it's boring – scrap it and start again but before you do, ask them if they have any suggestions.

If you do not have much contact with children, you could approach your local school. They may be willing to let you talk with the children, or listen to them read; this way you can ascertain what books or subjects they most like and why. You could volunteer at a local youth club or group. Do anything that puts you in touch with young readers. This information will help you not only with your research but it will give you a better understanding of what children like and don't like.

How to write your children's piece

Once you have determined the readership for your endeavours, and your topic, you need to think about how you are going to write your piece. Is it going to be a *serious, humorous, informative, challenging, stimulating, enlightening* or *entertaining*? Pay attention to the presentation or layout. Is it going to be a straightforward piece of text, or could you make it a type of game… a quiz perhaps?

Young-readers like interaction. Asking questions in your text helps children feel like they are a part of the story – it also gives them an opportunity to stay connected and think about the topic.

Writing for young adults

As mentioned earlier, the *teenage* or *young adult* market appeals to those who are just into that age group right through to those who push at its edges, representing young people between the ages of around 12 to their early 20s.

Capturing the attention of teenage and young adult readers is a tricky one. According to *The Reading Agency*, 44% of young people aged between 16 and 24 don't read for pleasure, and 41% of 11 to 15-year-olds in England do not participate in reading and writing activities in their spare time (not including homework). Add to this how non-fiction topics have to compete with the fiction market and you will see your opportunities for writing non-fiction shrink even further.

However, young adults have an exceptionally wide spectrum of interests. You will notice there is a vast difference between magazine topics aged at children and those published for teenagers and young adults, including more publications covering sport, hobbies, gaming, film, music, fashion, hair, and make-up.

Many publications that target this age group have in-house staff to provide the majority of their copy but that doesn't mean to say they are able to cover everything. They will report on the obvious stories, particularly pertaining to current events and issues affecting young people. *Seventeen Magazine* recently featured articles about *What your selfie says about you* and *The best way to dump someone*. They will most likely cover a young actor or celebrity story, say one of the young performers from a television soap such as *Hollyoaks*. But, it is unlikely that they would know if a youngster from your town has just landed a part in a major new film. This may well be of interest, especially if your interviewee has something relevant to say about the other actors he will be working with. As I have stressed before, you must *find* the alternatives. Find the stories that staff writers aren't going to come up with, and something they couldn't easily write themselves, if you want to break into this market.

Use your locality as a vantage point – has a local girl just released a single in the charts? Has a teenager you know just received an award or scholarship for something unusual? Is there something in your local area that would be of interest to youngsters – a new training facility for canoeists perhaps? A new skate park or dance academy?

Although romance and relationships are particularly pertinent to young people of all ages – and there is an awful lot of scope for that sort of material – teenagers have a lot of other pursuits. Your task is

Chapter 11

to find out more about those interests and stimulate them with *entertaining, catchy,* and *lively* writing that will enthuse and motivate them.

Then there is everything to do with change. Think about how many things will change for youngsters between the ages of 10 and 20. Not only changes to their bodies but their outlook too.

YA Author, Mary Kole says:

> *Remember the electricity of adolescence? You have your first love, your first heartbreak, your first truly selfless act, your first betrayal, your first seriously bad decision, your first moment of profound pride, the first time you're a hero. These milestones space out as we age, but when you're a teenager, they all happen in very close proximity to one another.*

Mary Kole, Writer's Digest

Like writing for children, being able to write for teenagers and young adults means thinking like one, and using the sort of language they use. Cat Clarke, author of *The Lost and Found*, says she listens to teenagers talking on the bus. *"I often watch how teenagers behave in coffee shops, and try and listen to their conversations. But then I genuinely love to people watch."*

Being aware of what interests today's youngsters is just part of the process. Being able to understand what makes them tick will help you to write authentically for this age group. There are topics that children of the millennium face that previous generations didn't, such as cyberbullying, their online image, and self-confidence, plus other social media led topics. Today's youngsters are much more aware of world events, current affairs and politics because of social media.

Returning to an individual's personal life journey, major events such as exams, leaving school, going to college or university, a first job, money, cars, setting up a home, or perhaps even moving in with a partner are all relevant. Plus, there's more – relationships, sex and contraception, drugs, alcohol, bars, clubs and parties, same gender holidays... the list goes on. I have found that today's youngsters are much more aware of same-gender relationships, transgender issues, racism, disabilities, and other social issues than ever before.

In a *BBC Breakfast* interview, Joanna Trollope spoke about leaving university during the 1960s, and how her job options were limited to nursing, teaching or working in the Civil Service. Today, young people have much wider career choices; they are told they can be anything or do anything they choose to do. Options means decisions for teenagers to make, issues and concerns to overcome, or difficulties they need to be aware of. If you've got teenage kids what do you worry about for them? Can you use this information and put it across in a *non-preachy* yet informative, and entertaining way? Yes, you can! And the way to do it is through your research. Read what other writers are writing for this age group, study how they are doing it, and give it a go yourself.

Patrick Ness, author of *The Rest of Us Just Live Here*, says:

> *My teenage self is still hanging around; it's choosing to engage with him, writing books for him, seeing what he felt and needed that he wasn't getting. I genuinely think it's the simple action of taking a teenager seriously.*

One word of warning – if something doesn't interest you then don't even attempt it. If pop music drives you crazy, stay away from it. If you hate what your 15-year-old is wearing don't even go there – you will find it difficult to write enthusiastically or in a non-biased way, and your readers just won't understand.

Young reader markets

Your research into the existing children's market will help you decide what type of things you want to write, and for what age group. You could decide to stick with articles for magazines, online sites, or a blog. You might even attempt a larger project such as a book.

Your next step is to consult your *Children's W&A Yearbook*, as this will help you find the publications, editors or publishers you need to approach. When writing a book, it is a wise idea to get a publisher onboard at the ideas stage; you probably don't want to write a complete book and find that no-one wants to publish it. You could also use the Yearbook to help generate ideas.

Chapter 11

When writing articles, make a shortlist of your targets and do additional research. Check that contact details are up-to-date and correct, and always review magazine, blog and periodical websites, as this is the mostly likely place you will find the most recent information or latest trends. The last thing you want is to pitch an idea to an editor if they have just run or published a similar story.

Follow each editor or publisher's guidelines and submit your query (usually by email). Keep your synopsis succinct, and remember to include brief but relevant information about yourself and any previously published work, especially for this genre.

Also, consider how the topics you have written about for a younger audience could be rewritten and submitted to a general interest or women's title. For example, if you have written a piece about leaving home to go to university, rewrite it from a parent's perspective. What impact will it have on the family when the eldest child heads off to university? Especially if they are the sort of youngster that has been very hands-on around the home, or is a carer for a parent.

What about an article on drugs? Parents often worry about this as much as youngsters do with regards to peer pressure – or if they get involved with the '*wrong crowd*'.

In turn, how much do parents know about what their youngsters are exposed to (especially when they have computers in their bedrooms and smartphones that they seem perpetually attached to)?

Where feasible or practical to do so, consider re-using the copy you have aimed at one age group to rewrite a new piece for another group. Of course, you will need to make the necessary adjustments to the language, style and content of your piece – to meet the needs of the younger or older reader – but with research and practice, you should be able to achieve this efficiently.

Remember – always look for the alternative ways to gain mileage from your work.

Chapter 12
Writing for Radio

Have you ever thought about writing for radio?

Novice writers often do not consider writing for radio as a viable outlet for their work. Sadly, they are missing a great opportunity. The market is hungry for stories from talented new writers, and broadcasters maintain they are just not receiving the quantity or quality of work needed to feed their requirements.

I guess writers bypass writing for radio because they think of being *published* as their goal. Nevertheless, being broadcast is the equivalent. Writers might also overlook the opportunities for writing for radio because they think it is a different beast altogether. I am here to tell you it is not.

The only fundamental difference between writing for radio and writing for print is that you are writing for the ear, not the eye. Listeners need to be able to understand what is being said the first time around – they aren't able to go back and listen again – unlike re-reading a sentence in a magazine.

The written content of a good radio script is conversational in style. The narration should sound as natural and relaxed as possible. When writing your script, use the words and phrases you would use in everyday conversations, and articulate as if you are telling a story to a friend.

Give your listeners the opportunity to imagine the people, places, and the events you refer to in your script. Include descriptions, interesting sounds, and give them a sense of time and place. Although many radio talks (particularly documentaries) will include sound effects to help create atmosphere, it is imperative that, wherever possible, you create imagery through your words and descriptions.

Just as you should read all your written work aloud before sending it off to an editor or publisher, this is more important for the copy or scripts you write for radio. Do not just read it aloud though. Use a recording device (most smartphones have this facility so you don't

Chapter 12

need to rush out and buy a digital voice recorder). Record yourself reading your piece aloud and then play it back. You are listening out for several things, so listen carefully and take notes.

Most importantly – does it *sound* right? Listen for any sentences that you stumbled over or which don't appear to flow properly. Is there a jump from one subject to another where connecting information might need to be included? Does it make sense? Does it have a definite beginning, middle and end? Will the beginning catch the listener's attention from the outset or is it too laboured?

It may help to have someone else read it aloud to you. Often, when we are familiar with a piece of work, we read what is in our heads not what is on paper. Having someone else read it aloud could help you to identify any problems with your piece, as you are focusing on how it sounds rather than how it is being read.

Radio talks

What is a radio talk?

A radio talk is what a magazine editor would call an article. Typically, radio talks are around 750 words in length. This equates to around 5 minutes of airtime but just as the copy length of magazine articles can vary, so do radio talks. Familiarise yourself by listening to radio talks that interest you, or refer to the broadcaster's submission guidelines. Note the duration of the broadcast and always endeavour to provide your copy to the same length, exactly as you would a word count for an article.

Radio talks cover all manner of subjects, whether that is something of personal interest to the author, a family story, or just a topic that the author feels listeners would relate to.

Biographical pieces are particularly popular. Providing well-researched copy about lesser known figures of historical or scientific importance, or a person with royal connections, or an author, an inventor, or a musician – can all prove successful. Someone with a colourful background, or who found fame through unintentional means. These are the types of stories that fascinate producers and listeners.

Often, the strategic move to having work accepted for radio can be linked to the author, a personal viewpoint or individual experience

164

they wish to share with the audience. If the story can be told with *style, wit,* and an *economy of words* – it can be written as a radio talk. That doesn't mean to say it should be about the author, or their life, but instead it could reflect an author's viewpoint on a subject.

For example:

The Long View – Gun Culture:

Jonathan Freedland examines gun culture – both now and in the 16th century when the wheel-lock pistol was a new and fearsome invention. The weapon of choice for well-to-do young aristocrats, pistols had also found their way onto the streets and into the hands of criminals – gun crime was up, people feared it, and the authorities were trying to quell the problem.

Historian, Lisa Jardine, reveals that policing difficulties, the celebration of the gun in popular culture, and the allure of carrying a weapon, were all issues then just as they are now. Jonathan Freedland also finds out about an audacious attempt to assassinate Elizabeth I using the new pistols and sees how Elizabethan attempts to legislate for guns mirror our own times.

It seems that the tension between an elite culture of hunting and shooting, and a popular culture of self-defence and street violence, is something the British have faced for centuries.

The above example highlights the author, Jonathan Freedland's viewpoint on gun culture as well as an extra insight from historian Lisa Jardine. The talk is further authenticated by revealing additional historical information sought during the research of the subject.

Jonathan Freedland is a journalist, author and broadcaster. He is the presenter of BBC Radio 4's contemporary history series.

Here is a different example, this time an introduction about Video Games.

Video Games – Jonathan Freedland puts the panic over video games into historical perspective by going back to the scandal surrounding the arrival of the early English novel.

Fears over the dangers of video games have been raised in Parliament and there is an ongoing debate as to whether they lead to irresponsible copycat behaviour and deprive the young of an active lifestyle. In the 1740's, similar concerns were raised when Samuel Richardson's novel 'Pamela' took the public imagination by storm. For the first-time, readers were entering a hyper-realistic world – one where a servant girl is being pursued by her master – and the line between reality and fiction became blurred; the novel's arrival also coincided with the introduction of the sofa to the nation's reading rooms, giving birth to the first 'couch potatoes'.

Jonathan retraces the footsteps of the 'Pamela' controversy via Richardson's printers near Fleet Street; an image from the novel buried deep in the Tate stores and beside an elegant 17th century sofa in a London town house.

Whilst exploring the shockwaves caused by 'Pamela' he also explores the controversy's parallels with today's debate about video games.

Both the above talks have been well-researched, include lots of facts, and have been substantiated by information obtained from other sources. This is what producers will be looking for.

Essentially, anything goes. Your talk for radio broadcasting could be about almost anything – a family tale, a local legend, or a piece of local history. Think about your own experiences or something that has happened to you that will be of interest to other people; an inexplicable event to which you have a possible explanation, historical parallels like the examples above, or an interesting ancestral tale. The ideas are endless.

How to get started

Revisit your other non-fiction work and ideas, either material you have written for magazines or online publications. Review an interview with a local person who has an interesting or unusual pastime or hobby. Could any of this material be used for a radio talk?

It is our interest in people, lives and relationships that intrigue listeners as much as readers, and a reason the broadcast of *Our Tune* ran from February 1979 until October 2015. Created and hosted by Simon Bates, listeners wrote to the host with never-ending accounts of their stories of love, romance, separation and divorce, and these tales of relationship love and woe had listeners tuning in for years.

What made the *Our Tune* broadcast so popular is the tone of the narrator's voice, the format of the stories, and the repetition of the *Our Tune* theme track. Each story started with an ear-catching paragraph of how the couple met or how their love blossomed before revealing the rest of the tale.

When writing your radio talk, you should do the same. You need an attention-grabbing headline and story starter to attract the attention of your listener. Cut to the tale and unfold the details in an interesting way. Keep your listener intrigued to the end and leave them wanting more.

Not all the *Our Tune* stories had a happy ending but most certainly offered hope. For some it was optimism that the lives of the individuals would improve, or faith that they would find love elsewhere; for others it was just the prospect that the love a couple had shared for 20 years or more, might continue for another 20.

In summary:

- A radio talk can be on any subject of general interest – and gossip is general interest. You must fully research your facts and state them clearly. Know your subject, and if you are giving your opinion make this clear.

- Write your story in about 1000 words to begin with then cut accordingly. Pay particular attention to the beginning.

- Listen to your own piece before sending it to a producer and, if you can, ask someone else to read it *to you*.

- Try your local radio station first, they are usually friendly and receptive to new ideas but don't be afraid of approaching the *BBC* either, they welcome new writing talent.

- Remember that a radio talk can easily be converted into a magazine article and vice-versa. The spoken and written word are simply two different formats for the writer to use as required.

Documentaries

A documentary is a much fuller story than a talk and normally uses recorded material cut into the narrative such as music, sounds, and interview pieces or expert opinions – all tailored to fit the broadcasting time allocated. The difficulty here is that you are not likely to be successful with a documentary unless you have managed to interest a producer and you co-work on the project.

You may have more success with a documentary idea if you pitch to local radio stations on subjects that will interest local listeners. If you manage to get accepted and build a portfolio of work, this will help you to open the doors to the likes of the *BBC* and other national radio broadcasters. Remember to consult your *W&A Yearbook*, as it includes listings of broadcasters and other significant bodies relevant to radio and the broadcasting industry.

The best way to approach a producer or broadcaster for documentaries is by a query letter, email, or telephone call. Clearly express your aims. There's no need to make any recordings but do state what you plan to include by way of other supporting material. Your intention is to attract his interest.

However, once again, you should listen to (and analyse) a few documentaries that have been broadcast, to get a feel for the genre, before you even think about your query submission. This will help you ascertain the type of documentaries producers may be interested in. Try the *BBC Radio* website and tune in for replays or use podcasts and download them. *BBC Radio 4* is particularly good as it has a very broad range of radio talks and documentaries. Even if you are male, don't be afraid to tune into *Women's Hour*, as they broadcast material on a variety of very interesting subjects suitable for the ears of both genders.

Many documentaries are produced by in-house staff at the *BBC* and local radio stations but you might just hit upon an idea that appeals and they wish to explore further.

Here are two extracted examples of radio documentaries. The first was broadcast for *BBC Radio Suffolk* and the second for national radio. Given the geographical differences, it is clear why each one was used for the respective audiences, and illustrates how you could adapt your work to suit the relevant listeners' markets.

Shingle is Special

The *Suffolk Coast and Heaths Partnership is keen to raise awareness about the special wildlife to be found on Suffolk's shingle beaches.*

Sea birds such as the Little Tern and rare shingle plants such as the Sea Pea are under threat as a result of human activity.

Little Terns are migratory seabirds that nest on shingle beaches in Suffolk between April and July each year. These birds have become increasingly rare as disturbance, mainly by walkers, dogs and predators have threatened their breeding sites.

Suffolk's shingle beaches also support some of the largest concentrations of shingle plants to be found anywhere in the world.

However, a recent survey by English Nature found that all Suffolk's shingle beach SSSIs (Sites of Special Scientific Interest) were in unsatisfactory condition, mainly due to trampling by beach visitors. The plants are specially adapted to the harsh conditions found on our beaches but are often low-growing, making them very vulnerable to being walked on.

Malcolm Farrow, Communications Officer with the Suffolk Coast and Heaths Unit said: "At this time of year, flowering shingle plants are one of the most amazing and spectacular sights to be seen on our coast but they are very easily damaged. Please help us to protect these rare and vulnerable plants by avoiding walking near them.

Please also keep a look out for Little Terns and other shingle nesting birds. Little Terns usually nest in small groups and are quite noisy so they should be easy to spot. But other shingle-nesting birds such as Ringed Plovers can be much harder to see, so please be careful, keep any dogs under close control and avoid any areas that have been fenced off to protect shingle wildlife."

Call That Justice

First broadcast October 2006

Every day, tens of thousands of children around the world wake up behind bars. Many of them will have committed no offence. BBC investigates children's rights in justice systems around the world.

Almost every country in the world has committed itself to respecting the human rights of children. But in reality, the signatures on the UN

169

Convention on the Rights of the Child, are not worth the paper they are written on.

There is overwhelming evidence that countries in both the developed and developing world are guilty of child abuse on a massive scale. These are not isolated incidents, but rather an everyday occurrence.

For many of those children, being sent to jail spells the beginning of months and sometimes years of suffering. Often denied legal representation or contact with parents, they are forced to share cells with hardened adult criminals.

These are the children the world forgot. In many places, violence, sexual abuse and even torture of juveniles is commonplace.

This hard-hitting three-part series uncovers a global scandal about the neglect and abuse of children's rights within the justice system, around the world.

Part One: Pakistan

Six years ago, the government of Pakistan introduced new laws to protect the rights of children in conflict with the law.

Yet far from obtaining justice, many such children still fall prey to physical and sexual abuse at the hands of police and adult prisoners.

They are victims of a justice system that is inefficient, corrupt and uncaring.

In short, radio talks and documentaries should not be overlooked as a viable route to sell your work. Don't forget to revisit your notes and the research material you have collated for your written articles and features and re-use it to write for radio. It will be necessary to rewrite your copy to suit radio audiences and listeners rather than readers but having spent all that time researching and writing an article, with a little adaptation, it could just as easily be heard on the radio, giving you double the rewards for your effort.

Writing radio adverts

Although we are yet to discover how to write for business, it seems pertinent to mention writing radio adverts in this section.

If you have some experience in PR or marketing you may already have a flair for copywriting, and you could utilise your skills to write radio adverts.

Successful radio adverts do however, need careful planning and execution. Most are less than a minute long. Being able to get across enough information, in just a few seconds, so your listener understands the message is crucial. And not easy to do.

Ignore for a moment, all the legal jargon that is required by the *Advertising Standards Agency (ASA)* – you know the stuff they say in a nanosecond at the end of the advert, about terms and conditions. Concentrate, instead, on the main body of your advert. It must be punchy and engaging. It needs a message – a hook – upon which listeners will grasp the concept of the product or service you are attempting to attract them to.

Although you may think many radio adverts are a bit cheesy, and let's be fair, many are, they are written to a format. They will typically have some sort of musical intro or background. Some will try to be humorous or have a humorous slant, most are simply persuasive – *the must-haves* – you simply can't be without, types. There are also *info-commercials* but generally most radio adverts are trying to sell you something.

An info-commercial is usually written to inform rather than to sell something. Party political broadcasts, new Government legislation that affects the populous, or health advice is often given in info-commercials. Info-commercials are generally longer in airtime than the typical length of commercial or advertisement.

The crucial part of writing your advert is the timing. Once you have written your copy you should practice reading it, and remember to *time* yourself reading. The average reading speed is 120 – 150 words per minute so that gives you an idea of how few words you can allow yourself to get your message across.

This is an example of an advert I wrote. This is around 100 words of spoken text so just under a minute. Full airtime would have been a minute with the musical intro.

Chapter 12

Lexden Wood Golf Club – Heart Radio Commercial

Music:	*In (upbeat)*
MVO:	*Still playing golf?*
FVO:	*Yes, and loving it. Have you tried Lexden Wood Golf Club they've got everything for the golfer?*
MVO:	*Everything?*
FVO:	*Yes, everything and it's all included in the membership... unlimited use of the golf course, nine-hole academy course, and driving range.*
MVO:	*What about a shop?*
FVO:	*It's a new American Golf superstore, with a price match guarantee on all products – and so well stocked. I spend nearly as much time in there as I do on the course.*
MVO:	*So, I can get everything for the golfer?*
FVO:	*Yes – even my birthday present!*
MVO:	*Lexden Wood Golf Course, everything for the golfer and more. Go to Lexdenwood.com*

Note: FVO – female voice over. MVO – male voice over. You might have a child voice over, which is likely to be BVO or GVO, or you could actually use character names, if more relevant. Also note: all names are written in capital letters and for each person speaking a new line/carriage return is required. Directions such as music intro would be written in italics for the producer to differentiate between characters and dialogue and the directions.

If this category of writing appeals, or you have some copywriting experience, put together some ideas and contact your local radio station. With only a few exceptions, almost all local radio stations rely on radio advertising for revenue, and many would welcome some new writing talent. I would recommend listening to their current client adverts and see if you can write something different. Many radio advertisers regularly advertise with the same local station, and producing new ideas is something their existing bank of copywriters often find tricky.

Chapter 13
Online Writing

Throughout this book, we have already mentioned various aspects of online writing. Social media has cropped up a lot, and blogging has been seen as particularly popular for food and travel writers. What we are now about to discover are the benefits of writing website copy, while also exploring other online markets too.

Social media

Although social media, per se, does not offer opportunities for writers to write in any extended form, or earn directly, it is an important aspect of many marketing activities and plays a vital role in the digital strategies of many of today's businesses, however large or small.

Social media has, in fact, opened the marketing gateway for many small and independent businesses that could not otherwise afford to compete with their corporate counterparts. It can also be used as a relatively inexpensive way to reach a much wider audience and has fewer geographical restrictions compared to other sales and marketing activities, such as newspaper or directory advertising, or cold-calling.

As a writer, you might want to use social media to market your own work, whether that is articles or books. Creating an online profile is much easier and less costly than creating a website, and with features and applications already inbuilt, you can use these add-ons to sell your completed work.

You can also use your social media profiles to connect with other writers and people associated with the business of writing. This is invaluable to you, especially in the early days of your writing career. You can learn from others, access courses and workshops, and find writing opportunities or jobs. Many editors and publishers also use social media, affording you an excellent means of communicating with the right people in the industry.

Chapter 13

As part of your social media profile, you can write and publish your mini-biography. This is your first test. How tightly can you write about yourself and your writing endeavours that will encourage others to connect with you? Whether you are a published writer, or yet-to-be published, don't undersell yourself but don't oversell yourself either. Keep your profile succinct but let your personality and character shine through. If you are genuinely quite humorous and quirky, then be so. If you prefer a more professional approach – then write professionally. Your mini-biography should reflect you.

Blogging

What is a blog?

A blog is essentially a webpage hosted on a website that contains, *news*, *comments* or *articles*, written in an inclusive and *search-engine* friendly way. The blog itself can be the actual landing page of the website if, for example, your blog is hosted on a blog platform like *blogger.com* or *blogspot.com*.

One of the fundamental differences between a website and a blog page is that the overall content of a website may not change very often, whereas a blog page is usually updated with new content more frequently.

Typically, blog pages are run by an individual. In some cases, it could be updated by a group of people. Equally, many businesses use copywriters to write and post their blog content.

Evidently, the content of a blog is far less formal than the conventional content found on websites, and more *conversational* in style. As we discovered in writing food blogs, often the writer draws readers in by including some personal experiences as part of the blog content too. Companies often use blogs as a method to profile staff. This enables the company to appear more approachable and friendly. Some companies use case studies for their blog content, including details of completed jobs; again, this indicates *'real life'* and *'real-time'* style content.

Writer bloggers might write about the difficulties of getting over writer's block, or use their blog to familiarise readers with a subject they are developing for their next book – perhaps teasing them with a few carefully selected excerpts. Some offer hints and tips to help you improve your writing skills or advise you on how to get published.

As a writer, it is not essential to write a blog. Many do but just as many do not. Some writers believe blogging is a good way to promote their writing or raise their author profile – and it is. For others, it is a distraction, and they would rather concentrate on their other writing pursuits.

If you are an avid journal writer then blogging might be used as an extension of this. It's good practice and may help you write on a regular basis. It could also help you to write more succinctly and for public consumption.

If you do decide to write a blog, you do not have to blog every day. Some bloggers blog daily, some weekly, and others less frequently. However, if you are planning on using your blog page as a portal to gain exposure for your writing, you will need to blog frequently to build and gain an audience. It is pointless writing a blog every day when only your mum reads it. Your aim is to build an audience of readers who are interested in *what* you say and the *way* you say it.

Publishing a blog that is *accurate, timely, relevant,* and *informative* will not only help you build your audience – it could earn you recognition as an authoritative source; this will help you open the doors to other publishing opportunities.

Personal blogs allow the writer to write about many different topics, and this is fine if you have no interest in making money from your blog, or if you just love writing. If you are serious about writing for publication and you are using a blog to gain exposure, it is advisable to keep your blog *themed*. This enables you to share your knowledge and expertise for a specific subject, and in a more structured way.

It is advisable, therefore, to create a different blog for different themes or topics, as your audience will only grow if the subjects you write about are relevant to them. It is so much easier to start and maintain a blog if you are passionate about the topic. You can create a one-page blog, and that page can have many *sub-blogs*, but each one should be given its own title or reference, enabling readers to find it more easily. You might enjoy keeping Koi Carp and chickens. It is unlikely that many other readers who keep Koi Carp would also be interested in keeping chickens.

That said, as readers, we are drawn to blogs because of their subject matter, but also because we enjoy the blogger's *voice* and *perspective*. So, contrary to what I have just told you – *multi-topic* blogs can be successful. Providing that your perspective is consistent, readers will follow you from idea to idea, just as a friend would one day listen to your adventures of mountain climbing and the next your newfound love of cave diving. However, your multi-topic blogs, aside from being diverse, must be reader friendly and well-organised. *Category pages, tags, shortcodes* or *custom image widgets* are blog page tools to help you organise your posts and multi-topic blogs.

There are numerous websites and blog sites that provide you with all the information you need to create and develop your blog – *www.theblogbuilders.com* or *www.theblogstarter.com* – to name but two. Whilst we won't go into the technical side of creating a blog, I will give you a little advice on the writing of your content for your blog.

Whatever topic you choose to write about, your content should be relevant. It should be *relevant* to your subject and relevant for your reader. You may be writing a travel blog – from the outset you need to decide if you are going to focus on one element of a journey per blog entry or post, or if each blog post will reveal lots of different aspects of your trip. To write a blog applicable to your readers, first, ascertain who your readers are. If you have a loyal following of readers already, you can find out a lot about them from the comments they may leave on your posts, or by looking at any blogs they have written, or from their social media profiles. If you are writing a blog for the first time, you should think about the type of audience you want to attract. Are you writing for young parents or OAPs, the middle classes or gap year students? By identifying your readership, you will be able to tailor your copy to gain more readers of a similar type. Suffice it to say, that does not mean that you cannot write for a much broader readership – you can.

Once again, it comes back to your research.

To write successful blogs, you should read a variety of different blogs by other bloggers. You can gauge which ones are more successful by the audience numbers they have engaged, and by the quantity and type of comments their blog posts receive.

Writing *tightly* and *succinctly* will improve the effectiveness of your blogs. Keep your ideas simple and clear and try to avoid tangents. Writing this way, however, does not mean your blog should be less entertaining or engaging. In fact, it is the reverse. You must work harder to write in an enthusiastic and appealing manner using fewer words!

Aim for quality, not quantity. There is no magic word-count for writing a successful blog but there is a formula to help you write your blog for the best engagement, courtesy of Joe Bunting of The Write Practice:

75-300 words. Super-short posts are best for generating discussion. They rarely get many shares on social media, and they're horrible for SEO, but if you want a lot of comments, write short posts!

300-600 words. The standard blogging length, recommended by many "expert" bloggers. Good middle-ground for social shares and comments. Too short to gain much authority or search engine-love.

750 words. This is the standard length for professional journalism, especially newspapers. I find that it's pretty good for getting links from other bloggers and shares on social media.

1000-1500 words. You'll get fewer comments at this length but a lot more shares on social media, especially if you've written a post that actually solves someone's problem. That being said, I've written posts this long and gotten 100+ comments, so it really depends on the topic and your audience.

2,450 words. The highest-ranking articles on Google are most often 2,450 words. If you want to rank well on search engines (and thus get thousands of new readers per month), this is the best length to write. However, make sure you write about a topic that people are actually searching for. It would be a shame to write a book-length blog post on a topic no one ever searches for!

Building your audience

So how do you build your audience and gain readership?

Chapter 13

You may be familiar with the term *Google* rankings. When people are searching for information about a particular topic or product, they type a word or string of words into their search bar; these are known as *keywords*. *Google* analyses the keywords it finds in the background content of lots of websites to give the searcher the best possible matches. Some years ago, to rank higher in the listings produced by *Google*, webmasters would load their sites with keywords to draw visitors.

Today, Google is more interested in the semantics. It wants to see regular content change, and is looking for phrases rather than keywords. It is also looking for activity on websites such as clickthroughs via links that take the viewer to other pages.

Alison Withers, Multimedia Reputations

The more interactive your website or blog, the higher the chances of Google recognising it as a meaningful and valuable site, thus improving your position in the relevant search listings.

In addition to content or phrases that may bring readers to your site and blog, social media plays an important part too. Putting keywords or teasers on social media feeds with a link to your blog will take readers from social media to your website and blog. On *Facebook*, Tyler Wagner posted a video clip with the headline: *'Why You Need To Write A Book Now' If you're interested in achieving results like you heard on this video, apply here: Http://bt.ly.......*

From the link, viewers can read the blog and *share it* (they may also share the social media post – and you want this to happen). What you do not want to do is copy and paste your whole blog post into a social media feed. Although some readers will share it, your aim is to drive them to your website. You want to entice them to sign up for the other blogs you write, and perhaps read the previous blog posts you have already posted. Your goal is to build a loyal following of readers. This is what will make your blogging activities more successful and help you to build that all-important audience.

> *A note about sign-ups – although it is common for websites to encourage you to sign up for a newsletter by entering your email, you can encourage readers to sign up to receive notifications of your latest blog. These tools are available on your blog page settings. However, sign-ups can be more successful if you are giving away free content. For example, if you have written a series of factsheets on writing – 'From page to publication' – readers can sign up to receive these fact sheets at periodic stages. Your aim here might be to give them enough information to get started but your ultimate goal is to encourage them to buy your new book on the same or a similar topic.*

DO share other people's posts and blogs. If you have found a blog interesting, and particularly if it is about subjects you write about, do share.

> *Sharing other people's blogs that bear some relevance to your blog topics can add weight to your blog site. Third party endorsements, multi-shares and comments you leave on other people's posts and blogs can also help drive readers back to your site. But – don't spam.*

Aisleen Marley, Marley Bird Communications

Websites

Over the last ten years, website content has changed dramatically. Nowadays, there is a widespread need for well-written high-quality copy, with a variety of keywords strategically placed to engage the reader, rather than the keyword-heavy 'gloop' that was common just a decade ago.

Despite the changes, many business owners still undervalue the quality of their website copy. Many will spend thousands of pounds on having their website developed and yet give little thought to the actual content. In my experience, most website developers can't and won't provide the copy, and it falls back to the website owner to manage and provide it. This can often lead to a lengthy delay in a new or updated website being launched.

This is a good opportunity for you. There is still a strong market for good website content copywriters. Whether you offer your services as a freelance copywriter to local business owners, website designers, or you apply to agencies offering this service – the demand is still high.

As well as being able to write engaging content, you will need to be aware of SEO and the keywords and phrases relevant to the industry and the pages of content you will be writing. *And, this applies to both blog content and copy for any other website pages.*

As always, you are still writing for your reader, not the business, and you should put yourself in the reader's mind. What information do they need to know about this business, product or service? What questions might they need the answers to? If they buy said product or service, will it resolve their need or issue?

Keep your copy *succinct* and *on point*. Use bullet points to break up long paragraphs of text. Better still, write shorter sentences and paragraphs to help your reader find the information they are looking for *quickly*. Include links to other pages to help readers navigate around the site and to easily locate the information they are looking for – such as delivery information, T&Cs, or goods returns.

E-commerce websites work in a slightly different way. These are more product, less content-based, sales sites. E-commerce sites are all about the sales.

Browse lots of different sites to analyse their set up. View some e-commerce sites, such as your favourite online fashion stores but also look at service companies or information sites, to gauge how and why they have written the content in the way they have. Make notes on the word count of copy in different areas of the site, and log which sites you favoured more and why. This will help you ascertain how best to write the website content for client e-commerce sites. Familiarise yourself with the style and type of language used and see if you can identify keywords and phrases. Also, observe any *headlines* or *calls to action*. It is useful also to understand how and why the links are placed where they are. See if you can spot blog content too. It may not always be obvious that a page is a blog and sometimes the buttons to the page will be tagged something other than 'blog'. They could be labelled as *'latest news' 'new products'* or even *'case studies'*.

If the site has social media buttons, and most do, have a look at their posts and see how many link back to the website and vice versa.

The more information you can gather about websites the easier you will find it to write the content for them.

Other online markets

As you have now come to appreciate, many people do not have the skills or the inclination to write, but the fact you are reading this book implies you do. This is a good thing from both perspectives as it leaves space for those who want to write to find work (writing about the stuff other people are not able to write about, or which they choose not to write about). Even better, despite the extensive changes to the world of publishing that we discovered early on in this book, the internet has provided us writers with many new prospects.

I am actually quite envious of today's writers. In the early years of my freelance writing career, query submissions, article ideas, and carefully crafted covering letters were printed off and sent via *Royal Mail*, accompanied by a self-addressed and stamped envelope. Then, I would sit and eagerly await the positive replies or the dreaded rejection letters. Writers' markets consisted of newspapers, magazines, and if we could get it, work for private clients. Freelance writers had to generate their own ideas, meticulously study their markets, and pitch those ideas to editors in the hope they may bite.

Then along came the internet. Submissions and queries could be sent via email, (and any responses were often received within a matter of days – not weeks) while companies were crying out for copywriters to write website content. In the last decade or so, the internet has changed again. Today, *outsourcing, job searching,* and the openings afforded to writers have never been more bountiful.

In addition to writing content for online magazines and eZines, blogs and websites, or even ghostwriting autobiographies (for *Storyterrace*), there are numerous possibilities to write for other online markets. And, the beauty of this type of work is that you don't have to come up with the ideas! The customers already know what they want. All you have to do is research the content, facts, and information – often some of this will be provided by the customer – and then write and submit your word-perfect copy, in the style and manner in which the customer has requested. Easy – right?

Chapter 13

Well, there is an art to it – otherwise everybody would be doing it!

Individuals and companies have all sorts of requirements for text. In addition to website content, blogs, and other online copy, good freelance writers are sought for articles, reports, whitepapers, tender proposals, business profiles, and marketing materials including brochures and manuals.

Just search online for *'freelance writing opportunities'* or *'freelance writing jobs'* and an abundance of sites will appear.

Peopleperhour.com, Freelancer.co.uk, Textbroker.co.uk, Upwork.com, Fiverr.com and *Lowpricearticles.com* amongst others offer writing services for customers.

On some of the sites, the customer uploads their content requirements and freelance writers pitch for the work. The customer then chooses who they want to write their content. On other sites, the content requirement is matched to selected writers from their bank of registered freelancers.

In most cases, it is assumed that the customer will have some idea of what they are looking for, including how much content they need and its purpose. Your job is to write the content to match their requirements. In other instances, customers may be a little vaguer, so carry out any necessary research to provide the copy to meet the industry norm. If the content's purpose is clear, this should enable you to seek out other material along similar lines. The amount of research you need to do will depend upon the subject matter and the technical aspects of the job.

The rates that customers pay, and the amount of money that writers receive, varies from site to site, and by the job specification. In the case of *Textbroker,* for example, clients pay different amounts depending on the rating level of the writer they wish to engage. As a writer, your level is set by *Textbroker* during your application process. As *Textbroker* explains: "your registration text is given an initial rating between 2 to 4 stars by our experienced editors. As a quality assurance feature, all authors are re-evaluated when their first five articles are submitted. These articles are then rated between 2-5 stars." In turn, your rating will evolve as the number of satisfactorily completed jobs increases, and as more customers review and rate the quality of your work.

For the writer, different sites have their own sets of standards and requirements. Some will ask you to supply copies of written work; others may ask you to complete a written or grammar test. In turn, there are no restrictions about who else you can write for or how many other of these types of sites you can register with. It is worth trying out a few to see which one suits you best, whether that is based on the type of work or the earnings per word or per job. Most of these sites manage the process directly, including how and when the writer gets paid – and that can be a great advantage to you as a freelancer, even though the rates per word or per job can be on the low side, especially when you first start.

One of the downsides of this type of work is the rates of pay. They are often low. Some agencies pay per word, and this can be less than a couple of pence, others will pay per article, but that could be as little as £10 - £15 for 500 words. To make a sensible living as a freelance writer, you would have to provide a lot of copy, and pay is a reason, perhaps, why others in the industry refer to them as *'content mills'* – the implication being that a mass of writers churn out endless amounts of copy. However, on the upside, as a novice writer, writing this type of work will help you develop and improve your writing skills, and help you to compile a comprehensive writing portfolio. Many writers see these sites as a means to an end. Others, who can only write part time, find them an enjoyable and varied means of generating a side income.

If you are looking for more regular freelance writing work or a content writing career, try *Freelancewriting.com*, *Indeed.com* and other job boards. *Freelancewriting.com* is a website that advertises writing jobs and opportunities in journalism, copywriting, content writing and (as they call it) *'blogging gigs'*. The site lists specific jobs from across the industry and in every arena from health and beauty writers and editors to content marketing vacancies. On *Indeed* and other similar job sites, you might also find the occasional full or part-time writing roles advertised.

It can be said that if I had started my freelance writing career ten years later than I did, my journey would have been very different. Would it have been easier? I'm not sure. Yes, the opportunities may be far greater with writing online providing a viable way to earn a living as a writer, but nothing really beats writing what you choose to write about and having your work accepted for publication, especially when you've sent something on spec. By the time, I had written commercial copy for clients, and been subject to their requirements for more years than I care to remember, I could not wait to get back to writing about the topics I wanted to write about – without deadlines, without constraint, and without the hassle!

Overall, compiling a portfolio of published work can give you a sense of accomplishment and, if topped off with a by-line or two, you'll have something very tangible to be proud of.

Basically, what I am trying to say is, don't rule out one market over another. Aim for balance. If you write articles for publication, you will have something to show when applying to the online agencies and their customers, and vice versa.

Chapter 14
Writing for Business

There are two reasons you might want to write for business purposes. The first, is to offer your services as a freelance copywriter. The second, you are the owner of a business and you enjoy the challenge of writing your own copy or, perhaps, because it is more affordable for you to do so.

Irrespective of your reasons, the information relayed in this chapter relates to both scenarios, without exception.

What it takes to be a great commercial copywriter

If you're looking for a career as a professional writer, commercial copywriting can be a great career path, with plentiful sources of work. Whether it's right for you though, depends on many factors that can seem to have nothing in common with creative talent, and indeed, can challenge a naturally creative mind.

The first challenge will be in the subject matter, which will come in myriad themes. For instance, you may know nothing about technology in healthcare, but if you are commissioned to write a 1000-word feature, including an expert case study, with a deadline of a matter of days, you'll need to be prepared.

This is where the right research will pay dividends. First, think about your reader; particularly look at the publication you are writing for, and its 'house style'. Get a feel for the pace and content that will be expected from your article, look at the way the paragraphs, sub headings, images and pull quotes are laid out. This is the template you'll need to work from.

In commercial writing, statistics are your friend, and a key part of your article research. Look at studies relating to your subject and the headline statistics that will add credibility and gravitas to your article. Take care here though, always check your statistics are accurate, and record your sources for reference.

Remember, you don't need to know everything about the field, just the subject you are writing about. Use the same beginning, middle and conclusions you would articulate in any other piece of writing.

If your article includes case studies or interviews, plan your questions in advance to lead the interviewee towards the content you need. It can be nerve-wracking the first few times you interview someone, and you'll need to appear confident and in control of the process. It can help to send the questions in advance, so your interview subject has some time to think about the answers they will give.

Remember, they may be nervous too, so prior communication will put you both at ease.

As a commercial writer, you'll usually work to short deadlines, be expected to source interviews and images, and take responsibility for the whole process. If you're writing for a publication on behalf of a company, you may also have the challenge of lots of different opinions and expectations around your work. This goes back again to the researching and planning that will enable you to be assertive in negotiating with clients and keeping your article 'fit for purpose'.

Commercial writing can seem like it is devoid of any creativity, but I believe it's the opposite. You'll need inspiration, originality and resourcefulness, challenging your writing talents in new ways with every assignment. You'll learn that even the most seemingly boring subject can be interesting and even fascinating when you delve in to it. You'll have the opportunity to meet new people and explore a diverse range of subjects.

Always remember: write for your reader, research your subject, and be confident in dealing with your commercial clients. Enjoy the process and watch your career grow.

Kate Everett, professional copywriter, The Write Impression LLP

Commercial writing & copywriting

Commercial writing is writing for businesses. A commercial writer, writes *copy* or *text* to help businesses communicate with their customers, and perhaps more importantly, with potential customers. Commercial writing is also known as copywriting but I adore the following quote, which describes copywriting in a slightly different way.

Copywriting is the art and science of strategically delivering words (whether written or spoken) that get people to take some form of action.

Copywriters are some of the highest-paid writers in the world.

Copyblogger.com

Whether you call yourself a commercial writer or a copywriter, the writing principles are basically the same. You are writing to inform the reader but often you are writing to *sell*. It could be to sell a *concept, product*, or a *service. Keep this notion pinned to the back of your mind.*

Companies need a multitude of copy and for a variety of reasons. Most are trying to sell us something. However, sales and marketing copy isn't that straightforward. There are many tactics *marketers* employ to connect with consumers. Some of this will be direct sales copy, others will be enticement and engagement.

Being able to write commercial copy means you should always consider what you write as sales copy. The words and language you use ought to be *persuasive, upbeat*, and *positive*. There should always be some sort of *call-to-action*, even if you are writing an article. You might expect to see a call-to-action in advertising material but it is equally important in press releases, articles, and webcopy. Your text should lead the reader to find out more information, or better still – want to buy.

A call to action – in a marketing sense – means a piece of content intended to stimulate the reader to perform a specific act, through instruction or command.

One of the trickier elements of writing commercial copy is being able to write for more than one audience. Everything I have told you so far in this book, about writing for publication, is to be aimed at your reader. Right?

Well, here's the difference. If you are pitching work to an editor or publisher you are writing *for them* as well as their readers. Nevertheless, they understand their readers' needs – so you are essentially ticking two boxes at once. When your client is the business owner, however, you are required to satisfy him with your knowledge and facts about his business or product (and provide well-written sales copy) but you are *writing for his audience – not him –* and that is the tricky bit.

Chapter 14

Every time you write about his company, his products or services, you should imagine yourself as a customer or potential customer. And, you need to be very aware of how much knowledge that customer might have or might need. This is going to be very different from what your client might expect to read. If you are a business owner, and writing your own copy or marketing materials, this can prove problematic for you too. When you know your business inside out, you can lose sight of what your customers might need to know. Or, you might make assumptions that they know more than they do. *Jargon* and *acronyms* can easily be littered throughout your copy, and while you and your workforce understand what they mean – your lay reader may have absolutely no idea!

Many people find it difficult to write about themselves, so the advantages of using a freelance copywriter is that they have an outside perspective, and can often appreciate what readers (or customers, for that matter) should know.

As a commercial writer, I was occasionally asked by new clients, *'How can you write about my business when you don't know as much about it as I do'. My answer was always the same. 'It's my job. To be a good copywriter I write for the reader – your customer. Being detached from your business means I have a fresh pair of eyes. I have to understand what it is you do and how you do it – and relay that message, in jargon-free, simple terms, and at the same time persuade them that they need your services.*

Another common mistake, for both owner writers and novice writers, is to try and include too much information all in one piece. This is most frequently evident in press releases.

One of my many writing roles included editing press releases for a county magazine. I had to plough through copy of more than 1000 words, in some instances, and condense the information into 150-word 'business highlights', 'what's on' guides, and 'art news' pages.

What this illustrates is that much of the copy provided was irrelevant, and the crux of the matter, once drawn out from the rest of the text, could be said in much fewer words.

Equally, webcopy and even articles, can include all sorts of tangents, where the writer is trying to include everything about the business, all in one place. Besides boring your reader to death, or them failing to understand your message, if you have included everything in one piece – what more is there left to say? By breaking down the content into shorter samples, whether that is press releases, social media posts, blogs, or supplementary webpages, you are giving the reader lots of snippets of information that they can more easily absorb. This will also enable the reader to build a more structured picture of the business, and its products and services.

Let's now look at some of the copywriting services other businesses may require and how you can provide them.

Direct advertising

A lot of companies engage the services of advertising agencies to provide the copy for advertising materials such as billboards, posters, or leaflets. Businesses with smaller budgets tend to turn to copywriters for help.

There is a lot of written material, theories and evidence, based on human behaviour and psychology that explains *how we buy*. This is quite evident in the headlines used on marketing materials.

Simple and direct

Writing a headline that gets to the crux of the matter without trying to sound intriguing or clever.

Kate Atkins lost 2 stone in five weeks with Slimmer's World

What is the benefit?

Readers want to satisfy a need. The promise here is to convince them that your content will satisfy that need.

Lose 2 stone in five weeks

Announcement

Make an announcement with exciting news. We are curious beings. Bringing exciting news to your readers will grab their attention.

I lost 2 stone in weight and married the man of my dreams

How to

Focus on the needs and wants of your reader. It may not be enough to tell them how to do something, you may have to reveal the final benefit or result to get them to bite.

Chapter 14

How to lose 2 stone and keep it off

Question

Asking questions is always a great way to get your reader involved. Keep your question relevant to the theme of your content but also bear in mind the benefits to the reader.

Do you want to lose weight?

Command or direct

Telling your reader what to do is an effective tactic. However, you need to bear in mind the *'why'* factor. If you provide a command, how will it benefit the audience?

Stop faddy dieting and lose weight with us

Results and solutions

If your readers are looking for something, they want to know what the results or solutions will be. If you just said, *'Lose 2 stone'* they might ask *why* or *how?* If you tell them that they can do it in *5 easy steps* – it makes more sense to them.

Lose 2 stone in 5 easy steps

The statements above are typical of headlines used by slimming companies for advertising materials but you can use the format for writing headlines for any product or service. Be conscious of the readers' *needs*, the *benefits* to them, and the *results*.

One thing is for sure when compiling advertising copy – less is often more. In turn, depending on the subject matter, a little humour can work, a play on words can be effective, but equally, a strong but simple message might be just what is needed. Asking questions at the start of the campaign, or including numbers and statistics, can be powerful triggers too. Essentially, the purpose of a sales message is to solve the problems people have, even before they realise that they have a problem or a need.

Have you thought about the income you'll have to live on in later life?

Are you aware your pension or state pension won't be worth what you think?

Do you know what you can do about it?

The above example is asking questions of the reader. It is intended to draw the reader's attention to their pension, something they may not think about often, and then prompt them to do something about it – because, *it may not be worth as much as they think*. This illustrates a problem for the reader, a potential problem they were unaware of… until now.

For investments 'as safe as houses' talk to Asset Enterprise Partnership. The investment property specialists you can trust!

In this example, the copywriter is using the adage, *'as safe as houses'* to draw the consumer's attention to buying property as a sound investment. But, because investments can be risky, and consumers can be nervous about investing, the final strapline *'The investment property specialists you can trust!'* is used to reassure them. A *call-to-action* is also a prominent part of the text *'talk to'*.

If you are considering writing advertising material of this kind, it is worth doing your research to understand the science behind how consumers buy.

'Instant Advertising' by Bradley J Sugars, Founder of Action Coach, is worth a read and 'Lovemarks' is a cracking book about branding, by Kevin Roberts, the Worldwide CEO of Saatchi & Saatchi.

Search the internet for key tips and techniques, read other books on *consumer behaviour*, and study *sales literature* that comes your way. Despite the attempts of many to rid ourselves of *junk mail* – before you discard yours, take a closer look. Try to ascertain the message. Are you drawn in? If so, why? Was there a call to action? And, would you buy?

If you don't like it – why not? Could you improve it?

Now try for yourself!

Articles

Throughout this book, we have learned a fair amount about writing articles. Writing articles for business does not really differ from what you have already discovered. You need to have some idea of the audience or market you are writing the article for, before putting all the other principles into play. A strong headline, plus opening paragraph and start to your article, is needed to attract your reader.

Chapter 14

The middle should be packed with facts and information relating to the theme or subject matter, and your ending should come to a strong conclusion with one fundamental difference – you now include a *call-to-action*.

You could be writing an article for a magazine, or for a company website. You might be providing it for a third-party customer through an online writing agency. Whatever the case, study the target, which is ultimately the audience. Write your copy in an appropriate format for your target audience and ensure your word count is in-line with the other published articles. Pack your content with facts, and detailed information about the company's product or service, and stick to the theme or subject at hand.

Your article could be an interview-style piece, it could be a new product or service, or it could be about a recently completed contract. Where possible, include quotes from key members of staff, such as the managing director or project manager, or even from relevant outside sources, such as a member of a registered body for the industry you are writing about, or alternatively, a satisfied customer. As per before, numerical facts and statistics are always worth including, as are comparisons or developments in the industry to which you are referring, but always check these with reliable or primary sources.

In most cases, your article will be written in the third person, and this is always the preferred approach. However, some profile or interview articles will be required in the first-person voice. If you are unsure, check with the publication before you commence writing.

Where possible, your articles should be positive and upbeat. Steer clear of referring to things the company cannot provide, or comparisons with competitors, as this can draw a reader's attention to something the company is unable to deliver, thus losing them business or worse – *a sale*. Instead, focus on what they are good at, or excel at. Look for the company's *USP* – what makes them great at what they do and why? How do they separate themselves from the competition, or what is it they can do (or provide for their customers) that their competitors cannot?

USP – is the unique selling proposition or unique selling point in marketing. It was first proposed as a theory to explain a pattern in successful advertising campaigns of the early 1940s. Campaigns using USPs made exclusive propositions to customers that convinced them to switch brands.

Do not ignore negative elements if there is something to be gained from addressing the issue. If, for example, something went wrong during a construction process but through a new development or a member of staff's innovations the issue was overcome, then concentrate on how it was resolved – positively.

Alternatively, you could be writing about new legislation that could affect the business or industry you are writing for. In this case, do your best to include elements of both sides of the story.

For example:

The computerisation of crop-spraying tractors will reduce the number of traditional farming jobs. However, what the industry will require, is young farmers with more scientific or IT skills, which in turn, could lead to an increase in the number of young people wanting to work in the industry.

Press releases

The construction of a press release is very different to an article. For a start, a press release is a *newsworthy* story written for the media. The purpose of a press release (or news release, as it is otherwise known) is to pique the interest of a journalist or publication. Ideally, what businesses want is for a press release to be picked up by the media and then run as a much bigger story. A press release should intrigue a journalist enough to carry this through. At the very least, you can hope that your press release is published with the content you have provided, but if they do follow up your story, that's always a bonus.

Press releases should have an urgency about them, but this can mean they have a limited *shelf-life*. Obviously, a product launch or an event has a relevant date to which it refers, but the content of press releases tends to deal with the *present*. Articles can be written in a way that makes them less time-critical, or so that content is less likely to date. But, when writing press releases, you want your copy to be timely – so it is published more quickly. Press releases sitting in editor's inboxes can be easily forgotten if they aren't destined for a specific date or issue.

> *Tip: Think about issue deadlines. It is pointless sending a press release about an event in the month of the event or even, the month before. Most monthly publications have at least a two month copy deadline. If you do not think your press release will meet the deadline, write a post event release, ready for the following issue instead.*

If the content of your release is less time critical, find a way to make it relevant today. Use other topics or current issues to peg your story to. Hang your copy on the back of other companies' headlines and announcements.

As ISA Interest Rates Drop, Investors should be encouraged to consider Asset Backed Investments

The latest financial forecast reports that the average return on ISAs has already dropped from 2.57% to 1.16% in two years. Investment property company, Asset Enterprise Partnership, asks, in light of these latest figures, why investors are not being encouraged to consider asset-backed investments instead.

Being newsworthy is *the most* fundamental element of writing a successful press release. Next, consider what is *new* about your story, or if there is anything unusual or unexpected about it. If you think about the things you like to read, watch, and listen to in the media, it is likely you are most interested in something you haven't heard before. If you can deliver information that others will find useful, helpful, or surprising it will increase your chances of publication. You might be excited about the launch of a new product, or the appointment of a new managing director but will anyone else? Find a way to write about these topics that will be of interest to others.

Unlike much of your other work, where a catchy title is relevant, what your press release must have is a *killer headline*. Journalists' email inboxes are overflowing with potential material and you don't want yours to get lost in the clutter. Labelling your email with *press release* or *story idea* is okay – but follow this with a killer headline and you're almost guaranteed the recipient will at least be intrigued enough to open it.

New shop opening closes High Street

Stampede as High Tech Store Launches New Product

Revolutionary Robot Makes the Tea

Besides a killer headline, your press release should be *succinct, upbeat*, and have a *purpose*. The purpose may be to draw the reader's attention to an important matter. It may be to encourage them to buy something, or attend an event, or just to raise brand awareness – but finding its purpose will help you to structure your copy.

There is a straightforward format to writing a good press release:

1. Write a killer headline.

2. The opening paragraph should give an indication of what the press release is about. Include key tips or summarise the subject in the lead sentence.

3. As you write the main body of the press release, pack it with facts but leave waffle out of it. (Journalists and editors hate having to edit press releases).

4. Include relevant quotes. Write quotes to provide insight or opinion, and ensure they sound like a real person said them.

5. Keep to a single theme per release and avoid tangents.

6. Make your press release 'page ready'. Keep your formatting simple, your font size and type as standard, and avoid bold fonts and italics unless absolutely necessary.

7. Photographs can significantly increase your chances of having your press release published. Include good quality or high resolution, clear and in focus, photographs relevant to your topic, or source stock images from photo libraries. If sourcing stock images, ensure you are buying the correct rights for commercial reproduction.

8. Always include contact details and relevant purchase information for both the editor and readers.

We all appreciate that the media can be a very powerful medium. However, what a press release won't do is generate frantic calls from buyers or have the press pounding at your door asking for more information. Sadly, many new and small business owners think that by sending out one press release, the media are going to be eagerly lapping up their story and fighting other journalists to be the first to publish. This very rarely happens.

Despite the hundreds, perhaps thousands, of press releases my colleagues and I wrote on behalf of clients, in only one instance did we have to tackle a media frenzy over the launch of a new and innovative product. In the majority of cases, we would be hopeful to get published in half a dozen carefully selected publications. And, that is the key. You cannot just email your press release to all and sundry in the hope they will publish what you've written because you think it's a wonderful product or an amazing announcement – let's be real – they won't. All of your articles, features, and press releases must be submitted to a list of selected journalists working at specific newspapers and magazines (hardcopy and online), and other media contacts such as for radio and TV. Some industries are niche and may only have one or two magazines dedicated to their industry – and the business editors of the daily newspapers are inundated with press release copy from every PR agency across the country. This is what your client or business is up against.

If the core audience is local to your client or business, focus on building a good database of *relevant* local publications and include industry-specific titles pertinent to the business. In your database, include the contact details and information for the journalist or editor you will be emailing your press releases to.

If your target audience is nationwide, or even global, then consider using a *newswire* service.

There are several PR newswire services and agencies that will distribute press releases on behalf of companies and individuals but these are costly. Larger PR agencies often subscribe to these newswire services for more favourable rates and a better value service, but some also offer a *'one-off'* or *'pay-as-you-go'* type facility. One of the many benefits of newswire companies is that they provide the latest and most up to date contact details for almost every journalist of every publication in the UK, and for every industry. In many cases, they offer an overseas service too, covering the likes of the USA or Europe.

Specialist titles or trade and industry publications are often not available to the general public. Some are sold to subscribers only, others through industry-specific organisations. This can hinder your chances of finding them. The company you are writing for may already subscribe or receive relevant trade publications, so grab a copy or two, and do your magazine analysis. It is also worth asking your client if they have a list of publications they would like to appear in. This can help you target your press releases appropriately. Also, find out if particular newswire services hold the details of these trade publications too.

It is also more likely that journalists will pick up your press releases on maybe the second or third release. Editors and journalists like to see some consistency from copywriters and PR agencies. They like to be sure of the longevity of a company or business they are looking to support through, let's be honest, *FREE* publicity. Often, what they want to see is some reciprocal business. In other words, *advertising opportunities.* Publishers are more likely to publish press releases submitted from the companies that regularly advertise with them over a newbie trying his luck.

Editors will also instantly dismiss press releases which are blatant *sales* or *advertising copy.* Of course, we all know that press releases are used to raise brand or product awareness but to reiterate the beginning of this section: *a press release must appear newsworthy.* It is necessary to have a story behind the backbone of the release, otherwise you will fail to attract any media attention. If this happens, your client may not see the value in you writing this type of material for him again.

Chapter 14

Another word of warning: do not be too precious about your headline or the content of your press release. A journalist may even by-line the text with his own name, making no reference to you as the writer at all. This is normal. If you distribute a press release, you are giving editors and journalists carte blanche to publish without copyright restrictions. This means they can pull apart your copy, and reword and rewrite it to fit their own means, and publish without seeking your permission. Essentially, every publication wants to print an original, untold story, and they know other journalists have received your release and may also choose to cover it. Every publication will want to put their own spin on it, so that it appeals to their readers, and because they want to run a fresh story. The only grounds for complaint you may have, is if they publish incorrect information – but remember, you haven't paid for the space, so be wary of making too much of a fuss if you want them to publish press releases from you in the future. Needless to say, if they have published detrimental facts or inaccuracies then do make them aware – politely!

Brochures

Personally, I always enjoyed writing client brochures. Writing articles and press releases means coming up with a constant flow of copy ideas and finding markets to publish into. Writing brochures for clients gave me the opportunity to understand their business or product in depth, and write a substantial amount of copy. As a project, compiling brochures also meant I was often responsible for the brochure layout, the sourcing of images or photographs, and page layouts. This challenged my creative skills in different ways.

Brochures can be anything from a couple of pages long to small booklets. Some are folder-style with card inserts and others are bound and beautifully published.

Often, clients need brochures for handouts at business fairs, seminars or events. Sometimes, they are sent to existing clients to keep them informed of new products or services. If a company has rebranded and wants to refresh all its stationery, that might include new brochures too.

Because brochures can be very costly to produce, it's not only your copywriting skills that businesses need to engage; there are photographs to source, graphic designers might be required to design and produce the cover and inside pages, and there are also printing costs to be considered. Page count affects costs across all these areas, so it is very important that you do your best to keep your copy brief. If the client is more flexible about his approach, you should still be conscious of keeping your copy tight, relevant, and succinct – he will thank you for it.

Corporate brochures are designed to inform the reader about the products or services of the company. There is no room for waffle or padding. Be conscious of what the industry calls *'white space'* – interpreted, this means lots of page space around the text. This makes it easier for readers to read and comprehend the messages. *Short paragraphs, bullet points,* and *pull quotes* are techniques which can be used to enhance the white space and help readers navigate through your text. Visuals such as graphics, diagrams, and photographs help break up large amounts of text and can also aid the reader.

Writing brochure copy can also mean breaking the text into subsections, much like writing chapters of a book, or piecing together several articles. Each page may have its own headline or sub-headings. It may contain interview-style pieces into key staff or even suppliers, or case studies. If the client is looking for inspiration for his brochure copy, these are some of the methods you can suggest, to make it more interesting and engaging.

Some brochures may, in fact, just be product catalogues. Although the content you provide for catalogues may be somewhat restrictive, it still requires a tremendous amount of time and effort to produce relevant copy that is 100% accurate.

White papers

White papers are authoritative reports associated with business, technology, even the government; they are reports that provide information or proposals about a specific issue. White papers often present the issuing body's philosophy on a matter; they are written to help readers understand an issue, solve a problem, or make an informed decision.

When used for sales and marketing purposes, white papers can be written to entice or persuade potential customers of the benefits of buying a specific product or service. These documents are designed to be read before a sale, and are not the same as user manuals or technical documents that provide after-sales support.

The language used in sales and marketing white papers is as you would expect, designed to be persuasive, and influence current and potential customers' decisions. This could be between a manufacturer and wholesaler, or wholesaler and a retailer, but not necessarily the end user.

There is a fundamental difference between writing a white paper and say a brochure or other sales literature. Sales literature such as brochures are often eye-catching, colourful, and contain graphics, calls-to-action, and persuasive language and nuances. White papers are more structured, providing factual evidence relating to new methodologies or problem-solving. You would expect white papers to consist of several thousand words, probably not less than 2,500 and be written in a more academic and formal style.

Tender proposals

Tenders are an important activity underpinning the success of many companies but they can be a precarious undertaking. This is why many forward-thinking companies use copywriters to assist with their tender applications. However, you really need to have some degree of experience to take on the responsibility of such a task, or at the very least, have the confidence to tackle it. If writing and preparing tender documents is, or has been, a task to which you have some experience (say a part of your previous job) it could be something worth pursuing as a copywriter. Potentially, it is a very lucrative market for the right person.

Tender documents require anything between 2,000 and 20,000 words, depending on the size of the project and its complexity. Often the deadlines can be tight and you need enough time to prepare case studies, talk to staff, fact-find, and compile procedural documents or supporting evidence. If procedural documents or compliance paperwork don't exist, you may also have to prepare them for inclusion.

Often, clients will call upon copywriters at the last minute to produce the documents needed, when they realise the size of the task and the timeline! Be honest about what you are able to deliver and the time-frame required to deliver it. That doesn't mean turning down the job, you might just need extra manpower to help complete it on time. *Missing the deadline is one of the biggest reasons tender bids fail.*

Do not underestimate the complexity of this type of project or the reliance on others to complete the task thoroughly and on time.

Tip: It is worth pre-preparing a stakeholder plan. Make a list of all the names and positions of key staff, and note what they do and their contact details; that way you'll know who to approach to help you complete each element of the document.

There are a number of pitfalls to be aware of when preparing a tender document for a client. For a start, there are many different *points of failure* that could result in your client's application being unsuccessful, and this may have nothing to do with you or your work on the tender.

Confidence is the key to taking on a project like this. If you are preparing a tender that is worth £5 million to your client and it fails, whether that has anything to do with you or not – it could be perceived that you've lost them £5 million.

Preparing tenders can be very costly for your client. It's a time-consuming project for you and you need to price accordingly to complete the task. Again, be aware of the client's losses if the tender fails. *It could be worth agreeing a slightly lower fixed fee for the job plus a small percentage of the tender value if it wins.* You are taking a risk but so is the client.

It can also be cost-effective for your client if they bid for several tenders as much of the text written for one tender could be reworded and used for another.

Just because a tender bid is an official document doesn't mean it should be written in a flat tone. Some of the most successful tenders have been won based (in part) on the spirit and enthusiasm for the project being bid on. If your copy is written creatively, without waffle but with fervour and passion, it will make the process of reading so much more enjoyable for the recipient. If it's a close call between two companies, it could make the difference between your client winning or losing the contract.

Handbooks

Irrespective of the size of the business, any company that employs staff should produce a *company handbook*, even if it is only a few pages long.

A handbook should provide employees with information relating to the company, its working procedures, and the expectations it has regarding staff. In *Morrison's* (the supermarket chain) handbook, for example, there is information relating to *staff development and training*, and the opportunities for staff to advance their careers through gaining an *NVQ in Retailing*.

A handbook should include everything other than what is contained in the employee's contract. *A contract is between the employer and a single employee, detailing contracted hours of work, pay, holiday entitlement and any other benefits relevant only to that person.* The handbook contains information that relates to all staff, irrespective of their position. It is a guideline about the conduct and procedures the company expects all members of staff to follow, and what they should do when faced with specific situations, such as a health and safety issue or something as simple as the sounding of the fire alarm. Uniform specifications or acceptable work-wear are often mentioned, and it should contain the contact details of relevant key staff or departments such as the person or department responsible for HR (Human Resources). The handbook may also contain details of the company's mission statement or any charities it supports and how, and if, staff are expected to participate in company organised charity events. It may also tell the history of the company or its future growth plans.

From the handbook, employees should have everything they need to know about their employer, how inclusive they are as a company, and what is expected of them as an employee.

Handbooks can be really interesting documents to write. As a copywriter, you should aim to produce factually correct details but try to avoid making the information too dry. Enthusiasm for the company they are working for can help employees feel engaged with their employer, so keep your copy as light as you can.

Digital Marketing

I have previously mentioned *digital marketing*, but what is it?

Simply, digital marketing is an umbrella term for the promotion of products or services using one or more forms of electronic media or digital technologies. Although, we often refer to digital marketing as being internet-based – smartphones, media display type advertising (videos, vlogging, and short films), plus other digital mediums, are also included in this category.

Each element of digital marketing can be used as a standalone marketing tool. However, digital marketing works best when you combine several elements together. This might involve producing a *YouTube* video and embedding it on your website, alongside your social media streams, and profile pages.

Websites

Let's start with websites. Websites provide a digital platform where companies or individuals can display text, graphics and videos. E-commerce websites also enable viewers to purchase products or services.

In pretty much every category we have explored, there has been a formula to follow and it is the same for writing website copy. Every website you visit starts with a *home* or *landing page*, with the addition of top or side menus or tabs that take you to other pages, such as: *about us, products or services* (in various formats), and *contact*. Home pages, generally, may have less text and more graphics but as you work your way through the different pages or tabs you are likely to find more text. Often, landing pages will contain a few lines of text with an option to *view more* or *read more*, via a *button* that expands your reading pane or takes you to another page altogether.

There is no upper limit on the number of additional pages a website can have, or how much copy can be supplied on each page. Just visit *HMRC's* website and you'll see what I mean! The content provided on this site is phenomenal and from every page there is a link to another, and another, and another.

What is important here is that the website is easy to navigate. Pages are clearly labelled so that viewers can move from page to page without issues, or without getting thrown out of the website

Chapter 14

altogether. *Back buttons* or *back to* options should always be considered. Writing for a website is very similar to writing for any multi-form document whether a book, brochure, or white paper – just think of the binding being different. Structure is key.

We have explored writing webcopy as part of the previous chapter and this included blogs. Also, mentioned previously was the need for webcopy and blogs to be carefully constructed using *keywords* and *tags*, to enable search engines to find the copy relevant to viewers' search criteria – its *SEO*.

When writing copy for websites you should familiarise yourself with the keywords or potential search phrases relevant to the industry or trade. Think of some questions that would lead you to the website if you typed them into *Google* and build the relevant keywords into your copy. You should also provide the website designer with a separate list of specific keywords to ensure they are correctly tagged in the background text (or, as it is otherwise known, the backend) of the website.

> *Tip: website graphics and images should also be captioned with keywords for SEO purposes, including company logos, which often get overlooked.*

FAQ (frequently asked questions) pages are particularly useful for SEO, and they can save companies a lot of time by tackling repetitive queries head on. Talk to people who take phone calls within the business and compile a list of the most frequently asked questions they receive to produce a page for the website. When reading an existing client website, make a note of questions you find yourself inadvertently asking, and if you can't find the answers or information you need easily, elsewhere on the site, consider adding them to the FAQ page.

As a copywriter, you will have very little input into the design and layout of the website but you should be provided with a detailed outline of the pages they wish to include, indicating where text is needed. How much copy is needed for each page will vary and you may have to take an educated guess based on a current site, or other copywriting tasks you have already completed for the client. Ask for the build schedule too. The most frustrating delay to websites going live is the wait for copy either from the copywriter, or its signoff from the company owner. Give yourself enough time to write the copy, for the client to proofread it, and for you to make any editorial changes. Build in extra time for yourself, in case, during the writing process, it is evident that additional pages of text will be required.

Writing website copy can be demanding but it can also be a very rewarding process. If you enjoy the challenge of getting to the nuts and bolts of a business, its products or services, and seeing the visual results of your work (even though your name won't be mentioned anywhere on the site) then offer your services.

And, remember to write it from the *potential customer's perspective* not your client's.

Newsletters and E-marketing

E-marketing refers to applications and marketing activities sent via electronic media. Essentially, e-marketing encompasses internet marketing and digital marketing, or a combination of the two, but more generally it refers to email marketing, such as e-newsletters, and that is what we will consider here.

As emails have replaced printed and mailed content, companies have embraced the advantages of reducing marketing budgets and costs by emailing newsletter content instead. Newsletters have always been a popular means of giving customers up-to-date information by way of sound bites or short articles. Newsletters often contain at least three or four *'newsy'* items such as the content used for press releases or, indeed, what you now read in company blogs. Each article is usually only a few hundred to maybe 500 words long and the content varies between staff announcements, new product information, or other significant changes the business might have gone through since its last update.

Newsletter content is basically written to provide an insight into what is happening within a company, and is typically aimed at customers. Often, staff members are also kept informed of a company's comings and goings in this way too.

Traditionally, newsletters (partly due to cost) were produced infrequently, perhaps monthly, quarterly, half-yearly or annually but once they became electronic, the frequency of newsletters soon increased.

Chapter 14

> *Note: An alternative to an e-newsletter is an E-shot. These are often heavily sales-driven, sent once or many times a day, and only contain information relating to one product or a couple of selected products.*

When companies use *sign-up* forms, *e-newsletters* and *e-shots* are often to what they refer.

The content for e-newsletters and e-shots can be read within the email itself, sometimes as an attachment, and sometimes as a link from the original message (e.g. To view this email as a web page, go here). Commonly, the attachment will be a PDF.

A PDF is a Portable Document Format File – often containing text and images. Background colours, fonts and the layout of pdfs are often more user-friendly and attractive than documents produced in something like Word.

E-mail templates for e-newsletters are something entirely different. They look like PDFs but they are sent as part of the body of the email not an attachment – and usually originate from marketing software such as Mailchimp or Campaign Monitor.

When writing content for e-newsletters, it is advisable to write several articles or news pieces in full and upload these to the news pages or blog pages on the company's website. Then, for longer stories, use only the headline and the opening paragraph or two of the article copy within the e-newsletter and provide a *'read more'* option as a clickable hyperlink, to reveal the story in full via the webpage. Not only does this help keep the newsletter uncluttered, but it also enables readers to choose which stories they would like to read in depth, and which ones they would prefer to skip. Equally importantly, it allows the newsletter creator to track the opened stories, giving them vital information as to its popularity; such data can provide further *marketing* or *follow-up* sales opportunities.

As mentioned above, you can use the content you have written for press releases, articles and blogs and tweak the copy to fit the newsletter style and format. If you have already written and posted a blog, it is easy to provide the opening for the newsletter, from where the reader can *click through* to the story on the blog page.

While the blog copy may very well fit the style and voice of the newsletter, it is unlikely you can do the same with a press release or article written for a media publication. Unless you are providing a comment and link to the published article itself (this could be on the company website or the website of the publication), you will have to rewrite the press release or article copy to meet the needs of your newsletter readers. The reason for doing so is *familiarity*.

When writing for the press and a wider audience, essentially you don't know who they are, and you are making assumptions based on your research and other criteria. For example, you would never use the word 'you' in a press release (e.g. a press release about a new self-help book would never say "you will learn…", it would say "the reader will learn…") When writing copy for a company newsletter, however, you should have a much better understanding of the audience, and perhaps consider writing in the second person rather than the third, as required for the press.

The value of writing in the second person (where appropriate) is that it offers a more personal connection with the reader.

I would also recommend including no more than six different articles or news stories in any e-newsletter. This is enough information for any reader. The frequency of the newsletters should also be carefully considered, as people can be easily turned off by overly-frequent communications. *What nobody wants to see is readers unsubscribing.*

Social Media

As part of any 21st Century company's digital marketing strategy, social media is way up there, and writing social media posts alongside blogs, and other content, can be a creative way of generating income.

What social media posts need to do is *engage* with the reader. Consumers do not like being directly sold to but, through engagement, can be drawn in and persuaded. Perhaps.

To write good posts for use on *Facebook* or *Twitter* you should have a basic understanding of the rules. This includes the number of words or characters allowed, plus the use of images and acceptable language (this last one isn't going to apply because you are a professional writer – right?).

Chapter 14

I found it best to write out a list of say 20 or 30 posts at a time, varying the content and message to attract readers. Once written, these posts could be scheduled for release at different times on different days, depending on the parameters set during the posting process.

Social media posts can be scheduled through online platforms such as Hootsuite or TweetDeck.

The benefit of writing numerous posts at once was that one idea could lead to another, and when you are in the writing *zone* of a particular client's copy, it is easier and less time-consuming to produce multiple posts than manage them on a one-by-one basis. This formula works particularly well if you are working on a specific campaign or theme, but can be equally effective if you have lots of different messages to share with the readers.

Examples:

At @assetenterprise we work with seasoned property investors looking for the best possible returns (Hyperlink to webpage)

What we can't guarantee is that your investments are 100% secure but we do guarantee to look after your interests (Hyperlink to webpage)

*Are you looking for an alternative to ISAs? Investment Property Specialists @assetenterprise can help call ** ** *** *** (Hyperlink to webpage)*

We @assetenterprise have an established and growing portfolio of investment properties with a proven track record (Hyperlink to webpage)

Varying the order or words, adding different statistics or numbers, or hanging on the back of other posts can also help you create multiple posts along similar lines.

Where possible, use important dates or historical events, the seasons, festivals, and other relevant means to add timely content to your posts. Obviously, new product launches are always good; the same goes for excellent customer reviews.

Do remember to include *hyperlinks* on each post that takes readers to a relevant webpage, blog, or other information available on the company website – this interactivity is loved by *Google*. Use teasers to encourage readers to click on links. Competitions and prize giveaways work exceptionally well to entice readers to like your social media pages or sign-up to receive emails and other information. They also encourage reader engagement and post sharing opportunities.

Writing books for business

Writing books is a topic we have not yet explored in any great detail. If you are an expert in your field or have a specialist interest, we have already discussed how your knowledge might not just work for writing articles but also for writing a book. In the following chapter, *Submission and Publication*, I will share the relevant information you need to prepare your book for submission. However, just before we get too far ahead of ourselves, let us spend a little time looking at the opportunities for writing about business for business, or using your skills and experience from your profession to write for the business market.

Writing books for business is basically broken down into three categories: *books relating to specific trades or industries, 'how to' business books,* and *self-help/motivational style books.*

The first category, *specific trade and industry books,* speaks for itself. This is a very niche area, and potentially a very small market, but that doesn't mean to say it is a market that is not worth pursuing, especially if the content can appeal to a wider audience. For example, take the licensing trade or being a publican. In years past, many people romanticised about becoming publicans. This indicated that there was a need for books about running pubs. Equally, today, there are still numerous books being published about *running a restaurant* or *retailing.*

Books about writing are also an obvious scenario; *I am a writer and I am writing a book about writing,* and this will stand against the abundance of other books on every conceivable writing opportunity, from freelance writing and copywriting to ghostwriting, writing your memoirs, or writing for business. But, did you know there are also books about the *book publishing* industry and about *book shops?*

Other industries may have less market appeal, clearly. If authors have the knowledge and experience of a specific trade or industry, and they believe there is enough information and interest in the topic – why wouldn't they pursue writing a book on the subject?

The more niche the topic, though, the less likely a traditional publisher will be willing to gamble on its success. Nevertheless, with self-publishing facilities now widely available and the option to sell e-books and sell through online portals such as *Amazon*, it has never been easier to have a book published.

How to books for business can cover every conceivable topic from *preparing a business plan to managing accounts. How to succeed at networking, How to boost your sales, A guide to Telemarketing, Business Processes, Being a Great Boss,* or *A Guide to Successful Staff Management* – these, and many more are the types of *how to* books you can find about running a business.

Some, obviously, contain generalisations about running a business, while others focus on areas of expertise, and this could help you establish a theme for your business book. How much knowledge do you have about a certain sphere of business? For example, you may be an accountant – what information could you share to help other people manage their business finances in a more streamlined or profitable way? You could focus on the most common problems business owners face, and how they can overcome them. You could concentrate on the importance of maintaining good bookkeeping records, or provide information on tax avoidance schemes and the pitfalls of using them.

Equally, if your career has been in HR, you could write a handbook for smaller companies on how to deal with the most common staff issues or how to get the most out of your workforce. Basically, the ideas are endless. Try and generate original ideas but try not to be too niche. Think about things you have learned during your career. What would you have loved to have known at the start of your career? This sort of analysis may help you identify gaps in the market.

Self-help and motivational-style books are mostly written by self-confessed entrepreneurs, motivational speakers, and business coaches, in particular. These kinds of people are very good at self-promotion, and is the reason (I believe) why so many of them have written books about *what they do, how they do it,* and *how you can do it too.*

Self-help and motivational business books are also more commonly self-published.

Previously, I referred to a book called *Instant Advertising* by Bradley J Sugars. The Australian-born author, now a multi-millionaire, is the founder and CEO of *Action Coach*, a franchise that offers business coaching services. Bradley's collection of books encompasses specialist subjects such as *Instant Cashflow, Instant Sales,* and *Instant Promotions*, to more generalist titles such as *The Business Coach* and *Billionaire in Training.*

The very nature of what Bradley, and many others like him, do on a day-to-day basis is about encouraging others, building self-confidence, and providing a *can-do* attitude, and this kind of approach bodes well for book content. Highly motivated, driven individuals are great at standing up in a crowd and saying, *'Look how successful I am at what I do'* and this form of attitude can motivate others into believing they can *have it* and *do it* too – *so buy the book and learn how!*

Self-help and motivational books are often about positive thinking and behaviours, a mindset many writers and authors need to have.

Whatever type of writing you do, it should be entertaining and engaging to keep your readers interested; nobody is going to read something written by a *sourpuss*, or a book based on negative thoughts.

The content of your business book, (even if the topic might be considered a little dry by some), should be written positively and have a purpose. Your aim is to stimulate your reader into some sort of action. It should educate them on being able to adapt your strategies or methods, or so they can learn from your mistakes in order to make their own business more successful. You should include epic failures or moments of despair if you were able to turn problems on their heads and resolve them.

Much like the writing of your memoirs, you should be honest and open. You should not make yourself the superhero of your business but instead reveal the difficulties you had to overcome, to reach your goal or achieve the results you did.

Anyone can write about their business, their trade or industry. Anyone, who has the inclination to write a full-length book can write a book for business. The art of writing a successful book is finding the right content and being able to write it to stimulate and excite readers – then finding the means and methods to market it.

In this chapter, not only have you learned about how to write *marketing content* you now know how to *write a book* – so you should be able to fuse together the information and methods to *write* and *sell* your own book. But first, you need to discover how to get it published. *Read on*!

Chapter 15
Book Submission and Publication

Throughout this book, we have touched on the many options open to you for writing a non-fiction book.

Your first decision is to decide what topic you will write about, and then the type of book you want to write. For example. The topic of this book is about writing non-fiction but one of the first decisions I had to make was what type of non-fiction book I wanted it to be. I could have written it *textbook style*, giving you shorter snippets of information followed by assignments, exercises, or tasks to complete. I could have written it *reference style* with details about the history of writing and mentioned scholarly writers, or I could have written it as an *autobiography* or *memoir*.

Instead, I chose to write it as an information or *self-help* guide to enable you to read it chapter by chapter, and then put into practice the advice I have shared, without the interruption of stopping to complete exercises. My hope is that as you read the book, various parts of it have inspired you to pause and take some notes, or perhaps put into practice some of the techniques that have encouraged or motivated you.

Here is a recap of the genres your book could fall into:

- Specialist – cats, dogs, aeroplanes

- Hobbyist – arts, crafts, sport and recreation like walking or sailing

- Historical – period histories, people, events

- Textbooks – school books, learning aids

- Listings – book of quotations, clichés

- Dictionaries – dictionaries/thesaurus

- Reference – Writers' & Artists' Yearbook, Willing's Press Guide, Guinness Book of Records

- Biographies – author writes life story of another person

- Autobiographies – author writes own life story

- Memoirs – diary or journal quotes

- Books for business – specific trade and industry, how to, self-help & motivational

Preparing your book

In the same vein as writing magazine articles and features, you should write about what you know, or use your specialist knowledge. That said, it is no good planning to write about a subject when there are 20 recently published ones on the bookshelves of your local bookstore or library. First, ascertain whether there are any gaps in your market. For example, there may be plenty of books on *cars*, per se, but there may not be a recent one on *Supercars* specifically, and if you know there are 50,000 supercar owners in the UK alone, you can offer a publisher a good reason to publish your book.

But, before you begin typing away on the ins and outs of your specialist subject, you need to do your research.

- Identify the gaps in the market for the type of book you want to write.

- Identify, as best you can, how many readers might be interested in your title, e.g. 50,000 supercar owners.

- Find suitable publishers. It is no good sending your non-fiction manuscript to a publisher of fiction, or even a non-fiction publisher who specialises in historical publications or just biographies. Find the publishers who are interested in the book you are proposing to write.

- Make a list of all the publishers of other books whose topics are similar to yours.

- Check your W&A Yearbook for publisher details and note the subjects they cover.

- Write a preliminary email to the first publisher on your list to ascertain whether they are interested in your idea. Unlike fiction books, which are sent from publisher to publisher or agent to agent before acceptance, before you commit time and energy to writing a non-fiction title it is best to secure a commission from a publisher. There are many ways in which the publisher will want the book's content developed and supplied and they may differ vastly from your first thoughts or ideas. The last thing you will want to do is completely re-write the whole thing because the publisher wants it in a different format.

- Secure a deal, whenever possible, before you begin writing.

Ben Smart is a micro-moth enthusiast. It's a specialist hobby, and something he has been interested in for over 10 years. Over the last couple of years, Ben has put together a 216-page guide to locating the early stages of micro-moths in the north-west of England. Published in 2017, Ben's book, *Micro-moth Field Tips: A Guide to Finding the Early Stages in Lancashire and Cheshire*, is certainly very niche. Ben is also a photography enthusiast, enabling him to provide most of the 600 photo illustrations included in the book.

Ben established a need for the book through posts on *Facebook* groups, and not just in Lancashire and Cheshire; interest was coming in from a wider audience, such as enthusiasts from Europe. He was also aware that a book on a similar topic had not been published since 1905, and that one did not contain images.

A specialist book of this nature also needs a specialist publisher, and so Ben approached the *Lancashire and Cheshire Fauna Society (LCFS)*, as they had published several titles relating to birds, butterflies and moths. At first, the society was sceptical about the project until Ben could demonstrate the interest he had received from across the UK and Europe. In association with the *Lancashire Branch of Butterfly Conservation* and the *LCFS*, an agreement was made to co-publish.

Ben also sought the help of other European entomologists to provide additional information, clarifications and photographs, in return for a credit or acknowledgement in his book.

The above illustrates that even though you may have a very specialist interest (which may only appeal to a very niche market) it is still possible to convince a publisher to believe in your project and support your work, providing you can demonstrate a need or enough interest from book buyers.

Chapter 15

Entertain your reader

The language and style of your book are the key components to how successful it will be. You have more opportunity to use descriptive material when writing a book over an article, but this is certainly no excuse for writing in a boring or finicky way. Inexperienced writers who are overly-enthusiastic about their specialist topic, have a tendency to overwrite, and provide too much detail. Being economical with the words in your book is needed as much as it is with your articles and features. You may not have the restrictions of a word-count but every published page has a cost, and that cost is something that publishers are very aware of.

In turn, even though your subject might not be of appeal to the mass market, you should endeavour to make it lively and entertaining, to gain the attention of those with only a passing interest in the topic. Practice writing in an interesting and entertaining way, preferably with shorter but informative sentences. Make your work as easy to read as possible – for all levels of reader.

Ensure all your facts are correct and write authoritatively, ensuring your reader has confidence in your knowledge. Write in a way that your work cannot be faulted by someone who knows a great deal more about the subject than you, while still making sure that your language is appealing to readers of different levels. Where you can, and if necessary, use information from specialists in the field in which you are writing, and give credit where credit is due.

Credits will include references to information from other published work, photographs supplied by, or copyright owned by, or from whom permission to use was granted. Remember that just because something may have been provided free of charge, this does not mean you should not acknowledge the source; on the contrary.

If you can, supply the illustrations or offer the publisher details as to where photographs or illustrations may be available from.

Marketing yourself

Very few people can honestly say that they can confidently talk about themselves or shout about their abilities or achievements. The majority of us are quite modest, especially creatives like writers. The only exception I have witnessed, contrary to this, is those who appear to be natural sales people, motivational speakers, and entrepreneurs. For the rest of us, promoting ourselves doesn't come naturally and being able to sell ourselves and our books without sounding arrogant, egotistical, or big-headed, takes some work. However, if you want to convince a publisher to take you on – *selling yourself* is as important as selling your work.

Publishers will want to have confidence in you and your project. They will want to know that you can deliver what you are proposing, and that you are able to do your bit to help the sale of your book.

Besides carefully crafting your biography or personal profile, which includes detailing all your relevant accolades and achievements, your experience, and how you acquired your knowledge, you need to find other ways of making yourself marketable. Do not include irrelevant information or a CV detailing your life's work or the endless jobs you have undertaken, unless they bear some relevance to the venture you are proposing.

Building your social media presence and followers are ways to gain exposure. Gauging interest in the topic(s) you want to write about through dedicated webpages, forums and other groups, is another. Having a website and writing and posting blogs on the same themes as your book can also demonstrate an interest in your topic. Being able to give talks, seminars or provide workshops or courses on your chosen subject, can all help to raise your profile and generate additional supporters.

When writing about yourself, write as tightly and conservatively as you can – as this demonstrates your writing style. This is relevant, as it gives the publisher an insight into you and the way you write. Do not over-sell yourself, or tell untruths. Being an authoritative non-fiction writer is about being able to deliver facts – accurately and without elaboration.

If you have little or no previously published work, that doesn't mean to say publishers will reject you – we all start somewhere. But, what they do want to see is that you are able to commit to the project you are proposing and that you can write, and write well. *Everything* you send them – from the query email, the book or chapter synopsis, and your mini-biography – will tell them all they need to know about you as a writer and your abilities.

Chapter 15

How to present your idea

You have chosen your topic, picked a suitable publisher, now you need to pitch your idea. You need to tell him *why* you think there is likely to be a great demand for your book; quote the figures you have found *e.g. 50,000 supercar owners in the UK*, as well as others who might also be interested; for example, supercar manufacturers, supercar clubs, etc. In fact, any other individuals or organisations you can think of. This information is imperative. The publisher will want to know that if he invests significant sums of money in publishing your book that there will be enough market interest in it for him to earn back his investment with profits.

Next, tell him why you are the best person to write the book, giving any relevant qualifications or credentials that illustrate your knowledge and experience. It could be that you have written for *Car Magazine* for the last five years, or that you used to test drive Lotus prototypes and wrote the technical manuals. Only include what is relevant though.

It would also be prudent to include a *chapter listing, approximate word count*, and *a sample chapter*, or at least part thereof. Plan the book as you see it, working in a logical order.

Example:

What a Drive

Chapter 1. Introduction

Chapter 2. Supercars of the 1960s

Chapter 3. 1970s

Chapter 4. 1980s

Chapter 5. 1990s

Chapter 6. 2000s

Chapter 7. The Specials

Chapter 8. Other prototypes

Chapter 9. Supercars of the Future

Chapter 10. Where to drive your supercar

Chapter 11. Getting the most from your supercar

Chapter 12. Rallies and other events

Appendix

List of useful addresses

List of Supercar organisations

Just to recap what you should be sending to a publisher for your non-fiction book:

- A covering email giving brief details of the book idea and a brief personal profile, complete with your full name, a pseudonym if you use one, and your contact and address details

- A synopsis

- Sample chapter listing

- A sample chapter or part thereof

Sample synopsis:

What a Drive

The proposed book – written for all supercar lovers, not just for men – will be a beautifully illustrated publication. Aimed at both current supercar owners as well as those interested in supercars generally, it will contain information on all the iconic supercars manufactured between the 1960s and post-2000. Five chapters will each cover a decade of supercar production with model specifications, manufacturer details, performance, and the personal histories of owning the illustrated models.

The cars illustrated, complete with photographs (to be supplied) of the different models, will cover everything from the elegantly distinguished E-type Jaguar to the Aston Martin DB9. Further chapters will include prototype models that never made production.

'What a Drive' will be the most up-to-date book of its type, appealing to individuals and car manufacturers alike, not to mention car clubs, groups and associations associated with the car industry, and particularly lovers of high-performance supercars.

I propose to complete 12 chapters, as listed separately, and estimate that each chapter will be on average 2,000 to 3,000 words plus, with at least one picture per model, although in some cases it would be prudent to show more.

Chapter 15

The introductory chapter will explain how the supercar came about and how our fascination for speed and the need to push technology to the limits has ensured the continued production of these much-loved high-performance road machines. It will mention some of the most important individuals and manufacturers in the production of said cars.

Further information at the end of the book will provide useful names and addresses of motoring organisations and supercar clubs from around the UK, and in some cases beyond.

Now write your first chapter or part thereof.

Just before you eagerly hit send to the first publisher on your list, do yourself the biggest favour, and check absolutely everything you have written – again. This is your one and only chance to make a first impression – so do it well. Is your submission error and typo free? Is your spelling and grammar correct? Are technical terms or scientific names spelt correctly? Are your facts accurate?

When you are satisfied that your submission is the best it can be, send everything as attachments to the first publisher on your list. Then *forget* about it for a while and write something else. If you have not received a response, allow six to eight weeks before following up with a query email or telephone call, but if you happen to receive a rejection – take on board any advice given and approach the next publisher on your list.

Rejection is, regrettably, a very real experience that every author and writer experiences but it is how you deal with that rejection that will set you apart from other writers. Do not get despondent or demotivated. Use the experience positively instead. If the publisher does not think you are right for them, the chances are they were not right for you. So, find one who is. Do not give up. Perseverance is another attribute writers must possess. Revisit your original proposal and supplementary documents. Is everything presented as it should be? Is it all spelt correctly and properly laid out? Does your submission tell the publisher what he needs to know about you and your project? Can you incorporate the feedback you received from any previous rejections? Could you include any supplementary information that might convince the next publisher to take you on?

Take your time and look at your proposal with fresh eyes before resubmitting to the next publisher on your list.

Editing

Just before we look at the different ways your book could be published, it is worth mentioning here a little about editing.

Editing is an important part of the pre-publication process, whether you are publishing via a traditional publisher, or taking the route of self-publishing, and should even be considered before submission of your idea, where appropriate to do so.

Essentially, there are four main editorial stages, which involve refining your copy to ensure it is thoroughly readable, mistake free, and ready for publication.

1. *Manuscript review* – this initial review and critique assesses the overall strengths and weaknesses of your work.

2. *Structural assessment* – looks at pace, writing style, language and technical aspects.

3. *Copy-editing* – focuses on the detail. The copy-editor will be looking at the consistency of your text, as well as spelling, grammar and punctuation.

4. *Proofreading* – this is a final check of the layout and format and should also pick up any elements of the previous checks that have been missed or overlooked.

If your work is accepted for publication, it is usually part of the publisher's remit to provide the editorial services. In some cases, such as academic publishing, authors are now asked to arrange and/or pay for their own copy-editing. Under normal circumstances, you will not be asked to pay for this service. Beware of publishers who ask you to pay for the editing or publishing of your book, as these are likely to be vanity publishers. This is different from self-publishing. There are legitimate companies who offer to assist you in the publishing of your work who do not fall into traditional publishing or vanity publishing categories. *See the next section for an explanation.*

As an author, you might want to engage the services of an editor or proof-reader before submitting your work to a publisher, and in my opinion this is an absolute necessity if you decide to self-publish. Irrespective of how good you might think your work is, or how accurate your spelling, punctuation and grammar might be, don't underestimate the fact that everybody makes mistakes. Too many self-published books which have not had outside editorial oversight have been produced by authors cutting costs to save money. This is a big mistake. If you want the contents of your book to be taken seriously, it is essential that you do everything possible to ensure they are professionally edited, formatted and published.

> *Note: not all editors are the same. What you are looking for is an editor that has some experience or knowledge in the field you are writing about. An obvious one is whether they edit non-fiction or fiction. When choosing an editor, check their credentials and seek references, if necessary.*

Publishing the traditional way

There are some authors who will only ever consider self-publishing their work, and they will have their reasons for doing so. There are others who should consider self-publishing due to the nature or topic of their book, or because they have a captive audience – such as some of the self-help, motivational type books, or the sharing of ones' memoirs with family and friends.

For every other writer, traditional publishing is what they seek. But what is traditional publishing?

Let us first understand the different types of publishing, then you can explore the right process for you.

- *Traditional publishing* – refers to the long-established system of getting a book deal. This means the publishing company buys the 'rights' to an author's manuscript and provides the necessary support to see the book through from the first draft to the booksellers' shelves.

- *Self-publishing* – The author manages the publishing process allowing her complete control of the entire creative process, from writing and editing to publishing and promoting – and, at her own expense.

- *Indie-publishing* – Usually this means a smaller publishing house whose remit is to sell books to consumers, rather than selling services to authors. Being an indie author does allow you more creative control, and works well if you are writing for niche markets. Indie-publishing appears to fill the gap between traditional and self-publishing.

- *Vanity publishing* – avoid at all costs! Vanity publishers will take your money in return for a published book. This is very different from paying for the services of companies to help you self-publish or become an indie-author. Vanity publishers usually charge large amounts of money to publish your book and, in return, you are likely to get a poorly edited, formatted and published book that will be of little use to you except to light a fire.

In the earlier part of this chapter, we learned about preparing your book submission, selecting your publisher and submitting your proposal. This is relevant if you want to be traditionally published.

Traditionally published does not mean *one size fits all*. I have spoken to many traditionally published authors, and each of their stories is different. Even my own experiences of being traditionally published have been different again. Each publishing house works in a slightly different way and will have its own processes and departments with which you have to work. Some will want complete control of everything, others will want to work *with you* to produce the best possible book.

Having submitted your idea, and a publisher has shown eager enthusiasm for your project, the negotiation process will start.

In the first instance, you should receive a *contract* or *publishing agreement* outlining the publisher's proposal. This will include how much advance they will pay, if any, what *rights* they are purchasing including other media such as TV or film, what percentage you will earn from the sale of each book, the completion dates or chapter deadlines for your draft copy, any contractual commitments and other specifications.

Rights: As an author, it is advisable for you to retain the copyright of your work. In return for various payments, you license to the publisher, primarily exclusively, the right to publish multiple copies of printed books and/or eBooks as readable text. You can license your rights outright or in part; for example, English language rights but not other languages. You can grant exclusive and non-exclusive rights. Where possible, license but do not 'assign' your rights. Assignation is almost impossible to reverse. Most publishers will want 'all

Chapter 15

rights' and 'world rights', but it is up to you or your agent to negotiate if you want to retain certain rights.

Every contract you receive will be different, and the onus is on you to check that you are happy with the contents. It is always advisable to have an experienced legal adviser check the terms of your contract before signing. *The Writer's Guild*, the *NUJ* or the *Society of Authors* will review your contract if you are a member. It is my opinion that it is worth joining at least one of these organisations, especially if you are offered a publishing contract, and to use their contract review service.

> *Tip: Advance payments have changed over the years. As a new author, any advance offered is likely to be minimal, and in most cases non-existent. If you can demonstrate a need for an advance, or a higher one than initially offered because of extenuating circumstances (e.g. your research is going to entail lots of overseas trips), then do ask, otherwise be prepared to take what is on offer. Know that any advance paid will be deducted from the royalty payments of your sales, meaning if your book is a slow starter or fails to attract the necessary sales to pay back your advance, you will earn nothing more.*

The benefits of being traditionally published are worth the heartache of finding a publisher to take you on, in the first place. If you are dealing with a reputable publishing house, they will manage the whole process for you. Once your draft copy is submitted, an editor should be appointed to work with you to produce the best possible copy. It should include being professionally proofread for spelling and grammatical mistakes, as well as verifying your content. The publisher will format the pages, provide the cover graphics, and help you write the synopsis and book blurb, as well as your author profile. Further to this, they should be providing marketing services and have established contacts within the industry to get your book on the shelves of reputable booksellers.

It is, however, still necessary for you to consider self-promotion where possible, and to work in conjunction with the publisher's marketing activities. Book signings, giving talks, or attending book fairs is an important part of helping to maximise your book's sales, as is the use of social media and websites.

Self-publishing

In recent years, technology has paved the way for a boom in book publishing; never before has it been easier for authors to take control of their work and pursue self-publishing as a viable option to get their books to market.

Many authors take the self-publishing route, having thrust their submission or manuscript under the nose of every conceivable publisher and agent without success. Other authors believe that having control of the whole publishing process means more to them than being a traditionally published author. Some authors believe they can earn more from selling their books independently than by receiving royalty payments from publishers. A smaller number of authors, usually those writing for very niche markets, or as we have established in the previous chapter – specialist business books – choose self-publishing in the first instance.

These are all valid reasons for self-publishing. However, any author pursuing the self-publishing route for the first time is swimming in dicey water. *Beware* naive author, *beware*.

There is still an air of snobbiness associated with publishing, and coupled with the thousands if not tens of thousands of badly written, non-edited, and poorly printed self-published books, one can see why.

Besides the self-inflated egos of many self-published authors and the unscrupulous companies offering highly-priced but poorly managed services to unsuspecting authors, there are equally as many well-respected, best-selling and award-winning self-published titles that are proving the critics wrong. There are equally as many very respectable companies assisting authors with self-publishing advice and services.

If you do decide to take the self-publishing route, it is not one to be taken lightly. It is going to cost you money, and if done properly, a lot of it. But, if you want to be taken seriously as a published author then you should only consider publishing your book to the best of your abilities (finances allowing, obviously). After all, you haven't slaved for months or years to complete your copy, for the end result to be trash-worthy.

Chapter 15

Before we delve into the different processes of self-publishing, it is also fair to point out that there are always compromises and options that can minimise the outlay. The advances in digital printing technology no longer require authors or publishers, for that matter, to publish high volumes of hardback or paperback books, nor do they need to provide storage. *Print on demand* (POD) services mean exactly that. As a book is sold, say on *Amazon*, as few as one book is printed and ultimately sent to the buyer. Equally, eBooks require no hardcopy printing at all, again minimising the initial outlay of providing a copy. It is worth noting, however, that the printing of books via POD is more costly per book, when compared to an offset/litho print run of say 1,500 books or more. *The higher volume of books printed at the same time reduces the costs per book significantly, so bear this in mind too.*

By now you should be a dab-hand at research. There are hundreds of authors who have trodden the self-publishing route before you, and many more that will follow. Read what other self-published authors have to say about the process. The *W&A Yearbook* has several sections on publishing and self-publishing, written by various contributing authors, all with valid and valuable advice for the unsuspecting first-time author. There are books on the subject, blogs and other resources available to authors, so take heed… they could save you hours of fruitless work and a fortune in monetary terms.

Author Shelia Steptoe chose to self-publish two books: *Before I get Old and Wrinkly (2006)* and *Master Your Own Destiny (2013)* and she said, she would self-publish again.

"Before I get Old and Wrinkly was written initially as a letter to my estranged daughter," said Shelia, *"but other people who read the contents encouraged me to publish it."* After significant research, Sheila was put in touch with AuthorHouse, a self-publishing company that provides publishing services to authors. *"What I liked about AuthorHouse especially, was they offered a print-on-demand service, without the obligation of having to purchase a minimum number of books. They can do everything a traditional publisher can do – at a cost. They offered a set price package with the option to add more services if I required. The number of pages or words determined the price."*

"AuthorHouse gave me typeset and font options. This was my first mistake. Looking at a word or two in a particular font is not the same as seeing a whole page written in it. The font size I chose for my first book was too big. They

could have done the cover as well but I did my own. They could have provided the editing and proofreading services, but again I chose to use my own – this was lesson number two. Editing costs a fortune but if you want a quality book you have to have it properly edited," advises Sheila.

"Unfortunately, PR and marketing services are all extra costs too."

"However, the benefits of self-publishing in this way gave me control of the process, and I do like to be in control," Sheila said. "I did speak to a publisher but I was put off by the fact that even if we got to the publishing stage, the publisher could still decide not to publish – that wasn't an option for me."

"I learned a lot from self-publishing my first book, and I liked the fact that I had choices and the online publishing facility. A lot of self-publishing companies don't offer POD and demand the author buys a minimum number of upfront copies. There are many companies looking to profit from unsuspecting authors and because of this, self-published books are being devalued if there is no quality control. So be careful which company you use."

If you do not want to pay for the services of a company offering self-publishing assistance, you can manage the process entirely on your own. There is an abundance of facilities available to authors who wish to self-publish, with numerous online or desktop programs to help you with the design and layout of your book. You can then send your PDF files to a printer of your choice to have it published.

Be very cautious of this process, especially if it is your first time, as it can be a minefield for anyone who isn't computer savvy. Anne-Louise Hall used *CreateSpace* to help with the layout of her first book, *Blue Tits in the Arctic*. She spent countless hours trying to get the page layouts right, and still ended up with the chapter headings in the wrong place. However, she did say it was a relatively easy process and she liked the fact that she got a free proof and could have had it published by printers of her own choosing.

Printers' costs will vary, so do get quotes before you agree to have a set number of copies published. It is also advisable to ask to see samples of other books they have published. I would stay clear of any printing company that hasn't previously published books, as it is more complex than most imagine.

So, let us have a look at what is involved in self-publishing a book to see if this is the route for you.

Chapter 15

1. Once you have finalised your title, you will need an ISBN number. An ISBN (an International Standard Book Number) is used to identify a book and is used by publishers, booksellers and libraries for stock listing, ordering, and stock control. It is not a legal requirement to have an ISBN but in order for your book to be trackable, and that includes book sales – which means royalty payments – every book should have a unique ISBN. *ISBNs are also used by the British Library under the PLR (Public Lending Rights) register to calculate fees owed to writers and other creatives whose books (print, audio and eBook) are lent from public libraries. Payments are made annually, and the amount authors receive is proportionate to the number of times their book was borrowed during the previous year, which runs July to June.*

ISBN numbers and more information about ISBNs are available from *www.isbn.nielsenbook.co.uk*. The price of ISBNs is subject to review so it is best to check the website for details. At the time of publication, the price was £89 per ISBN or £149 per block of 10.

If you are going to publish only one book in only one format, the single ISBN will be enough. If you plan to publish more than one book, or to publish a revised edition of the original, or if you are going to publish your book in different formats (such as paperback and eBook), you will need a different ISBN for each version and each format, so 10 ISBNs would be more suitable. Unused ISBNs remain valid indefinitely.

2. When you are completely happy with your copy, pay for it to be edited. If you are using the services of a self-publishing company they should provide this service, albeit at a cost; if not, you will have to find a suitable copy-editor.

Firstly, check that the editor is experienced in the genre you are writing. You should ask for references, and don't just assume that because they have some author *'names'* on their website that they are valid. The editing and proofreading of your book is an area you should not skip or scrimp on. The value of your book rides on the quality of your content, and this can determine whether your book sells well or fails to make the grade.

Editing is costly, as it takes many man hours to read, reread and modify your copy, so do shop around for comparable prices, but also be wary of those whose prices are too low. Often, we get what we pay for. If you can, agree a fixed price rather than per word or per page, and agree timescales. Novice authors can have an unrealistic view of these costs. Imagine how long it would take to read your manuscript carefully, then multiply that by two or three readthroughs, and then multiply that again by a sensible hourly rate, and that should give you some indication of the costs involved. Essentially though, the editor you choose to work with should be selected on the quality of their work, and their experience, not just on price.

3. Your cover. Equally important to your book's sales potential is the quality of your cover. Again, use experienced graphic designers, preferably book cover designers to produce a quality cover. Many readers do judge a book by its cover – capturing their attention in the first instance is imperative.

4. Book blurb and author biography. The writing of the back-cover synopsis of your book is as important as the copy itself. In just a couple of hundred words, you must sell your book to the reader. This is your one opportunity, so it pays dividends to choose your words with care and precision. What reasons would your reader have for buying your book? Why *yours* and not a competing title? Your author biography is equally important – briefly write about your credentials to persuade the reader why they should buy your book.

5. Font, typeset and layout come next. Use a professional online or desktop publishing program to help you get this right. Again, the quality and reputation of your book will be evaluated on how professional it looks.

6. Indexing must be accurate. There are companies and individuals who can provide index servicing, but this will only be necessary if your indexing is complicated. While writing your book, you should be keeping notes on chapter headings, sub-headings and additional headings – which will help you prepare your index. When you have completely finished the copy, editing, and rewriting of your content – read everything again to ensure you pick up all the reference points that should be indexed.

7. Don't forget to include acknowledgments and sources. Every person or organisation that has helped in the preparation or content of your book should be acknowledged. Include research references and sources too.

8. Try not to be too eager to hit the *publish* button. Taking your time over the look and feel of your book could reap rewards. Rushing the process and making mistakes can be costly. *You only get one chance to make a good first impression!*

9. Pricing your book appropriately can be accomplished with research. Look at the price of other books on similar topics and which fit a similar size and style to yours. If you over-price your book, readers could be turned off. Equally, underpricing can devalue your book.

10. Prepare a budget or costing sheet. It is likely you will have underestimated the cost of self-publishing your book but you won't get a true picture of how much it is going to cost until you have collated the prices for each and every step. Don't forget to include marketing and PR costs in your budget. What is it going to cost you to host a launch party, to attend book fairs or book-signings? Are you going to write your own press releases or use a PR and marketing company to help you? There are costs associated with hosting and designing your website, plus the design and printing of business or information cards, which should include your website address and social media author pages.

Work out how many books you need to sell to cover your costs. The price to publish Ben Smart's book on Micro-moths was in the region of £4,500, selling at an RRP of £16, the publishers need to sell just under 300 books to cover their costs. What this figure doesn't consider is any retailer or bookseller discounts. For booksellers to make their profit, publishers need to reduce the wholesale price by anything from 25% to 60%. On this basis, even if we take an average of 40%, in this instance the LCFS would have to sell close to an additional 200 books just to break even.

How many books you have published initially is an important decision. Even if you opt for a POD service, you cannot go to book-signings or book-fairs without numerous copies of your book to sell. Bookshops often work on a sale or return basis, meaning you may have to leave two or three copies with each bookshop, without earning any money until they are sold.

Try not to be too over-enthusiastic about the number of copies you are likely to sell. Speak to other authors and booksellers, or the organisers of book fairs to gauge how much interest you are likely to get. Even if they expect a couple of thousand attendees at the event, what percentage will actually come to your stand? Of those that do – how many will buy a copy of your book? If 2,000 people attend and 5% visit your stand that's 100 people, of which maybe 25% may buy from you. That's only 25 copies. What you don't want is hundreds of copies printed and stacked up in the corner or your house or garage waiting to be sold. Start with a smaller number, you can always order more.

Note: Don't expect every member of your family or your friends to buy a copy either. Some will buy a copy out of loyalty but most will not. Many authors are often upset when family and friends show little enthusiasm for a book they have slaved over and talked about for years. It isn't personal – and don't take it that way. It may not be a topic or genre they are interested in. They may not wish to offend you if the content doesn't appeal to them. There are many reasons family and friends don't support their author relatives and friends but you did not write your book for them – you wrote it for the wider audience.

One last point to make on self-publishing. Even if you have conscientiously worked out the costs of self-publishing, there may be extra hidden or additional costs that arise. If they are significantly higher than you anticipated or can afford, be realistic about the services you can cut back on. It would be better to postpone publication until you've saved a little more than producing a poorly-designed and published book full or errors and inaccuracies – your reputation is at stake. Alternatively, see if you can get some pre-orders for your book. This could help fill the gap between what you have available and what you need to complete the project professionally.

Indie-publishing

Indie-publishing (independent publishing) is another way to get your book to market and there appears to be a small grey area about Indie-publishing. Different authors have their own opinions, but I will endeavour to do my best to explain it as I understand it.

With self-publishing, you can take one of two routes. 1. You buy a publishing package from a company to help you through the process, and pay for and use some (or all) of their services. 2. You use something like *CreateSpace* and manage the whole process yourself.

Indie-publishing also offers two main options. 1. Indie-publishing is also like #2, above, but according to Indie-author, Katharine E Hamilton, there is one bigger factor… and that is you. You are your own publisher. That doesn't mean you actually print the books yourself but on the inside of the front cover it is your name that is listed as the publisher.

> *The author has complete control over the final product. I hired my own beta-readers. I hired my own editors. I hired my own cover artist. I chose how big my book is. I chose glossy or matte finish. I chose page colour. I chose the price. I chose my distribution channels. I chose my formats. The point: I CHOSE EVERYTHING.*
>
> Katharine Hamilton

You still use a company to create and print your book: *CreateSpace, Lulu,* or *IngramSpark*. These companies provide you with the basic set-up tools such as uploading your manuscript, uploading your cover, and uploading the ISBN number that you purchased. You manage the publication but you are also wholly responsible for the marketing! It is up to you to write your own press releases, manage your sales literature, organise your book signings, organise your stand at book fairs and events, and manage the distribution which includes getting your book to booksellers and into bookstores.

Besides having total control over absolutely every aspect of your book's production, you also keep all the royalties. That's what you earn after your costs. Remember that your costs will also include bookstore discounts and costs for selling on book sites like *Amazon* etc. Bookstore and retailer discounts can be significant.

What appealed to Katharine about this was that she earned about 70% royalties from her book sales compared to the 5%-10% she earned from her first three books, which she self-published through *AuthorHouse.*

The alternative option under the banner of Indie-publishing concerns *Independent Publishing Houses* or *Small Press Publishers,* as they are otherwise known. Indie-publishers are more commonly recognised for publishing works that are considered outside the mainstream media's remit. In other words, the content could be niche or doesn't fit neatly into the genres of mainstream book publishers. However, these works are considered desirable by non-traditional publishers and possibly worthy of a place in any high-street bookstore.

Some Indie-publishers work with authors in a similar way to traditional publishers. These independent or small press publishers require a query and submission in the first instance and only select a small number of books to publish each year. Other Indie-publishers offer author services for a fee, in much the same way as self-publishing with a company like *AuthorHouse*. The one fundamental difference is that where author services companies will take money from any writer wanting to publish their book, with little or no regard for the quality of the writing or content, some Indie-publishers will only work with authors whose work fits the criteria of their publishing house. Discerning Indie-publishers are generally more concerned with their reputation as a quality independent publishing house rather than printing all and sundry that comes their way.

Crowdfunding

Not a new concept by any means, but crowdfunding provides an ever-growing opportunity for writers with little or no means of finding a way to get published. Crowdfunded publishing works by getting others to pay for books yet to be published.

Authors who can attract enough support for their books through crowdfunding can get their book published in one of two ways. 1. Some crowdfunding publishers will support authors who are able to raise enough funds for the publication of their book, irrespective of the quality of its content. 2. Companies such as *Unbound* books, on the other hand, *"selects the books it publishes and is as much 'a gate-keeper' as any mainstream publisher"*, according to *Unbound* author, Alice Jolly.

Unbound is not a mainstream publisher, in that it does not pay advances and it does not pay royalties. Authors receive a 50% profit share on print editions and eBooks. If you are lucky enough to have your submission selected by *Unbound*, the onus is on you, as the author, to raise the agreed amount of money, through subscriptions or pledges, before the book can be published. The amount each author needs to raise depends on the budget that *Unbound* proposes; however, every aspect is up for negotiation, so the amounts vary from author to author.

Vanity publishing

Since the days when every man and his brother wanted to write a book, and mainstream or traditional publishing seemed near-impossible for 99% of those writers, unscrupulous individuals and companies found a way to remove the life savings of many wanna-be authors.

Traditional publishers *invest* in their authors by using their own money for the publishing costs. Vanity publishers insist on an upfront payment from authors to produce the book. This is not the same as self-publishing where authors still have some control over the publication process. Vanity publishers offer contracts, and they do manage the production process – but often with very little input from the author.

How do you spot a vanity publisher?

Mainstream publishers do not advertise for authors, and almost all never charge a client. Vanity publishers, on the other hand, commonly place advertisements, usually in writing-related magazines or websites, inviting authors to submit their manuscripts. Unsuspecting authors submit their manuscripts and almost all, without exception, receive an offer of acceptance – but, '*as an unknown author*', they will be asked to pay towards the costs.

Vanity publishers may indicate that they are selective about the authors they work with. However, during 22 years of research into the operations of vanity publishers, Jonathan Clifford was not able to find one author who had been turned down by a vanity publisher, irrespective of the quality of their work.

Authors can be easily misled by false flattery pertaining to their manuscript, or false information relating to other '*successful authors*' offered by the publisher. I was approached by a vanity publisher, who even sent a copy of another author's book in the hope of persuading me to sign up with them – if I had parted with the £1,900 they had asked for. I kept the book but sent a stinking letter pointing out that as an author, I expected to earn from the sale of my book and not pay for the privilege of having it published. In truth, countless authors have parted with anything from just under £2,000 to in excess of £20,000 for publication of their book, and that saddens me.

Besides the over-inflated fees for publication, many authors have no idea as to how many books will be printed for the fee. Some publishers only offer POD but without substantial marketing behind the book, who is going to buy it? Other authors have been led to believe they will receive a refund of their initial outlay once the book reaches a certain target figure – these targets are often unrealistic.

I was delighted to read that many authors have successfully sued vanity publishers, who were found guilty by the courts for *'gross misrepresentation of the services they offer'*. Sadly, too many other authors have sunk back into the shadows, embarrassed that they have been misled and swindled out of thousands of pounds.

The marketing claims of vanity publishers can all appear very realistic to the unsuspecting author, and now that they are hidden amongst the reputable companies who do offer quality services to authors looking to self-publish, it may be even more challenging to spot them. Nearly all reputable companies, organisations and publications associated with the writing industry do not support vanity publishing, and some will go to great lengths to make writers and authors aware of them.

For more information about vanity publishing visit Jonathan Clifford's website www.vanitypublishing.info – archived by the British Museum Library in 2009.

eBooks

An eBook is an electronic version of a book, which can be read on a computer or a specifically designed handheld device such as a *Kindle, iPad, Nook*, or other smart device. There need not be a print equivalent of the title.

Despite the boom of eBooks and eBook devices in the early noughties, and trade publishers declaring that digital sales made up around 30% of their total book revenue – the printed book version has been making a comeback in the last year or so. Although, it appears that the sale of eBooks may have plateaued, it is still a very strong market, and especially so for self-published authors.

It is quite rare to find any recently-published book on *Amazon* without an eBook version tagging along, and authors who think it may not be worth the time and effort of converting their book to an electronic version are clearly missing out on potential sales.

Author Joanne Penn reported that in the financial year 2014-2015, 88% of her book sales income came from eBooks. She also pointed out that she makes more profit per eBook because there are no printing or shipping costs involved. Readers can also buy immediately once they hear about the book, and sales are global.

Some authors opt for just eBook publishing and as it is *free* to self-publish on the most popular eBook platforms, you can see why this is popular when compared to printed copy publishing. There are some costs, such as editing and cover design, but the actual publishing is free. Online stores will take a percentage of the sale price, in the same way retailers do.

You will need to format your book into an eBook file before you can publish electronically and the edited manuscripts will need to be in either a *.mobi* format for *Amazon* or *.ePub* format for other stores. Even if your book was published before the introduction of eBooks, it is still possible to have your books scanned from print back into *Word*, so you can retrospectively produce an eBook.

Kindle uploads via *Amazon* or *Scrivener* software from *Literature and Latte*, are both popular tools to help you format and publish your eBook.

If you are less confident with technology, or your book contains things like images, maps, tables, or graphs you may want to enlist the help of a professional book formatter.

Children's books which are image-heavy can be produced through *Kindle Kids Book Creator*, whilst *Kindle Comic Creator* is best for comics or graphic-heavy novels. *Kindle Edu* is recommended for textbooks.

Once you have your files in the appropriate eBook format, you need to consider which platforms to sell your eBooks from. You can opt for an exclusive with *Amazon KDP Select*, which includes *Kindle Unlimited* but to be honest, you should consider attracting the widest audience possible by having your book listed on numerous eBook sites. *Draft2Digital* and *Smashwords* can handle the distribution to other digital stores but in addition to *Amazon KDP* consider *Kobo Writing Life* and *iBooks*.

Each digital platform will look slightly different. They will also require slightly different information but most will want something along the lines of the following:

- Book name or title – enter the exact title of the book as shown on the cover.

- Subtitle – this is optional but more often used for non-fiction books. Keep it keyword relevant though.

- Series title and volume – an absolute must if your book is part of a series, as series titles will be linked together, giving customers a choice to download the other books in the series.

- Edition number – one of the benefits of eBooks is being able to update the content. If you spot a typo or other error, or the content of your book needs updating, you can easily do this and upload the latest edition. In this case, always supply an edition number.

- Description – the most powerful sales tool in your kit. This is the blurb you have written for the back of your book, or your synopsis. It is what sells the content. Remember to include the keywords and phrases readers will use as their search terms.

- ISBN – It is recommended that you have an ISBN as highlighted earlier in this chapter but it is not a legal requirement, so the choice is yours. Remember an eBook must have a different ISBN to your printed version.

- Language – It is likely that your books will be in English but if you do publish in other languages you can list them here.

- Publishing rights – Public domain books are out of copyright. It is important therefore, to establish that your book is not a public domain work and that you hold the necessary publishing rights.

- Categories – this is also important so that your book is listed in all the relevant categories. Each platform will have different category options but you should have a clear idea about the most obvious category or genre to list your book appropriately.

- Keywords – equally as important as categories. Keyword research should help you identify the relevant keywords so that readers can find your book online.

eBook publishing really is not as complicated as it might sound, and it is here to stay; avoiding it will only keep money from your pocket – so embrace it. Thousands of authors have taken the eBook leap of faith and are reaping the rewards. Many others have written or blogged about it, giving you all the information you need to make a successful launch of it. Worst-case scenario – pay someone else to do it for you – it'll be worth it!

Audiobooks

If you thought eBooks was hard enough to grasp, what about audiobooks? With the launch of *Amazon's Audible*, suddenly there is a real need for authors to consider turning their books into audiobooks. However, the process is complicated, and it's not as simple as just voice-recording your book – there is a whole lot more to it than that.

The popularity of audiobooks is not just for the fiction market. Authors of non-fiction books have woken up to the idea that their books are worth translating into audio format. And, not just because it gives them another income stream – *although, you could receive up to 70% of what your audiobook earns* – it's that readers have limited time. The attraction of audiobooks is being able to listen to a book whilst on the go – or when doing something else.

As Audible states:

'Listening is the new reading. Listen anytime, anywhere. Perfect for your commute, drive, workout or just before bed.'

But, just before you rush off to set up your voice recorder, we should explore the process in a little more detail.

First of all, check that you own the *rights* to your content. If you have assigned *all rights* to your publisher, you need to have a conversation with them in the first instance about the digital rights to your book. In most cases, for traditionally published titles, the publisher will manage the process. If not, it will require both technical expertise and talent to produce an audiobook to a professional quality and standard, and to satisfy the criteria of seller sites such as *Audible* and *iTunes*.

If you do have good technical skills, you are a quick learner, and you have a voice for radio (or know someone who does), you could save yourself a small fortune in production costs. For the rest of us, we are going to need to hire some professionals.

As you can imagine, there are already numerous companies geared up and ready to help you create your audiobooks such as *Author's Republic* or *Voices for Books*, or *ACX (Audiobook Creation Exchange)* a subsidiary of *Amazon Audible*. ACX is a marketplace designed for authors, narrators and audio producers, with a view to encouraging artists to create and publish more audio works.

The other alternative is to look for companies like *Creative Content* who are eBook and audiobook publishers. *Strathmore, Oasis* or *Podium Publishing* are also audiobook publishers worth considering.

Whether you are going it alone, or working with an audio publisher, here are a few things to consider.

- For works of non-fiction, you can add credibility to your work if you are the author-narrator. However, if your voice really isn't radio-friendly, voiceover actors are available for hire. If recording yourself, it is advisable to practise, practise, practise.

- Your manuscript will not translate perfectly into an audio book. Because we read aloud differently to reading in our heads, your manuscript will need to be rewritten as a marked-up script. Review your copy one line at a time and make annotations to indicate natural pauses or to emphasise certain words. You may also need to rework clunky or long sentences.

- There are literally hundreds of different combinations of hardware and software you can use to create your audiobook, so it will take you a bit of time to find the right ones for you. Research other writers who have created their own audiobooks or view YouTube videos, there are plenty online.

- Audiobook retailers demand that audiobooks are studio-quality productions and whilst you don't need to rent a studio, you will need (irrespective of where you make the recording) a really high-quality microphone.

- To maximise the sales potential of your audiobook, you may need to use an aggregator to list it on all the relevant audiobook sites including *Audible, iTunes,* and *Audiobooks. Author's Republic* offers to help you sell your audiobook through more than 30 major retailers, library providers and distributors, but they claim more are being added every month.

- Your audiobook will also require a different ISBN number from your printed version and your eBook.

Whether you are technology savvy, or you prefer to shy away from anything technical, this is not the time to be a shrinking violet. The sales opportunities open to authors now far exceed simple print books, and if you resist the digital age – the only person to lose out is *you*. Oh, and perhaps your publisher too.

Chapter 16
Legalities, Plagiarism and Copyright

The time has come to tell you about some of the less inspiring stuff because this chapter deals with some very important legal matters. However, I will do my best to make it anything other than a dull read.

As a writer or author, you will have certain legal obligations to adhere to… from managing your tax affairs to ensuring your work is not plagiarised from other authors. You will also need to consider carefully what and how you write about other people, to avoid writing anything defamatory. This is particularly important when writing memoirs, autobiographies, and biographies.

Defamation is the expression of an untrue insinuation against a person's reputation.

Lawontheweb.co.uk

Defamation is essentially divided into two areas: slander and libel. *Slander* is usually a momentary form of defamatory communication, such as speech. *Libel* is a more permanent defamatory form, mostly the written word. You cannot defame a deceased person. The press sometimes find themselves in court for libel, but equally, people using defamatory language against others on social media can find themselves in trouble too.

Defamation is not limited to individuals either. Companies whose profits or reputations have been damaged can also claim. Groups, however, who are not considered as a legal entity cannot claim for defamation. So, a group of disabled people who are written about, for example, cannot claim for defamation unless they are individually identified.

While on the subject of defamation, we should consider the laws on privacy and confidentiality.

Chapter 16

As a writer, the law also regards you as a publisher because you cause your work to be published. Whether you are writing an article, a blog, a press release, or other works of non-fiction, you need to ensure you are not infringing on the *privacy rights* of others. Generally speaking, everyone has the *right* to a reasonable expectation of *privacy* in respect of information divulged, whether that is disclosed formally, orally, or overheard. It also relates to information contained in correspondence, journals, telephone calls and emails, and social media – if it concerns family details, medical information, financial aspects, sexual preferences or orientations, or other details deemed to be of a private nature.

Be warned – it is likely that as an author, you will give a warranty to a book publisher that nothing contained in your work will infringe the *privacy* or *confidentiality rights* of any third person, and, if it does, you will fully indemnify the publisher. Book publishers often have insurance cover and may carry out pre-publication checks, but this insurance is unlikely to benefit the author, and it may fall to the author to compensate for any claims.

The law of privacy also relates to photographs, and long lens photography is often considered particularly *intrusive*. Photographs can also be considered as more powerful in that they can be used to mislead; often a picture can *'present an idea'* or *'story'* whether or not it is shown out of context. It is advisable, therefore, to steer clear of photographs that appear to depict sexual behaviours or relationships, actions intended to titillate, or private family activities.

If in doubt, either leave it out or seek legal advice – BEFORE PUBLICATION.

Writers also have an obligation to ensure the information they retain on their computers and devices is *data protected*. Writers who *process* information that could identify a living individual are considered as *data controllers* which, in simple terms, means that they are subject to the *Data Protection Act 1998*. The DPA defines *'processing'* broadly, but it covers the *collation, storage* and the *use* of information; this includes *publication*. This might all sound a bit scary, but essentially the principles relate to how personal data is processed and the security measures taken to protect the information retained. An individual has the right to seek compensation from a data controller who causes them damage or distress as a result of the unlawful processing of personal data. This could, in fact, even relate to the careless loss of a mobile phone that contains the private contact details of an individual. Data security is even more important if you're an avid journalist with access to high profile personalities as you have a 'duty of care' to protect those people whose numbers are stored in your phone or on a computer database.

The *British Government* now takes the real threat of personal data theft very seriously. Individuals and companies who don't take the necessary precautionary steps to protect the data they store on their computers and smartphone devices, are liable to face prosecution.

Encryption software is available to protect data stored on electronic devices including mobile phones and tablets, and this should be considered adequate enough to keep your data secure, in the event of loss or theft of the device. At the very minimum, I would always advise that secure passwords be used on all devices – phones, tablets, laptops.

Plagiarism

Plagiarism is to commit literary theft!

That may sound harsh but using the work of another, in any form, by copying it and passing it off as your own, is plagiarism and a serious offence.

This is not the same as paraphrasing. Taking a set of facts or opinions and rewording them, but keeping the original meaning and presenting the information in a new form is *paraphrasing* and a legitimate activity. Paraphrasing is also used to give *greater clarity* to the meaning of something (written or spoken).

Writers of all calibres are very protective of their work, and so they should be. Not only can there be financial implications and losses but it is also often a matter of principle. Individuals who have worked very hard to produce works for publication have a right to some protection of their work. As a writer, I am sure you are beginning to grasp the concept of how difficult writing can be; would you want someone else getting the credit for what you have written?

There have been a couple of occasions when I have advised you to not get too precious about not being credited for certain aspects of your writing (press releases, magazine submission ideas, etc.,) and explained the reasons why. However, plagiarising someone else's work or ideas is not the same.

> *Plagiarism is presenting someone else's work or ideas as your own, with or without their consent, by incorporating it into your work without full acknowledgement. All published and unpublished material, whether in manuscript, printed or electronic form, is covered under this definition. Plagiarism may be intentional or reckless, or unintentional. Under the regulations for examinations, intentional or reckless plagiarism is a disciplinary offence.*

Oxford University

As a writer, it is easy to find a piece of writing that eloquently expresses a thought or phrase you are trying to articulate. Often, there is a temptation to use that expression in its original form and if you do, this is plagiarism.

To avoid plagiarism, you can do one of two things. 1. You can use the phrases as a quotation, and you should put the quote in between quotation marks, and more importantly, *credit the source* (be that the writer or publication from where you found the content, or better still, its original source). *Giving incorrect information in relation to the source is also a transgression.* Or, 2. Re-write the phrase in such a way that it becomes your own piece in your own author voice and, therefore, an original piece of writing. *A note of caution – just changing the words is not enough. Plagiarism can also relate to the sentence structure. So merely changing a few words without changing the structure of a sentence will not do, unless you give credit to the source.*

The copying of many words or ideas from one source that makes up the majority of your work, whether you give credit or not, flouts the rules of *'fair dealing'* also known as *'fair use'*, which is equally considered as plagiarism or copyright infringement. See below for more information about copyright.

In its most general sense, fair use is any copying of copyrighted material done for a limited and 'transformative' purpose, such as to comment upon, criticize, or parody a copyrighted work. Such uses can be done without permission from the copyright owner. In other words, fair use is a defense against a claim of copyright infringement. If your use qualifies as a fair use, then it would not be considered an infringement.

Stanford University

What is *fair use*?

There are no hard and fast rules on *fair use*, which can make it extremely difficult for writers, editors and publishers to quantify. *Fair use* is a legal concept that allows brief excerpts of copyright material to be quoted verbatim without the need for *permission from* or *payment to* the copyright holder. Often, *fair use* is considered acceptable when used for the criticism of work, for commentary, for news reporting, for teaching, or research.

Using a paragraph or two from a book may constitute fair use but using 300 words from a 1,000-word magazine article is likely to raise more than a few eyebrows. However, *fair use* may not just relate to the amount of copy or text one has used in one's work but also the *value* of the text. If you use a few lines of a chorus from a song that happens to be one of the biggest tracks of the last decade, you could still find yourself in trouble.

Effect of the use upon the potential market for or value of the copyrighted work: Here, courts review whether, and to what extent, the unlicensed use harms the existing or future market for the copyright owner's original work. In assessing this factor, courts consider whether the use is hurting the current market for the original work (for example, by displacing sales of the original) and/or whether the use could cause substantial harm if it were to become widespread.

Copyright.gov

The use of images, video and other media in your work that belongs to another, without receiving proper permission is also plagiarism and breaks copyright laws. When buying images or other media from stock libraries or other sellers, ensure you obtain or buy the correct *rights* to publish commercially, whether that is for a magazine, book or online.

Basically, if you intend to make a profit by reproducing and reselling copyrighted works or a proportion of them, then fair use is highly unlikely to give you justification or protection. Other factors to be considered include the size or extent of the passage of material reproduced, the length of time for which the material will be used, the number of copies of the reproduced work that will be distributed, and the effect of the use on the market value of the original copyrighted work.

Rights

I have mentioned *rights* in numerous different places so I will take just a few moments to explain some of your rights.

Moral rights – you can keep or waive your *moral rights*. Although the *rights* of authors differ greatly between countries, typically they include the *right to be identified as the author* and the right to object to changes being made to your work, or how the work is presented – for example, if it is *derogatory* or *damaging* to your reputation.

I would advise against waiving your *moral rights*, and this is a contractual clause in your publishing agreement to look out for. It would be more favourable for you to question why a publisher wants you to waive your moral rights, and if there is cause for concern, to ask for a disclaimer or clause that meets their wishes rather than *signing away* your moral rights wholesale. From a publisher's point of view, I can appreciate the reasons they may ask you to waive your moral rights. Some authors can be particularly precious about their works and consequently stifle the publisher's wishes to publish in a certain format. However, the biggest risk to you as the author is not being *identified* as the author, and very few authors would be happy about that, so make sure you insist upon it as a clause in your contract if they insist upon you assigning your moral rights!

First rights – More commonly used (but not exclusively) for the publication of magazine articles, is permission from the author to a publisher to publish exclusively the *'first publication'* of the works. First rights can be country specific: *First British serial rights, First US serial rights,* etc., or *First Worldwide rights.* The amount of money a publisher will offer you can also depend on the rights they are granted. Authors would expect to receive a higher fee for *First Worldwide Rights* over just *First British Rights*.

Second rights – If you have sold the *first rights* and another publisher or two wants to publish the same work, be that in its entirety or part thereof, as the copyright holder you can sell the *second rights* to publish in one or more publications. Publishers are aware that if they are paying for second rights, that the work has previously been published, and would therefore expect to pay a lower fee. However, if the work during first publication has garnered high acclaim, and publishers are falling over themselves to publish your work, there may be an opportunity for you to seek a higher fee. Before selling second rights though, do check any contractual agreement on the first rights as it may include exclusivity for a time period, say 12 or 24 months or longer, after publication. This means, you cannot sell the second rights until the time-period has elapsed. There is no upper limit to the number of times you can sell *second rights*.

Copyright

We touched on copyright above; it is an automatic right that exists under the law for any individual who creates literary, dramatic, musical, film, sound recordings, artistic or typographical arrangements. Works must be original (not directly copied or adapted from an existing work), and should exhibit some degree of labour and skill, or judgement, during their creation.

Copyright protects the creative work of individuals and prevents others from using it without their permission. This includes your works being translated, copied, publicly performed, transmitted, broadcast or adapted. This further means that others cannot distribute copies of your work, whether that is *free of charge* or *for sale*, they cannot *rent* or *lend* copies of your work, and they cannot put it on the internet, without your permission or that of your publisher.

As a writer, anything you write has automatic copyright protection. You do not have to apply or pay a fee, and there isn't a register in the UK for copyright works. In the USA, China, and India, it is optional to register some works, and in some countries it is mandatory. Copyright is internationally recognised, and international conventions guarantee a minimum level of protection in most countries, the most important of which is the *Berne Convention* – which is a framework agreement between nations in respect of *intellectual property rights*.

> *Intellectual property refers to creations of the mind: inventions; literary and artistic works; and symbols, names and images used in commerce. Intellectual property is divided into two categories: Industrial Property includes patents for inventions, trademarks, industrial designs and geographical indications, and Copyright, which covers literary works.*
>
> WIPO

Although, some writers recommend that you apply the copyright symbol © followed by your name and the date you wrote the work, this isn't a requirement to protect your copyright. As stated above, you have an *automatic right*. I have also read authors who say using the © symbol smacks of being an amateur or novice, and if you wrote it some years ago, publishers might assume it has been *'doing the rounds'* to other publishers or agents before them, during that period – but I don't believe that is the case.

> *You can sell or transfer your copyright to another party. Sometimes, publishers ask authors to assign their copyright. However, many people in the industry advise against selling or assigning your copyright. If a publisher asks you to assign your copyright, ask why. It could be that their concerns can be addressed in a clause in your publishing agreement or contract instead.*
>
> *Transferring copyright does not have to be all or nothing. The law allows you to transfer copyright to certain elements (e.g. print) while retaining the rights to others (e.g. movie adaptations).*

Articles from the *Society of Authors* and other writing organisations claim it is commonplace for many authors to feel coerced into assigning their copyright for fear of losing the publishing contract and, subsequently, many who have previously signed away their copyright have come to regret it.

In an interview published in Author Magazine, Horrid Henry author Francesca Simon, says 'I have never received a penny in royalties from Novel for the exploitation of their adaptation of my books.' This is because, when she sold publishers Orion her first Horrid Henry book in 1993, the deal 'included all those other rights' and they subsequently sold them to Novel.

Daily Mail

It is easy to appreciate why Ms. Simon is aggrieved when the animated *CITV* series, inspired by *Horrid Henry*, has been broadcast in 44 countries – with sales of the DVD topping 1.5 million. The character also spawned a film in 2011, starring Richard E. Grant, as well as computer games and other merchandising.

If you have any concerns about assigning your *rights* or breach of copyright, seek expert advice. The *SOA*, *The Writer's Guild*, and the *NUJ* offer help and guidance in relation to all matters regarding rights, publishing agreements, and contracts.

If you are worried about protecting your copyright, it is common advice to post an original or first draft copy to yourself. The package must be clearly date-stamped and remain unopened. On postal receipt, file it somewhere safe and secure. Alternatively, you can file a copy with a solicitor.

In most countries, copyright lasts for a minimum of life plus 50 years (or 70 in the UK) for most types of written, dramatic and artistic works, and at least 25 years for photographs. It can be different for other types of work.

However, the 1988 Copyright, Designs and Patents Act now states for literary, dramatic, musical or artistic works it's 70 years from the end of the calendar year in which the last remaining author of the work dies.

If the author is unknown, copyright will last for 70 years from the end of the calendar year in which the work was created, although if it is made available to the public during that time, (by publication, authorised performance, broadcast, exhibition, etc.), then the duration will be 70 years from the end of the year that the work was first made available.

Copyrightservice

Chapter 16

The ALCS, the CLA, the PLS, and the PLR

The ALCS

The *Authors' Licensing and Collecting Society (ALCS)* was founded in 1977 to represent the interests of all UK writers, and aims to ensure those writers are fairly compensated for any works that are copied, broadcast, or recorded.

The *ALCS* is committed to ensuring the rights of writers – both intellectual and moral rights – are fully respected and rewarded fairly. The *ALCS* represents writers of all calibres across print and broadcast media.

Ultimately, *ALCS* collects fees that would otherwise be difficult, time-consuming or legally impossible for writers to claim on an individual basis – money that is nonetheless due to them. Over time, *ALCS* has combined specialist knowledge with highly sophisticated systems that can track the works of writers against secondary use for which payment would be due. Their work extends across the world and international contracts and reciprocal agreements also ensure UK writers are duly compensated for any overseas use.

Membership to *ALCS* is open to all writers and successors of their estates for a modest one-off fee. However, members of the *Society of Authors*, the *Writers' Guild of Great Britain*, the *NUJ*, *Chartered Institute of Journalists*, and *British Association of Journalists* are granted FREE ordinary membership of *ALCS*. More information can be found on the ALCS.co.uk website.

The CLA

The *Copyright Licensing Agency (CLA)* helps customers legally access, copy and share published content, while also making sure that copyright owners are paid *royalties* for the use of their work.

Founded by its owners, *ALCS* and the *Publishing Licensing Society (PLS)*, the *CLA* predominately provides *rights, contents*, and *licensing services* to customers in the academic, professional, and public sectors. Businesses, charities, educational institutions, and public sector organisations are encouraged to buy licences from the *CLA* to simplify the access, management, and use of copyright content. They are the only way to obtain blanket clearance to make copies of the content these institutions want or need, rather than having to seek clearance from the copyright holder each time.

The money collected by the *CLA* is forwarded to the *PLS* and *ALCS* for distribution to the copyright owners in return for the use of their intellectual property.

The PLS

Publishers Licensing Society (PLS) (not to be confused with the PLR, which is explained next), provides a simple and cost-effective solution for collective licensing. This means individuals or organisations who wish to copy from published material can do so without breaking the law. Collective licensing eases the burden of direct licensing which would be otherwise inefficient and arduous. A blanket licence allows users to copy works from a broad range of material in return for a licence fee. The collected fees are then paid to the *rights* holders.

All UK and overseas-based publishers of books, magazines, journals and websites, can choose to sign up with the *PLS* to administer copying rights and to manage their works on a collective basis. There is no charge for signing up with *PLS*.

The PLR

Public Lending Rights (PLR) was established by the *Public Lending Right Act 1979*, which gave British authors a legal right to receive payment for the free lending of their books by public libraries.

The funding, provided by Central Government, ensures that payments are made to eligible authors, subject to how often their books are lent out from a selected sample of UK public libraries.

To qualify for payment, authors must apply to the PLR office which maintains a register of eligible authors and books. The Act established PLR as an intellectual property right, entirely separate from copyright.

To qualify for PLR in a book, you should be named on its title page or be entitled to a royalty payment from the publisher (but you do not have to own the copyright). When two or more contributors are involved they must divide the PLR between them.

PLR.uk.com

The ISBN number is used by these organisations to track works back to the copyright holders and authors.

Income tax

Now that you understand how and who may pay you all those lovely royalty payments, the Government is going to want a share of those earnings.

Here is where I put in a *disclaimer*. I am not an expert in tax affairs and cannot be held responsible for any taxable claims you make that are disallowable or illegal. My purpose here is to provide a guide on allowable income and expenses, as of May 2017. It is your responsibility to check with HMRC in respect of all current legislation.

Whether you write full or part-time, it's your only job, or it is one of many, if you earn from your writing then your income *IS* taxable – even, if you are writing casually and pay tax through PAYE as an employee. In the same vein, expenses you incur during your writing pursuits can be offset against income earned. However, if the expenses incurred, in connection with your writing, far exceed any income received, the resultant losses may be used to reclaim tax paid on other income.

A note of caution – HMRC fully appreciate losses may be used as a basis to reclaim tax and to that end, if you only receive the occasional small token payments for your writing it could be deemed as a hobby and HMRC may not consider this as taxable income. This means they will not accept your expenses either.

Income received is any monies you have been paid for writing-related activities, which could be reader's letters, articles, or advances and royalties received from book sales. It will also include any fees or payments received for giving talks or presentations, or for attending events. Some grants and bursaries, awards and prizes are subject to income tax too; others are not. Further guidance on this can be found in the *W&A Yearbook* and on the *hmrc.gov.uk* website.

If you do intend to declare your income then you should register as self-employed with *HMRC*. This will not affect any *PAYE* status you have, you will be given supplementary sheets relating to your earnings as an employee, as well as being self-employed, which are required to complete and file a *self-assessment tax return.*

Equally, if you are already self-employed and writing is a secondary business, you can complete a separate self-employed supplementary form for each self-employment, or if your business activities are registered in your own name (and not a business name), you can combine the income received and allowable expenses from each pursuit. You cannot double-claim expenses though. If you already claim expenses relating to your home office for business-related activities you cannot claim again for your writing, unless it is shared or split proportionally (e.g. 80% other business, 20% writing).

Allowable expenses relate to costs incurred by you to deliver your writing pursuits. They can include computer and printing equipment, printer cartridges and servicing of equipment, mobile, telephone and internet charges, subscriptions for software, stationery purchases, travel expenses including hotels (plus meals on overnight business trips), and fuel or public transport – for activities relating to research or conducting interviews, or attending events.

You can also offset the costs of buying books, magazines and magazine subscriptions, and other publications relating to the topics you are writing about. You can also offset the costs for any workshops or courses you pay for. You cannot claim back anything that is considered for dual purposes such as food or clothing. For telephone or mobile costs or vehicle costs (including tax, servicing, repairs and maintenance) where there is an element of personal usage or mileage, you must do your best to keep accurate records for business use, and only claim a proportion of the bills that relate to your business activities.

If you use a room in your home for your writing, you can offset a percentage of your utility bills such as electricity, gas, council tax, property insurance, rent, and mortgage interest but not mortgage payments. You can either add up the total amount of your bills for the year and divide by the number of rooms in your property *(then divide by 12 for the monthly amount),* or you can use the *flat rate scheme* based on the number of hours you work from home, providing it is more than 25 hours per month. For example, if you work 25 to 50 hours for your business at home, you can claim a £10 flat rate fee *per month* towards your home's running costs. Check the *gov.uk* website for more information and for applicable rates.

Chapter 16

Remember to include website development and hosting, graphic design charges for business cards and stationery, and any book launch or book signing expenses.

It is relatively simple to keep details of your income and outgoings, (although HMRC is changing the rules on self-assessment submission and filing, so do keep yourself regularly informed of these changes) but should you choose to use a bookkeeper or accountant, their fees are allowable expenses too. Your spouse or other family members can be paid by you for such services as these, or other administrative tasks, but you must clearly show that they are being paid. Your spouse is then responsible for declaring their income, unless you are paying them via PAYE.

What you cannot claim for is non-business driving or travel costs, fines, or travel between home and work. You cannot offset costs relating to your spouse or other companions unless they are actively involved in the business pursuit to which the expense relates.

As an author, you also have a dispensation option – it is called *'Averaging for creators of literary or artistic works'*. HMRC understands that it can take many years to write and publish a book, and earnings may take many years to materialise. However, writing your book and having it published or taking the self-publishing option means that you can incur several years' expenses and potential losses, and yet have much higher earnings in the year, or years, after publication.

Guidance on *'HS234 Averaging for creators of literary or artistic works'* is available on the gov.uk website.

Authors and artists who have fluctuating profits may pay a large amount of tax in a good year, and little or no tax in a bad year. A relief, introduced in the March 2001 Budget, allows such people to average their profits for successive tax years. This can reduce their total tax bill for the 2 years concerned. The relief replaces previous reliefs for spreading of royalties and sums received for the sale of works of art. The same sort of people will benefit but this relief is simpler and more people will be able to claim.

Averaging will only help you if the top rate of tax that you pay is different for each of the 2 years. For example, averaging:

- *will not help you if you pay higher rate tax (40%) each year*

- *may help you if you pay tax at the basic rate one year and higher rate the next*

- *may help you if you are liable to tax one year but your income falls so you are not liable the next*

gov.uk

* * *

Finale

Having just worked your way through all the dos and don'ts of writing and publishing, the legalities you need to adhere to, and understood your *rights* – do you still want to be a writer?

Of course, you do!

I hope you have found this journey a rewarding one, and as this journey ends for me – it is only the beginning of your new adventure.

I have provided you with the tools, I have given you the techniques, and I have even disclosed many tips of the trade. I now hope that you will use all that I have shared with you to find your own writing path, see yourself grow and your work flourish – and when you see your work published that you will think of my little book, and how it helped you achieve your goal, as it has helped me achieve mine.

Now, don't put it away or bury it on a bookshelf with all the other books you have collected. Keep it close to hand and refer to it as often as you need – it is a little gem – and it will be your writing companion. Use it well!

Index

Index

Index

Index

CPSIA information can be obtained
at www.ICGtesting.com
Printed in the USA
BVHW031405171122
652112BV00002B/86